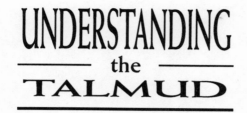

UNDERSTANDING
the
TALMUD

UNDERSTANDING
—— the ——
TALMUD

A Modern Reader's Guide for Study

EDWARD S. BORAZ

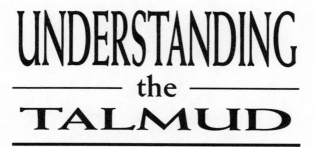

JASON ARONSON INC.
Northvale, New Jersey
London

The author gratefully acknowledges permission to quote from the following sources:

Tanakh—The Holy Scriptures: The New JPS Translation According to the Traditional Hebrew Text. Copyright © 1985 the Jewish Publication Society. Published by the Jewish Publication Society. Used by permission.

Talmud Bavli, vol. I of *Bava Metzia*, explained, translated, and punctuated by Rabbi Adin Steinsaltz. Copyright © 1983 Israel Institute for Talmudic Publications. Published by Israel Institute for Talmudic Publications. Used by permission.

The Talmud: The Steinsaltz Edition, vol. I, by Adin Steinsaltz, ed. Copyright © 1989 by Milta Books & The Israel Institute for Talmudic Publications. Reprinted by permission of Random House, Inc.

This book was set in 12 pt. Berkeley by Alpha Graphics of Pittsfield, New Hampshire.

Library of Congress Cataloging-in-Publication Data

Boraz, Edward S., 1952–
    Understanding the Talmud : a modern reader's guide for study / by
Edward S. Boraz.
        p.   cm.
    Includes bibliographical references and index.
    ISBN 1-56821-616-5 (alk. paper)
    1. Talmud—Introductions.   I. Title.
BM503.5.B67   1996
296.1'25061—dc20   96-5142
                                                      CIP

Manufactured in the United States of America. Jason Aronson Inc. offers books and cassettes. For information and catalog write to Jason Aronson Inc., 230 Livingston Street, Northvale, New Jersey 07647.

This book is dedicated to my parents,
Helen Mae Boraz and Martin L. Boraz,
may his memory be for a blessing,
and to my wife, Shari,
and children, Joshua and Rebecca,
who give me much happiness, joy, and love.

Contents

Preface   xiii
Acknowledgments   xvii

1   EXPLORING THE *MITZVAH* OF TALMUD STUDY   1

    The Duty to Understand   1
    The Historical Imperative   3
    Jewish Identity, Continuity, and Transcendence   4
    Talmud Study and the Growth of American Jewry   6
    The Talmud and *K'lal Yisrael*
        (The Community of Israel)   10
    Conclusion   11

2   UNDERSTANDING THE ROADBLOCKS: REMOVING THE BARRIERS   13

    Impediments to Comprehending the Talmud   13
    Removing the Roadblocks: A Journey through Time   14
    Building on the Steinsaltz Edition of the Talmud   24
    One Approach to Further Removing the Barriers:
        A Methodology to Integrate Torah with Talmud   26

3   THE DEVELOPMENT OF SACRED LITERATURE   31
    FROM THE RABBINIC VIEW

    Introduction on Methodology   31
    The Rabbinic Understanding of Torah   33

Torah as Pre-existent to Matter
The Definition of Torah
The Chain of Tradition: The Oral Law
    and Its Embodiment in the Mishnah
The Embodiment of the Oral Law into the Mishnah
Summary

4   THE HISTORICAL APPROACH: TOWARDS AN UNDERSTANDING   49
    OF THE CONTEMPORARY AND ANTECEDENT LITERARY GENRES
    OF THE TALMUD: SCRIPTURE, MIDRASH, MISHNAH, TOSEFTA,
    AND BARAITOT

Scripture   49
Midrash   53
    Origin and Development of Midrash Halakhah
    Nature of Midrash
    Mekhilta de-Rabbi Ishmael
    Sifra
    Sifre
Mishnah   61
    Mishnah Defined
    Historical Setting
    The Nature of the Mishnah
Evidence That the Mishnah Was an Edited Version   69
    of the Oral Law
    Tosefta
    Baraitot
Summary   70

5   THE HERMENEUTICS OF THE TALMUD   73

Introduction   73
Origin and Development   75
Kal V'chomer (KV): An a Fortiori Inference   76
    An Illustration of the KV from Scripture:
        the Story of Miriam
    Refutation of the Kal V'chomer
    The Importance of Preserving a Refuted KV
Binyan av Mishnei K'tuvim   84
Gezerah Shavah   87
K'lal U'phrat Ukhlal   88
Conclusion   89

6   THE TALMUD'S RESPONSE TO THE BARAITA OF RABBI HIYA   93

    I. The Rule and Rationale of Rabbi Hiya   94
    II. The Necessity For the KV   98
    III. KV Number 1   101
       A. ADM and WS Are Legally Analogous
         and Stand in a Relation of Minor to
         Major Importance Because the Former
         Does Not Require Payment, Whereas
         the Latter Does
       B. Challenge to KV Number 1: ADM Is
         Legally More Powerful Than WS
       C. Response and KV Number 2: WS Impose
         the Severe Penalty of Fines Whereas ADM
         Do Not: Thus They Do Stand in a Relation
         of Minor to Major Importance
    IV. The Relationship between Admissions   103
      and Witnesses
       A. Challenge: An Admission Charges a
         Litigant with Greater Religious
         Obligations Than the Testimony
         of Witnesses
       B. Response: Rabbi Hiya Relies on a
         Minority Opinion that Supports This KV
       C. Further Challenge: ADM Carries a
         Heavier Penalty Than the Rule of WS
       D. Response: Rabbi Hiya Relies on the
         Same Minority View of Rabbi Meier
       E. Challenge: In Contrast to the Testimony
         of Witnesses, an Admission Is Not
         Affected by Evidence That Contradicts
         or Refutes It. Therefore, ADM has Greater
         Legal Efficacy Than WS
    V. The Law of the Single Witness as a Basis for a KV   110
       A. Formulation of New KV Based on Rule of SW
       B. Challenge: The Single-Witness Rule Is
         Not Comparable to That of the Baraita
       C. Response: The Oath Imposed by the Single
         Witness May Serve as the Basis for
         Requiring the Defendant to Take the Oath
         on the Remainder

D. Challenge: The SW and WS Are Not
    Legally Analogous and Thus No KV
    Can Be Drawn
VI. A KV Derived from Two Rules: ADM and SW   115
A. A KV Based on the Common Element of
    Claim and Denial Found in the Cases of
    Both ADM and SW
B. Repetition of Previous Objection of a KV
    Based on SW
C. Response: Support That Aspect of the KV
    by the Use of the Case of ADM
D. Challenge: The Argument Is Circular
E. SW and ADM Share a Common Element
    that Is Also Found in the Case of WS, and
    This Might Serve as a Basis for a *Binyan Av*
    (an Extended Form of a KV) to Support
    Rabbi Hiya's Teaching
F. Challenge: A Presumption of Truthfulness
    Distinguishes the Cases of Both SW and
    ADM from the Case of WS
G. Response: But the Defendant in the Case
    of WS Is Presumed Truthful So as to
    Testify in Other Cases
H. Challenge: Unlike WS, ADM and SW Are
    Not Subject to the Law of Retaliation, and,
    Therefore, the *Binyan Av* Must Fail
I. Response: The Law of Retaliation Is Not
    a Sufficient Distinction So as to Render
    This KV Invalid
Observations   123
The Fuel of the Dialectic   124

7   THE SCRIPTURAL FOUNDATION FOR THE TALMUDIC DIALECTIC   127

Introduction   127
A. The Oath and Its Midrashic Explication   129
    The Role of Intent
    The Oath in the Context of Holiness
    The Perjurer Is the Moral Equivalent of a Thief
    The Oath, *Hilul Hashem*, and Repentance

B. The Scriptural Derivation for the Partial 143
Admission: Exodus 22:6–8
Introduction
The Legal Analogy between Bailment and Loan
The Duty to Loan
Concerning All Matters of Trespass
The Meaning of "This Is It"
"The Matter between Them Shall Be Brought
before *Elohim*": From Oracles to God to Judges
The Requirement to Pay Double
The Requirement to Accept the Oath
Summary
C. The Law of Witnesses: Exegesis of 155
Deuteronomy 19:15–20
By the Mouth of Two or Three Witnesses
Summary
Conclusion 159

8 THE SYNTHESIS OF THE SCRIPTURAL FOUNDATION WITH THE TALMUD 161

Introduction 161
I. The Rule and Rationale of Rabbi Hiya's Baraita 162
II. The Necessity for the KV 165
III. KV Number 1 167
A. ADM and WS are Legally Analogous
and Stand in a Relation of Minor to
Major Importance
IV. The Relationship between Admissions 168
and Witnesses
A. Challenge: An Admission Charges a Litigant
with Greater Religious Obligations
Than the Testimony of Witnesses
E. Challenge: An Admission Is Not Affected
by Evidence that Contradicts or Refutes It
V. The Law of the Single Witness (SW) As a Basis 171
for the KV
A. A Single Witness (SW) May Compel
a Defendant to Deny under Oath the
Substance of the Former's Testimony

VI. A KV from Two Rules: ADM and SW   173
   A. A KV Based on the Common Element
      of Claim and Denial Found in the
      Cases of Both ADM and SW
   E. Challenge: A Presumption of Truthfulness
      Distinguishes Both the Single Witness
      and Partial Admission from the Baraita
   F. Response: But the Defendant in the
      Baraita Is Presumed Truthful So as to
      Testify in Other Cases
   G. Challenge: Unlike WS, ADM and SW Are
      Not Subject to the Law of Retaliation and,
      Therefore, the Binyan Av Must Fail
   I. The Law of Retaliation Is Not a Sufficient
      Distinction So as to Render This
      KV Invalid
Conclusion   177
   The Values Embedded in the Scriptural Foundation

9 TALMUD AND SCRIPTURE: IMPLICATIONS OF A   181
  SCRIPTURAL METHODOLOGY IN THE UNDERSTANDING OF TALMUD

   The Philological Method: Benefits to Build On   181
   Scriptural Methodology: An Approach to   182
     Understanding the Talmud
   Implications of the Methodology   184
     The Meaning of Talmud
     The Function of Talmud
     The Challenge that Awaits Us

   Glossary   187
   Bibliography   197
   Index   201

Preface

Two summers ago, I had the privilege of studying privately with Dr. Ben Zion Wacholder, the distinguished holder of the Solomon J. Freehoff Chair of Talmud at the Hebrew Union College—Jewish Institute of Religion in Cincinnati, Ohio. He was trained in the *yeshivot* of Lithuania, a world which no longer exists.

We studied the Talmud *Bava Metziah*. He was and is a patient teacher, entertaining every question and every challenge to the text that I could think of. (I have a law degree, which qualifies me as one who is professionally trained in the art of asking questions). As we studied, it became clear that his vision of Talmud was that of a much larger work—an extension of the task that God began at Sinai. Scriptural passages, uncited in the text, clarified a Gemara that would have remained obscure, at least in my mind. The Talmud took on a metaphysical dimension that was exciting. An ancient dialogue became alive at his kitchen table as I read and he taught.

This book represents an attempt to give to you what was given to me that summer—an intellectual and spiritual adventure into the world of Torah; a meeting place where the human mind struggles to discern the divine will.

HOW TO STUDY THIS WORK

The educational model that I have employed is based on my learning sessions with Rabbi Wacholder, in which I was (and to some extent will always regard myself as) an untrained reader. Every question was entertained patiently, regardless of its simplicity or complexity. This book has adopted the same framework with regards to its intended audience. It assumes that one may have little background in the study of Talmud and is thus unfamiliar with much of the vocabulary and terminology that is frequently taken for granted. A reading knowledge of Hebrew is not necessary, though it would prove helpful.

In order for the reader to acquire the "vocabulary" of the text, patience is required. The uninitiated will encounter words or phrases that will require some reflection. However, the technical terminology (words appearing in italics) employed in each chapter is defined and explained in the glossary in order to enable the reader to have a better grasp of the ideas of the chapter. From time to time, it may be helpful to refer to the glossary of terms.

Nearly every example of a concept found in the passage is taken from the text itself for purposes of illustration. Thus, by the time the reader will have engaged the actual portion under consideration, he or she will have a grounding and a familiarity with its basic concepts and methodology. The purpose is to allow the reader the opportunity to absorb the arguments found in the portion and to reflect on the significance of each, as opposed to spending considerable time in simply understanding the words of the text.

WHY THE SELECTION FROM *BAVA METZIAH*

The selection is taken from a tractate (volume) of the Talmud entitled *Bava Metziah*—literally, the middle gate, which begins with a case in which litigants both claim ownership of a garment and no independent proof is available to establish the validity of either position. The specific section deals with the general issue of under what circumstances may an oath be imposed on a defendant and when it should be withheld.

On the surface, this issue is not one that a person would associate with religion. Indeed, this passage is difficult. Yet, it was chosen specifically to demonstrate that what may appear to be an exercise in scholasticism is in fact a search for that which is holy and sacred within the context of human relationships.

The goal of this work is to facilitate not only an entry into an ancient dialogue, but to allow the reader the opportunity to respond and to contribute to an ongoing work that began at Sinai and continues throughout time.

Acknowledgments

To Rabbi Bernard and Yetta Robinson, for guiding me towards the path of Torah and learning. Their love and support remains forever in my heart.

I want gratefully to acknowledge the help, assistance, and support that I received from Dr. Jeffrey Salloway. He is a man of great integrity and commitment whose friendship and encouragement have made this work possible.

I also want to thank Dr. Steven Ballaban for his editing and friendship as this project developed.

And finally to Anne Millen and Patricia Gladden for their support in reading parts of this work as the "untrained eye."

1

Exploring the *Mitzvah* of Talmud Study

THE DUTY TO UNDERSTAND

Mitzvah is a word filled with ambiguity. On the one hand, it means the doing of a good deed. When a person does something that helps another and has some implicit or explicit reference to the Torah, we often say "he [or she] did a *mitzvah*." It also has the technical meaning of a divine command.

These two associations of a "good act" and a "command" result in a psychic tension. Something that we do for someone else that makes us feel good is labeled a *mitzvah*. At the same time, we are commanded to do the act. An order to do something is generally met with resistance. When our parents told us to eat the broccoli or clean our rooms, most of us, at least inwardly, resisted. Nevertheless, we did what was asked. Only later, sometimes much later, did we learn the invaluable lessons of discipline, order, and health (see Robert Fulghum's *Everything I Ever Needed to Know, I Learned in Kindergarten*).

The simple answer to "why one ought to study Talmud" is that the act is a *mitzvah*. Yet, the study of Talmud may be so formidable, challenging, and complex, that one may ask, for what purpose? In the age of secular freedom, when we have complete access to literatures of any genre, one may rightfully ask, why this particular text?

Let us begin our work with the story of Sinai and its aftermath. When the Jews were asked whether they would accept the Torah and its commandments, the Bible tells us that they initially responded, נעשה [*naaseh*]—we will do it. We are then told of the ten commandments and statutes—very specific laws, quite complex—which the Jews were to implement. Moses then erects an altar, conducts a religious service, and reads the "Book of the Covenant" to the people. They respond, נעשה ונשמע ["(All that God has spoken,) we will do and we will understand."] The duty to comprehend with our intellect, spirit, and emotions—all that comprises our humanity, became part of this sacred covenant.

This new word ונשמע [*v'nishmah*] teaches that obedience is not enough in order for Divine law to endure. One must seek to understand the underlying reasons for the doing of a *mitzvah* if one is to fulfill it and for it to fulfill the individual. What then, at this particular time in our history, are the reasons for the importance of this commandment of Torah study that may be embraced through the study of Talmud? The term "Torah study" embraces many forms. It may focus on Scripture alone or include commentaries that are nearly a thousand years old. Torah study includes Midrash—homiletical studies on both the narrative and legal sections of Scripture. The specific form of Torah study that this book is concerned with is the Talmud, which means "learning."

The first response to this religious imperative for the modern Jew is paradigmatic. The Talmud's blend of legal, literary, ethical, and theological concerns, rejecting by its own structure rigid fundamentalism, provides us with real nourishment for our intellect and spirit as we confront the challenges of the twenty-first century. The dangers of easy answers to complex problems, often with disastrous consequences, have been present in every society throughout history. The Talmud's literary structure of argumentation, its commitment to complex levels of analysis, and its demand for logical consistency, enable us to see beyond the "quick fix." The text is devoted to searching and developing the ideal Jewish society—one founded on equality and justice.

To be sure, the Talmud was written in a historical context vastly different from the world we live in. Its solutions may not be entirely applicable to ours. But to its credit, the Talmud is not an abstract, religious work. It grows out of the needs of people in all spheres of life. The authors have created for us a valuable paradigm that may be utilized for meeting the challenges that confront us and our children. Their methodology nurtures ideals within a society of competing demands and interests. Thus, its study serves as a form of training in bringing the ideal into the real, whether within the American Jewish community or the larger American society, which espouses this virtue as well.

THE HISTORICAL IMPERATIVE

A second purpose has its roots in history and is particular to the Jewish people. Learning the classic Jewish texts in the *yeshivot* (schools of study) of both Western and Eastern Europe involved generations of traditions. The Talmud became part of the genetic code of our people. There, these texts were safely guarded. Elie Wiesel, survivor of Auschwitz and Nobel laureate, once wrote: "Did we keep the Torah alive for 4,000 years or did it keep us alive? One is linked to the other, one is justified by the other. The Torah is an endless chain in which we are links, living links in an endless chain suggesting eternity, for God's voice reverberates in it forever."[1]

Like the beautiful words in our liturgy, taken from Scripture and recited each Friday night, ושמרו בני ישראל את השבת—"and the children of Israel shall keep the Sabbath"—we might create a new prayer in response to the historical aspect of guarding the Talmud: ושמרו בני ישראל את התלמוד "And the Children of Israel shall guard the Talmud." Such a prayer echoes the words of Wiesel.

Fifty years ago an entire Jewish civilization was destroyed. The chain of tradition of which Elie Wiesel has written, and of which

---

1. "The Endless Chain," in *Against Silence: The Voice and Vision of Elie Wiesel*, ed. Irving Abrahamson (New York: Holocaust Library, 1985), p. 307.

our rabbis have spoken throughout the ages, was seriously weakened, if not altogether broken. Like a thread fallen onto the floor, the tapestry of our people ceased to be woven. Many of the quiltmakers, indeed its leading designers, perished, never to return.

True, there are still great Jewish scholars and many students of this literature. There are *yeshivot* in both the United States and Israel whose sole mission is its study and scholarship. But to the vast majority, the Talmud remains a word that symbolizes a mystical, yet inaccessible, Jewish work. The majority of us are like children, unsure of how to begin to sew. Instinctively, however, we know that we must try. The *mitzvah* of preserving and nurturing a history that began at Sinai, continuing to fifteen hundred years ago in the Jewish academies of Babylonia when the Talmud was written and then up to today, is ours to do. In so doing, we connect to an ancient and sacred dialogue in which our ancestors engaged to discern the complex divine message of Sinai.

JEWISH IDENTITY, CONTINUITY, AND TRANSCENDENCE

In the American Jewish community, we are struggling with the issues of Jewish identity and continuity in the wake of the 1990 Jewish Population Survey. Disaffiliation and assimilation in an age of secular freedom present a significant challenge to our Jewish institutions. Despite the richness of our history, the argument that one should identify with the Jewish people and continue its traditions and customs for their own sake is simply not a meaningful response in many instances.

Michael Lerner, in his book *Jewish Renewal: A Path to Healing and Transformation*, sets forth that one of the central tenets of Judaism is the struggle for transcendence.

> The struggle between our capacity for transcendence and compassion, on the one hand, and our tendency to embody and pass on the pain and cruelty of the past, on the other, is the central drama of human life and human history. That it finds expression in the Torah, should be no surprise, nor necessarily a basis for discounting the divinity and holiness of the Torah tradition. . . .

The Torah is a useful guide to life because it is both a record of grappling with reality from the standpoint of God, and a record of the way that we are still in the struggle. . . . That wrestling is never a finished product, but a path which a people has chosen to be on. . . . We have a Torah that is an ongoing process, in which each generation unpacks its meaning by allowing itself to hear the voice of God within it in the way that generation can bear.[2]

It is this struggle for transcendence that will give Jewish identity and continuity meaning regardless of the culture in which Jews find themselves. Our Jewish identity, continuity, and even reaffiliation will be furthered if we are able to access those sources that have historically transcended the culture of a given time and place.

The Talmud is one such source. Jacob Neusner, in his work *Invitation to the Talmud*, writes, "The Talmud is the single most influential document in the history of Judaism. It therefore must be read . . . as fundamentally and deeply religious literature."[3]

The Talmud functions to engage the reader of rabbinic literature on multiple levels of analysis in every area of human thought and practice. Its study results in an existential view of the world that becomes rich in meaning and purpose. Rabbi Adin Steinsaltz writes, "The ultimate purpose of Torah . . . is to provide a comprehensive world view, bringing out both the essential relationship of Torah to every subject, but also the subjects' connections with each other."[4]

For these two scholars, we see that Talmud study has both a religious and philosophic component. The fusion of religion and philosophy that is found in the Talmud results in a careful study of each aspect of human life, and at the same time connects that feature to the whole of the person and the world of which he/she is a part. Each commandment of the Torah is linked to another in

---

2. Michael Lerner, *Jewish Renewal* (New York: G. P. Putnam & Sons, 1994), p. 97.

3. Jacob Neusner, *Invitation to the Talmud* (San Francisco: Harper & Row, 1984), pp. 1–2.

4. Adin Steinsaltz, *The Talmud: The Steinsaltz Edition, A Reference Guide* (New York: Random House, 1989), p. 2.

a way that the reader is able to discern only from his or her personal encounter with the Talmud. These connections are what render the study of Talmud a most meaningful adventure. Talmudic study leads to transcendence.

These three reasons—(1) an approach to fuse the real with the ideal to create a better world; (2) the need to weld the weakened links of the chain of our tradition, to add to the depth of our Jewish identity and continuity, and thereby, (3) to move towards transcendence—underlie the *mitzvah* to study the Talmud. The purpose of this book is to guide those who seek not only to pick up the thread but to begin weaving into the fabric of Judaism their understanding which will enrich our tradition for generations to follow.

TALMUD STUDY AND THE GROWTH
OF AMERICAN JEWRY

Apart from the individual necessity for Talmud study, its study remains relevant regardless of movement affiliation. It exerts a powerful effect on each of the three major branches of Judaism. The foundation of Orthodox Jewry is the Torah, both Written and Oral, as understood by the Talmud and the subsequent rabbinic literature which followed its redaction in 600 C.E.

Conservative Jewry defines itself as a halakhic movement. Simply stated, *halakhot* (plural of *halakhah*) are the norms taught by the Jewish tradition. They deal with the question, "How should one live as a Jew?" These norms are elaborated both in the Bible and in their rabbinic interpretations in the classical Jewish texts of Mishnah, Talmud, and Midrash. *Emet V'Emunah: Statement of Principles of Conservative Judaism*, provides:

> The single greatest event in the history of God's revelation took place at Sinai, but was not limited to it. God's communication continued in the teaching of the Prophets and the biblical Sages, and in the activity of the Rabbis of the Mishnah and the Talmud, embodied in Halakhah and the Aggadah [law and lore]. The process of revelation did not end there; it remains alive in the Codes and Responsa [later rabbinic literature that codified the legal aspects

of the Talmud and applied to the problems of successive genera-
tions] to the present day.[5]

Having defined revelation as an ongoing historical process that
began at Sinai and has continued throughout millennia, the Conservative movement addresses the ethical component of *halakhah*
as embodied in Talmud and our sacred literatures: "It is a concrete
expression of our ongoing encounter with God. . . . It is a means of
identifying and preserving the moral conscience of individuals and
society by presenting cases for consideration and teaching Jews how
to think about them morally."[6]

The Talmud is thus a part of the revelatory process. Its nature
is that of an encounter between the human and the divine. The
resulting tension and its resolution renders the talmudic process
applicable to teaching us how to address the contemporary issues
of our time. Its study strengthens our moral consciousness by training us in how to analyze the reality of our time with the ideals that
we hold dear to our hearts.

Though historically emphasizing the prophetic message of
Judaism and regarding Talmud and resulting *halakhah* as nonbinding, the Reform movement nevertheless has regarded the latter as
sacred. This is evident in its Columbus Platform of 1937 and its
San Francisco Platform of 1976. The former provides:

> Revelation is a continuous process, confined to no one group and
> to no one age. Yet the people of Israel, through its prophets and
> sages, achieved unique insight in the realm of religious truth. The
> Torah, both written and oral, enshrines Israel's ever-growing con-
> sciousness of God and of the moral law. It preserves the historical
> precedents, sanctions and norms of Jewish life, and seeks to mold
> it in the patterns of goodness and of holiness.

Torah, for the Reform Jew, early on encompassed both the Oral
and Written Law. It associates these two aspects of Torah with the

---

5. *Emet Ve-Emunah: Statement of Principles of Conservative Judaism* (United
States of America: Jewish Theological Seminary of America, Rabbinical Assembly, and the United Synagogue of America, 1988), p. 20.

6. Ibid., pp. 20–21.

norms of Jewish life and thus renders them sacred. The San Francisco Platform of 1976 sharpens this definition of Torah as an inclusive ongoing process that seeks to reveal the divine intent.

> Torah results from the relationship between God and the Jewish people. The records of our earliest confrontations are uniquely important to us. Lawgivers and prophets, historians and poets gave us a heritage whose study is a religious imperative and whose practice is our chief means to holiness. Rabbis and teachers, philosophers and mystics, gifted Jews in every age amplified the Torah tradition. For millennia, the creation of Torah has not ceased and Jewish creativity in our time is adding to the chain of tradition.[7]

Torah, for the Reform Jew, as for his/her Conservative counterpart, results from the divine encounter. This encounter is not limited to the "experience" of God to one moment in time. Study of Torah and its amplification, for the Reform Jew, is the religious imperative to be done in every generation. Thus, moving towards an understanding of the rabbis of the Talmud (as well as other literatures) is vital to the Reform understanding of the Torah tradition.

Though similarities exist between the Reform and Conservative movements in relation to Torah, traditionally their respective views of the binding nature of halakhah have differed significantly. As we have seen, Conservative Jewry regards the halakhah that results from the talmudic inquiry to be "binding" in a definitive manner, though retaining flexibility. Reform regards Torah as an ongoing creative process and rejects the notion of a "binding Jewish norm."

A Reform Jew may, therefore, ask, "What practical result might emerge from the study of Talmud?" Rabbi Walter Jacob, while serving as president of the Central Conference of American Rabbis (CCAR), confronted the historical objection to halakhah[8] (laws and

---

7. Michael A. Meyer, *Response to Modernity: A History of the Reform Movement in Judaism* (New York: Oxford University Press, 1988), pp. 389, 391.

8. The term *halakhah* traditionally refers to laws, customs, or practices that are considered binding upon the Jewish community. In traditional Jewish communities, the *halakhah* is determined through an analysis of such sources

customs whose theoretical basis are found in the Talmud) within the Reform movement by asserting the need for standards to govern the movement. He wrote:

> When our founders [those of Reform Judaism] rebelled against a stagnant orthodoxy, they chose the high road of individual autonomy, selecting the best from our past to give Jewish content and meaning to our present-day lives. No one can fault this ideal, but it has not worked. We need direct standards—*mitzvot* [ethical observances]—and *halakhah* as we go beyond guidance to governance. The Reform Movement will be open to new ideas, but if we must choose between a Reform Judaism that provides guidance and governance, the latter must be our path. Such a path requires that we adopt measurable religious standards for our leaders, board members, and all our congregants.[9]

If Rabbi Jacob's position is advanced, the Talmud will become an important factor in the ongoing evolution of the Reform movement. Perhaps not so much for any conclusions that might be drawn from its arguments and pronouncements, the Talmud may prove a significant model for engaging in the divine inquiry. As part of that process, a "Reform *halakhah*," in the sense of normative standards, may emerge that will define the parameters of praxis within it.

Emphasizing the importance of the *mesoret* (received tradition), Rabbi Sheldon Zimmerman, President of the Central Conference of American Rabbis, in his 1993 address to the CCAR eloquently stated:

> When we become rabbis we take upon ourselves *shalshelet hakabbalah*, the chain of received teachings, link by link interconnected; *mesoret*, tradition in its broadest and best sense; serving as

---

as the Talmud, the *Shulkhan Arukh*, Maimonides's *Mishneh Torah*, and the "Four Columns" by Jacob ben Asher. The latter works, of Maimonides and Jacob ben Asher, are codifications of the *halakhah* by rabbinic scholars who lived during the Middle Ages. Reform Judaism rejected a "binding *halakhah*" in the course of its history and developed the notion of "individual autonomy" regarding religious praxis. See Meyer, *Response*, p. 393.

9. Walter Jacob, "Standards Now," *Reform Judaism* 21:1 (Fall 1992): 64.

kley kodesh—vessels and instruments of holiness. A good part of our authority resides in continuity with past generations, as well as in our capacity to be *poskim*, interpreters of today. . . .

It is from the covenantal relationship with God, Torah and *mitzvah* that we gain our right to speak and teach as rabbis. Without an essential link and connection to the covenant of Torah and *mitzvah*, we are not rabbis.

If you are a Rav [rabbi], there is tradition, loyalty, continuity, the *shalshelet* [chain of tradition]. Authority comes to us from these sources and we are bound to them. . . .[10]

Rabbi Zimmerman's address was directed to those of us who are rabbis. Yet, we can see that his remarks may have an impact on the direction of the Reform movement. Again, not in terms of whether Reform Jews will become *shomer shabbat* (one who strictly observes the Shabbat—for example, does not ride in an automobile) or *kashrut* (one who observes the dietary law) as defined by Orthodox Jewry, but that they will develop a sacred bond to a literature that all movements regard as hallowed.

THE TALMUD AND כלל ישראל *K'LAL YISRAEL* (THE COMMUNITY OF ISRAEL)

The fragmentation of the American Jewish community is of deep concern. Dr. Jack Wertheimer, Professor of History at the Jewish Theological Seminary of America, in his most recent work, *A People Divided: Judaism in Contemporary America*, writes:

As for organized religious life, the official movements of American Judaism struggle with internal dissent, even as they wage even harsher campaigns against their denominational foes. . . . Perhaps to compensate for such internal disunity and to create a common cause against external foes, each of the movements has embarked

---

10. Rabbi Sheldon Zimmerman, *Presidential Address 105th Annual Convention, Central Conference of American Rabbis* (Chicago: Central Conference of American Rabbis, 1994), p. 2.

on a program of more overt competition and criticism directed at other Jewish movements.

He concludes this segment by writing: "Shrill divisiveness [among all denominations] rather than pluralism, is the order of the day."[11]

One difficulty that has contributed to this fragmentation is the problem of sources that each group regards as sacred and the nature in which they are understood and hence practiced. While the written Torah is read by all within the major branches, the Talmud, in significant part, is an exegesis of the former. Those who study Talmud understand the Torah differently from those who engage in other forms of Torah study. To the extent that one engages in Talmud, regardless of movement affiliation, a part of this fragmentation may begin to heal. A Reform or Conservative Jew who studies the intricacies of the Talmud will gain a greater appreciation and hence sensitivity for those who are more traditional or Orthodox. Perhaps the stridency of the Orthodox will diminish, and its respect for those who are non-Orthodox will increase, when the latter are able to speak in the same "language" as the former, yet derive different lessons. Therefore, Talmud study can be a source for healing the divisiveness that Wertheimer describes within the American Jewish community. It has the potential to move us towards כלל ישראל *k'lal Yisrael*. In short, the influence of the Talmud is not merely one of historicity but may be regarded as manifest in the current development of all the major branches of Judaism and their underlying interdependency on one another.

CONCLUSION

In summary, the issue of "why study Talmud" is addressed on four levels. First, talmudic study is both a spiritual and intellectual endeavor that enriches the Jewish experience. Second, the history of

---

11. Jack Wertheimer, *A People Divided: Judaism in Contemporary America* (New York: Basic Books, a division of HarperCollins Publishers, 1993), p. 189.

our people, and the resulting loss of a culture that was significantly committed to this tradition of study, compel our collective Jewish consciousness to encounter these texts. Third, Jewish continuity and identity, if they are to be taken seriously, must be built on authentic foundations which seek to provide a means of transcendence from the strictures of society. Finally, though the three main branches of Judaism treat the Talmud differently in its theological dimension, nevertheless each characterizes it as sacred and its study as a religious imperative or "should." It has the potential to be a source of healing for the current state of fractionalization of the American Jewish community and thereby to move us towards the ideal of כלל ישראל *k'lal Yisrael.*

Let us now move to the more difficult issue of understanding the formidable roadblocks to Talmud study.

2

Understanding the Roadblocks: Removing the Barriers

IMPEDIMENTS TO COMPREHENDING THE TALMUD

Anyone untrained in the study of classic rabbinic literature may experience a high level of difficulty in comprehending a portion of Talmud. Possessing the intellectual capability of understanding the dialectics of the Talmud is not at issue. It is a matter of removing the obstacles, which may be generalized as follows.

There is the formidable problem of language. The Talmud actually consists of three languages. One is mishnaic Hebrew [as distinct from modern Hebrew]. Another is Aramaic. Finally, the classic commentaries to the Talmud are written in "medieval rabbinic Hebrew," which is a blend of both Hebrew and Aramaic. The language barrier alone is arduous.

The syntax of the Talmud is associative and its literary style terse. These factors give the appearance of a work that lacks an inner order. Its discourse seems to shift from one subject to another in ways that are not readily apparent. Often, the pronominal references are unclear, thus causing the reader to lose the "thread" that holds the discussion together. In addition, one would expect the Talmud to read as an essay on some aspect of religion. Instead, the reader encounters an argumentative text in which an assertion is made and then immediately challenged. A debate then ensues which loses the untrained and trained reader alike. In short, a talmudic passage seems scattered and diffused, rather than a well-reasoned dialectic inquiry.[1]

Most of the concepts throughout the Talmud are not defined. The Talmud does not provide the reader with a study guide, nor does it provide a pedagogy. Its authors assume their readership to be familiar with both its underlying methodology, such as its rules of logic, and the theological principles upon which it reaches its conclusions on a given topic.[2]

Finally, the work requires a strong facility for logic and abstraction.[3] As such, it creates a "world of discourse" that often appears independent from the concrete realities of a given time, place, or society.[4]

For these reasons, modern scholars have concluded that the intended audience of the Talmud's creators were rabbinic scholars and students.[5] These writers assumed the reader's thorough training in Scripture, Midrash, the hermeneutical principles of rabbinic exegesis, and Mishnah, as preliminary to their work. Without this foundation, an attempt to study Talmud would be analogous to the study of calculus without an understanding of algebra. One is hardly possible without the other. The Talmud has remained inaccessible to most, despite the growing level of interest and intellectual capability to study it. Tragically, when literature is unreadable, it becomes irrelevant.

REMOVING THE ROADBLOCKS: A JOURNEY THROUGH TIME

To guide the reader, a cursory historical survey of the development of the Talmud's Hebrew and English translations may be helpful

---

1. Neusner, *Invitation*, p. 20.

2. Steinsaltz, *The Talmud: A Reference Guide*, p. 7.

3. Ibid., p. 3.

4. Jacob Neusner, *Judaism: The Evidence of the Mishnah* (Chicago: University of Chicago Press, 1981), p. 245.

5. David Kraemer, *The Mind of the Talmud* (New York: Oxford University Press, 1990), p. 1.

at the outset. (The Talmud itself is written in Aramaic.) The Talmud is considered by most scholars to have been written from the period of 425 C.E. to 600 C.E. in what was then Babylonia (now Iraq). The following is a brief selection of the portion that forms the corpus of this work. Again, the purpose of this chapter is only to demonstrate the difficulties in encountering the text and the historical efforts to remove them (a translation to the following selection is given later on in this chapter).

תני רבי חייא מנה לי בידך והלה אומר אין לך בידי כלום והעדים
מעידים אותו שיש לו חמשים זוז נותן לו חמשים זוז וישבע על השאר
שלא תהא הודאת פיו גדולה מהעדאת עדים וחומר

After its redaction, the Talmud remained essentially in the hands of a few for over five hundred years. Its understanding was limited to the scholars of the Babylonian academies. Up to the eleventh century, Jews lived throughout Europe, particularly in Spain, France, and Germany, as well as in North Africa and in the Orient. The communities of the Diaspora would submit questions on Jewish laws that were important in their communities, sending them by messengers, to these schools for answers. The authorities in Babylonia would give a detailed response and then send it back to them by messenger. Often, when the letter arrived at its destination, a community celebration was held, highlighted by a public reading of the answer.

Up to this time, the Talmud itself, from what we know, lacked a formal written commentary that explicated the text. However, by the eleventh century, the Babylonian academies, because of economic and political circumstances, as well as the development of Jewish communities throughout the world, began to decline. At the same time, serious talmudic study began to emerge in a number of Jewish communities throughout both the Occident and the Orient. In the eleventh century, a rabbi in France, by the name of Rabbeinu Shlomo ben Yitzchak (Solomon ben Isaac of Troyes, 1040–1105) addressed the pressing need of providing a methodology for the study of Talmud. Known by the acronym "Rashi," he is one of the great literary figures of Jewry. His commentary is essen-

---

6. Talmud, *Bava Metziah*, 2a.

tial to understanding the talmudic discourse. Robert Seltzer, in his classic work *Jewish People, Jewish Thought: The Jewish Experience in History*, describes this achievement as follows: "Rashi's Talmud commentary is a masterpiece of conciseness and clarity, opening up the extremely condensed talmudic text to the average Jewish youth attending one of the schools that had been established in most Ashkenazic communities."[7]

The following is Rashi's commentary to the small segment that appeared above:

וישבע על השאר כדין מודה מקצת הטענה שאמרה תורה ישבע כדילפינן
בשבועות [דף לט:] מכי הוא זה ואע"ג דזה לא הודה הרי יש עדים במקצת
ולא תהא הודאת פיו גדולה לחייבו על השאר שבועה מהעדאת עדים: מקל
וחומר: לקמן מפרש מאי ק"ו

One should not experience frustration over the lack of translation. It's included here simply to show the need for clarification and thus the contribution of Rashi in explicating the text, rendering it accessible to the students of his time and place. As an aside, one may note that there are thirty-six words to the actual text, while Rashi's commentary contains forty-five. In such a small fragment, this may not seem significant. Spread out over thirty-nine volumes, Rashi's commentary, more likely than not, greatly exceeds the word-length of the Talmud.

There were other luminaries as well. The commentaries by the Alfasi, Tosafot, Rabbeinu Asher, and the Maharsha, found in any standard edition of the Talmud, are beyond the scope of this work. Their central purpose was to clarify seemingly contradictory passages, to state the *halakhah*, to disagree with a prior interpretation of the talmudic text (such as Rashi's), and to render congruent their community's practice to those set forth in the Talmud. Their work is distinct from Rashi's in that the latter was primarily concerned with understanding the *p'shat* (the plain meaning of the text), as opposed to other scholarly and communal concerns. Throughout the medieval, renaissance, and enlightenment periods, scholars

---

7. Robert Seltzer, *Jewish People, Jewish Thought: The Jewish Experience in History* (New York: Macmillan Publishing Company, 1980), p. 354.

were continuously studying and adding to the corpus of the talmudic literature.

Between 1520 and 1523, the standard page of the Talmud and its pagination system, as it is known today with the Mishnah and Gemara sections of the Talmud in the middle of the page surrounded by Rashi and Tosafot commentaries, was published in Venice by Daniel Bomberg, a Christian. The work became known as the Bomberg edition and an excerpt, which includes our *sugya* (portion), appears below.

The formal "Talmud" (that material written circa between 425 C.E. and 600 C.E.) is in the center. Our *sugya* (portion) begins seven lines from the bottom. The side closest to the binding (the right-hand side) consists of the Rashi. On the outer edge the left-hand side is the Tosafot, a collection of commentaries by an academy of scholars who lived in northern France and Germany from the twelfth to fourteenth centuries. The pagination system of the Bomberg is the standard still used to this day for citation and format.

Varying editions appeared throughout the Middle Ages. Then, between 1880 to 1886, the "Widow" and the Brothers Romm of Vilna, Lithuania—known as the Jerusalem of Eastern Europe because of its commitment to Jewish piety and learning—published what has come to be known as the "Vilna Edition of the Talmud."[8] It has become the standard text used throughout the world for Talmud study.[9] The same excerpt is set forth below, and the reader will note the similarities between the Bomberg and the Vilna. Both place the Gemara in the middle of the page with the Rashi on the side closest to the binding (the column on the right), while the Tosafot is on the outer edge of the page (the left column closest to the Gemara).

---

8. The widow's deceased husband was one of the owners of the publishing company. When he passed away, she, along with his brothers, continued his work. The publishing company became known as the Widow and Brothers Romm Publishing Company.

9. For a detailed explanation of the layout of the Talmud page, see Steinsaltz, *The Talmud: A Reference Guide*, pp. 48–59.

Naturally, the Vilna edition added to the Bomberg. For example, some words or phrases have parentheses in the main text. They indicate that some sources suggest that a particular word or phrase be deleted or emended. Opposite the line, outside of the main text, the variant or source is cited. There is also the commentary of Rabbenu Hananel, who lived in North Africa in the eleventh century. His father was a student of the *Geonim* (see glossary), scholars who studied the Talmud and wrote responses to questions of *halakhah* in the academies of Babylonia, where the Talmud was first written, between 600 and 1000. Finally, there is a series of citations entitled עין משפט נר מצוה—*ein mishpat ner mitzvah* (literally, "The eyes of the law are the the light of the commandment"). Created after the Bomberg and incorporated into Vilna, this important contribution refers the reader to those works which codified the laws articulated in the Talmud. For a detailed explanation of the intricacies of the talmudic page, one should consult *The Steinsaltz Talmud, A Reference Guide.*

In 1920, Lazarus Goldschmidt undertook the translation of the Talmud into German. His work represents the first complete effort to render the entire Talmud into another language. Not only did he provide the Aramaic text on the same page, but he noted variants in manuscripts which differed from the Vilna edition. Below is the same excerpt that we began with:

תני

רבי חייא מנה לי בידך והלה אומר אין לך בידי
כלום והעדים מעידים ·אותו שיש לו חמשים זוז נותן
לו חמשים·זוז וישבע על השאר שלא תהא הודאת
פיו גדולה מהעדאת עדים מקל וחומר

	הכל + M 35	חיא — M 34	עיר — M 33
P 39	עבדי M 38	אמי — M 37	רי — M 36
	זוז. — M 41	אותו — M 40	האמנתיו

R. Hija lehrte: [Spricht jemand zu einem:] ich habe eine Mine bei dir, und er-
widert dieser: du hast nichts bei mir, und Zeugen bekunden, dass er bei ihm fünfzig
Zuz habe, so muss er ihm fünfzig Zuz' zahlen und wegen der übrigen schwören,
denn [durch einen Schluss] vom Leichteren auf das Schwerere ist zu entnehmen, dass
das eigne Geständnis nicht bedeutender sein dürfe als eine Bekundung von Zeugen.

25. Der ganze Betrag.   26: Wenn beide den Preis bezahlt haben (ob. S. 461 Z. 7) u. ihnen
weder der Gegenstand noch der gezahlte Preis ausgeliefert wird, so erleidet der Beträger wol einen Schaden-
27. Cf. Bd. vij S. 773 Z. 8 ff.   28. Der Krämer u. der Lohnarbeiter.   29. Wenn der Schuldner
einen Teil der Schuld leugnet u. einen Teil eingesteht, so muss er einen Eid leisten.

The first complete English translation of the Talmud appeared
in 1935, published by Soncino Press, and edited by Dr. I. Epstein.
In 1960, a project was undertaken by the same publisher and editor to incorporate into one volume both the English translation and
the standard Vilna edition of the Talmud. The format would consist of the following: On one entire page was an exact reproduc-
tion of a page of the Vilna edition of the Talmud. The opposite page
was the English translation. Edited by Dr. I. Epstein and appropriately titled "The Soncino Talmud," this work is a formal translation. Colloquialisms are avoided, and it tends to be literal. Included
below is a translation of the Talmud text cited above:

R. Hiyya taught: [If one says to another,] "You have in your possession [1] a hundred zuz [a form of currency] belonging to me,"
and the other replies, "I have nothing belonging to you," while witnesses testify that the defendant has fifty "zuz" belonging to the
plaintiff; the defendant pays the plaintiff fifty zuz, and takes an oath
regarding the remainder [2], for the admission of a defendant ought
not to be more effective than the evidence of witnesses [3]; a rule
which could be proved by a Kal wa-homer [4].

[1] I.e., on loan. [2] He swears that he does not owe the fifty zuz. The evidence of the witness places the defendant in the same position as his own admission of part of the claim would have done. Shebu. 39[b]. [3] If therefore the defendant's partial admission necessitates his taking an oath on the rest, the evidence of the witnesses regarding the partial debt should at least have a similar effect. [4] V. Glos.[10]

This achievement rendered the Talmud accessible to English scholars and students of this literature. However, one might experience difficulties in studying this text on several levels. While this is the most literal of available English translations, it does contain 156 words, compared to the 36 in the original Aramaic. Though the text is heavily footnoted in order that the translation be as literal as possible, the reader must continuously reorient him/herself. The issue of relevancy is not addressed in the text. Who is R. Hiyya? From one's own experience and background, the taking of an oath is commonplace and, with very few exceptions, no one is precluded from doing so. Thus, why is such a teaching important? Why does the text compare the law of "admissions" to those of "witnesses"? What is an *a fortiori* ("Kal wa-homer") inference? Without an adequate background in Talmud study, this work, while monumental and extraordinary, is not altogether helpful to those who lack formalized training.

This remained the only complete English translation of the Talmud until 1989. Before examining this new work, a necessary step must be provided. Beginning in 1967, a Rabbi from Israel, Adin Steinsaltz, wrote a Hebrew commentary to a volume of the Talmud. His "commentary" differed from its predecessors, for it incorporated the actual words of the text. The technical terminology was explained clearly, the flow of the argument set out in clear steps, and necessary biblical references cited. Thus, if one understood modern Hebrew, one could follow the Aramaic text. The same passage cited in the Soncino is set forth below. In the Steinsaltz

---

10. Isadore Epstein, ed., *Hebrew–English Edition of the Babylonian Talmud*, trans. Maurice Simon (London: Soncino Press, 1960).

Hebrew Commentary, the words of the Talmud appear in bold and
slightly larger type, while the Steinsaltz commentary is usually not
in bold and always slightly smaller in typeset.

בַּ‏ תָּנֵי רַבִּי חִיָּיא:, ''מָנֶה לִי בְּיָדְדָ'' וְהַלָּה אוֹמֵר: אֵין
לְךָ בְּיָדִי כְּלוּם. וְהָעֵדִים מְעִידִים אוֹתוֹ שֶׁיֵּשׁ לוֹ חֲמִשִּׁים
זוּז ← נוֹתֵן לוֹ חֲמִשִּׁים זוּז, וְיִשָּׁבַע עַל הַשְּׁאָר, שֶׁלֹּא
תְּהֵא הוֹדָאַת פִּיו גְּדוֹלָה מֵהַעֲדָאַת עֵדִים, מִקַּל וָחוֹמֶר.[11]

בַּ‏ תני [שנה] ר' חייא בברייתא:
הטוען לחבירו ''מנה (מאה דינרים) לי
בידד'', שלוית ממני ולא פרעת, והלה
הנתבע אומר: אין לך בידי כלום,
והעדים מעידים אותו שיש לו
חמישים זוז (דינרים) – נותן לו
חמישים זוז, כפי שהעידו העדים וישבע
על השאר שאכן לא לוה ממנו את
חמישים הזה הנותרים. והסברה לביסוס
דין זה – שלא תהא הודאת פיו
גדולה מהודאת עדים, מקל וחומר.
שהרי הלכה היא שאדם המודה במקצת
הטענה שטוענים כנגדו – חייב להשבע
על מה שלא הודה בו. וכאן שעדים
מעידים שהוא חייב במקצת הטענה קל
וחומר הוא שצריך להשבע.

Even without an understanding of modern Hebrew, one can readily
appreciate the work of Rabbi Steinsaltz. The Aramaic, set forth in
bold, is then translated and explained in the Hebrew counterpart
so that syntax, pronominal references, and the flow of text are
greatly improved. Moreover, the actual Aramaic text, which appears
in the center of the page, contains Hebrew vowels and punctuation, unlike the standard Vilna edition. Thus, even if one knows
only how to read Hebrew, but does not understand it or the Aramaic, nevertheless, he/she at least has access to it. Steinsaltz's
modern Hebrew translation marked, in the judgment of this author, the first time in the history of our people that this type of
translation and explanation had been undertaken. Because of the
painstaking nature of the work, only nineteen volumes have been
published to date.

Recognizing this accomplishment, Random House undertook
in 1989 to publish the English edition of the Steinsaltz Talmud.
The format sets forth the Aramaic text of the Talmud, which again
contains the vowels and punctuation marks to aid the reader. On

---

11. *Talmud Bavli*, vol. I of *Bava Metzia*; explained, translated, and punctuated by Rabbi Adin Steinsaltz (Jerusalem: Israel Institute for Talmudic Publications, 1980), p. 15.

the inside margin, there is a literal English translation of the text and below it, Rashi's commentary. On the outside margin is Rabbi Steinsaltz's translation and commentary, which continuously guides the reader through the text. Following the format of the Steinsaltz Hebrew Talmud, the English edition sets forth the literal translation in bold, with Steinsaltz's commentary set in normal type. Below is the same excerpt from the Talmud *Bava Metziah* that has been previously set forth above.

Rabbi Hiyya taught the following baraita: In a case where one person claims against another, **"You owe me a maneh** (equal in value to 100 dinarim or zuz), that you borrowed from me and have not repaid," **and the other person says: "I owe you nothing," and witnesses testify that** the defendant owes the claimant **50 zuz (half a maneh), he** must pay the claimant 50 zuz, in accordance with the testimony of the witnesses, **and take an oath regarding the rest** of the money, asserting that he did not borrow the other fifty zuzim from the claimant. The premise upon which this ruling is based, is **that** a defendant's **own admission** should not be more effective than the testimony of witnesses, and this ruling can be proved by a **kal vahomer** (*a fortiori*) **inference.** For the law is that if one person claims that another owes him a certain sum of money, and the defendant admits that he owes the plaintiff part of the sum, the defendant must take an oath that he does not owe the plaintiff any more money. If an oath is required in the case of a partial admission, then here, in Rabbi Hiyya's case, where witnesses testify that the defendant owes the plaintiff part of his claim, there is even more reason that the defendant should be required to take an oath regarding the rest of the claim![12]

One can easily appreciate the advancement in rendering accessible the talmudic literature to a broader audience. The English is less formal. The "flow" of the text is improved. In short, it is a remarkable work that makes the Talmud available to the modern Jew. This translation and explication contains 268 words, over seven times the number contained in the original text.

---

12. *The Talmud: The Steinsaltz Edition*, vol. I, *Tractate Bava Metzia: Commentary by Rabbi Adin Steinsaltz* (New York: Random House, 1989), pp. 23–24.

It is also important to note the recent publication by Mesorah Publications, Ltd. Beginning in 1992 under the general editorship of Rabbi Hersh Goldwurm, Mesorah undertook to publish an English translation of the Talmud. To date, eleven volumes are in print. The format combines features of both the Steinsaltz and the Soncino translations. As in the latter, one page sets forth the standard Vilna edition of the Talmud. Unlike the Steinsaltz, the Mesorah does not punctuate or vowel the text of the Talmud. One who is unfamiliar with Aramaic or can read Hebrew only with vowels would be unable to read the text accurately. On the opposite page, there is a corresponding English translation that is similar to the Steinsaltz in its format of citing a phrase of the Talmud in boldface and then translating and explicating it in regular type. At the bottom of the English page, there are footnotes that serve as an additional aid.

Each of these works is monumental. Never before has there been such an undertaking to render what was once an obscure text accessible to such a broad audience.

BUILDING ON THE STEINSALTZ
EDITION OF THE TALMUD

Nevertheless, there has never been, nor will there ever be, a definitive work on the Talmud. From the time of its inception, scholars have written commentaries on it. Before Rashi, there was the Alfasi, and before him the literature of the Geonim, the scholars who lived in Babylonia who compiled volumes of works entitled "שאילות ותשובות"—literally, "Questions and Answers" on topics of halakhic praxis. A generation after Rashi, there was Maimonides, who wrote the *Mishneh Torah*, a codification of the laws of the Talmud, and the Tosafot, scholars who lived in northern France. The latter wrote critically on Rashi's commentary and on the text itself, pointing out seemingly contradictory passages found in a different volume and then attempting to reconcile them. Dr. Ben Zion Wacholder, holder of the Solomon J. Freehof Chair of Talmudic Studies at the Hebrew Union College—Jewish Institute of

Religion, has characterized the work of the Tosafot as a "third Talmud."

This process of writing commentary has continued to our own time. On the basis of a history that began fifteen hundred years ago and continues to today, one can safely say that no work is definitive. Instead, one work builds onto another.

There are several reasons for this phenomenon. One is that the dialogue in the Talmud, though regarded as sacred, never claims that its pronouncements are definitive. Another is that its literary style is argumentative. An assertion is made and then generally followed by a challenge, which usually takes one of two forms. The first is that the assertion contradicts the established law or custom and therefore appears incorrect. The second is one of logic. The assertion is then reformulated or the challenge itself considered to be invalid. Thus, the literary style of the Talmud invites commentary and interaction.

From this perspective, certain aspects of the Steinsaltz edition may benefit from further elaboration in order to address both the problem of the "relevance" of such a text to modern Jewish life and that of understanding the dialogue in significant part as commentary on the Torah. In addition, one must acknowledge and respond sensitively to the needs of the untrained reader and her/his encounter with the Talmud, regardless of which edition is studied.

The modern reader, in studying this particular text, may require further clarification based on the following. First, the laws that are stated in this *sugya* (Aramaic for a section of Talmud) pertaining to partial admissions and witnesses are not fully explicated in terms of their derivation from and relationship to Scripture. The absence of citations of Scripture or Midrash in the Aramaic text suggests that its authors assumed its audience to be entirely familiar with the rules and their derivation. Thus, these rules, which claim to be from the Torah though they are not precisely stated there, need further explanations as a background to the study of the *sugya*.

Second, the hermeneutic rule of the *kal v'chomer* is not explained in general terms, nor is there amplification of its significance in early rabbinic literature (such as Midrash and Mishnah) as a tool for deriving Jewish law from Scripture. The Steinsaltz edition clarifies the rule. However, the reader would benefit further by understanding the theoretical nature of the hermeneutic rules, their importance to the rabbinic task of interpreting Scripture, and the method through which they may be refuted.

The philological nature of the works by Soncino, Steinsaltz, and Mesorah, by design, limits the opportunity to explore the significance of such talmudic phrases "the Tanna of our Mishnah taught along similar lines" and the nature of the "oath" as stated in Scripture and understood midrashically by the Sages in the development of the rabbinic literature. These terms, undefined in the Talmud, though clarified within the context of the commentaries, are not examined independently. The reader, if provided such a background, would be able to understand the deep theological and ethical concerns that are encoded in this small, yet important, passage.

None of the above issues should be construed to mean that this author views their work in any manner as "deficient." To the contrary, their accomplishments are what have made this work possible. Their goal, as well as that of such other luminaries as Jacob Neusner, is to render the entire Talmud accessible. The methodologies of the Soncino, Steinsaltz, and Mesorah editions, based on their mission of providing complete access to the entire Talmud (a work which comprises thirty-nine volumes) for the modern reader, cannot possibly be expected to address these areas of inquiry.

The aim of this work is narrow: To develop a methodology that would explore in depth the related antecedent and contemporaneous literatures—of Scripture, Mishnah, and Midrash—of a small portion of Talmud. The purpose is to elucidate the universal and religious values that are embedded in the text, yet not readily apparent to the modern reader.

ONE APPROACH TO FURTHER REMOVING THE BARRIERS: A METHODOLOGY TO INTEGRATE TORAH WITH TALMUD

These needs may be addressed by acknowledging the current gap that exists between the modern reader and the Bavli's intended audience—that is, rabbinic scholars and students. In order to develop an appreciation for the underlying religious significance and ethical tensions of a talmudic passage, this work proposes that the modern reader would benefit from the following:

First, a reader must understand the hierarchy of Jewish classical texts, which begin with Scripture and its midrashic explication and extends to the oral traditions embodied in the Mishnah, Baraitot, and the Tosefta.[13] Second, the relevant passages from these sources, which underpin the talmudic inquiry of a given passage, should be made explicit to the extent possible. Third, an analysis of the appropriate hermeneutical principles (rules of logic) that are employed by the talmudic passage either to justify or to reconcile the elements of its dialectic inquiry would prove helpful, just as one might set forth the basic axioms and corollaries in the study of higher mathematics.

When combined, these elements would form a *scriptural foundation* upon which a penetrating reading of a *sugya* would be made possible. This *scriptural foundation* could then be integrated into the talmudic discourse at the appropriate points in the dialectic inquiry. The result would deepen the level of understanding and appreciation of the Talmud as a source for religious, spiritual, and ethical guidance for modern Jewry—an outcome that could give the reader the experience of "learning" Gemara.

Thus, the principle task of this work is to integrate those literatures that are both contemporaneous to and antecedent to the talmudic discourse. Chapter 3 will focus on the meaning of Torah and its study from the traditional rabbinic perspective. It will explore the essence and purpose of Torah in the context of the Sinaitic revelation, developing a rabbinic "theory" of Torah, as it were, in order for the reader to approach the talmudic text from a similar framework. Chapter 4 will examine the approach of modern scholarship with regard to the historical development of Scripture, Midrash, and Mishnah from the postbiblical era, beginning with

---

13. A collection of additional halakhic teachings of the tannaitic period (not included in the Mishnah), which traditionalists and some modern scholars attribute to Rabbi Hiya and Rabbi Hoshayah (circa 225). See chapter 3 and glossary.

Ezra (circa 458 B.C.E.), up to the editing of the Bavli (circa 600). The reader will have both the rabbinic and historical perspectives from which to read a passage of Talmud.

Chapter 5 will discuss the theory of rabbinic hermeneutics in the development of Jewish law, with a specific concentration on those rules that are used in the development of the selected *sugya* of this work. The examples of how these rules operate will be taken directly from the talmudic passage selected for this work.

With the requisite theoretical and technical background, the reader is ready to encounter a selected portion from the Talmud *Bava Metziah*, specifically 3a through 4a, in chapter 6. A translation of both the Gemara and Rashi's commentary is provided. The *sugya* is set out in outline form in order to aid the reader in understanding the flow of the text. The Gemara text is delineated in **bold** typeface, with "the Rashi" set forth directly underneath it, in italics. Below the Rashi, my own comments appear in order to further explain the flow of the text and to isolate those issues that suggest that an investigation into scriptural, midrashic, and mishnaic sources would be helpful to a more penetrating understanding of the passage.

Having worked through a passage, chapter 7 examines these issues in their scriptural, midrashic, and mishnaic contexts. For example, one such item is that of the oath. This chapter will explore the scriptural and midrashic understanding of the oath and the role it is designed to play in society. The aim here is to build a *scriptural foundation* that would provide the reader with the requisite knowledge that talmudic learning takes for granted. Chapter 8 then integrates this foundation with the *sugya* from *Bava Metziah* at 3(a)–4(a).

The main purpose of this work is to give clarity to material that is difficult by stressing the underlying religious themes of the text. It is hoped that the reader will get a spark of the rabbinic struggle to discern the "divine will." The student of the tradition will discern that the methodology of the Talmud rejects both dogmatism and fundamentalism, on the one hand, and ethics that respond only to the exigencies of the moment, on the other. The study of its process and assumptions will illustrate that the

Talmud's principal concern is with the dynamic and tension-filled relationship between the divine standard and its imposition on a humanity which strives for perfection within the limitations of time and space.

This fact alone, that our Sages struggled with the conflict between the ethical dilemmas of the human condition and the need to fulfill the "divine teaching" of Torah, renders the study of Talmud a vital area of inquiry for our time. Let us begin our task.

3

The Development of Sacred Literature from the Rabbinic View

INTRODUCTION ON METHODOLOGY

There are two approaches to analyzing the literatures that comprise the building blocks of the Talmud. One is to examine the philosophical treatment of these genres from the rabbinic perspective. Studying the rabbinic literature that preceded and followed in the tradition of the Talmud Bavli produces a sharper and more detailed image of how the authors perceived their task and their world. In literary terms, this approach would be considered intertextual—in other words, seeing the Talmud within the context of related literatures.

This chapter is devoted to creating this contextual framework of the authors by focusing on three aspects. First, the writers of the Talmud Bavli considered the study of Torah to be above all other pursuits in that it leads to real knowledge of God, of the universe, and of life.

Second, the definition of "Torah" encompassed the Written Law, the Oral Law, and their amplification. The imperative of Sinai was for humanity not only to embrace the teachings of the Torah, but also to render the Torah viable in each generation. When it is made vital, Torah becomes both significant and relevant. This has remained the sacred task of each generation of Jews ever since Sinai.

Third, however, meaning and viability are acknowledged by the rabbinic tradition to exist within a continuum of time. Each succeeding generation preserved and enhanced the "meaning of Torah" such that a tradition of learning evolved over a period of at least a thousand years before the writing of the Talmud. (Historical scholarship considered the Pentateuch to have been completed by the time of Ezra's return to Israel in circa 428 B.C.E. The Bavli was written over a period from 427 to 600.) It is, therefore, necessary to explain the ingredients of this *shalshelet hakabbalah* (chain of tradition), for it provides the requisite authority for the rabbis in each era to explore the meaning of Torah and to amplify its significance in all aspects of human endeavor.

The other approach to an understanding of the Bavli is one of historical scholarship. This method is more fully treated in chapter 4. By way of introduction, it examines the sources the authors used in the writing of the Talmud from a historic perspective. These sources consist of the written Torah, Midrash, the Mishnah, Baraitot, and the Tosefta. Much of this work is highly theoretical, given the absence of solid, authenticating evidence. Nevertheless, it will serve as an aid in placing each of these prior sources within its respective historical context and will suggest the following: First, most modern scholars agree that the written Torah was completed by the time of Ezra (circa 428 B.C.E.). Second, the interpretation of the Torah was developed in succeeding generations through the literary genre known as Midrash. Third, an oral tradition, consisting of laws, customs, and practices developed during the post-biblical era (400 B.C.E. to 200 C.E.), was edited by Rabbi Judah HaNasi in 200 C.E. as a result of social, political, and religious exigencies. This work became known as the Mishnah. Finally, certain interpretations, customs, and practices were excluded from the Mishnah during the editing process. These were embodied in the Baraitot and the Tosefta and served as an additional tool to the understanding of both the Mishnah and the development of the talmudic dialectic.

THE RABBINIC UNDERSTANDING OF TORAH

Torah as Preexistent to Matter

A midrash teaches:

> The Torah declares: 'I was the working tool of the Holy One, blessed be He.' [The midrash continues] In human practice, when a mortal king builds a palace, he builds it not with his own skill, but with the skill of an architect. The architect, moreover, does not build it out of his head, but employs plans and diagrams to know how to arrange the chambers and the wicket doors.
>
> Thus God consulted the Torah and created the world, while the Torah declares, *In the beginning God created Heaven and Earth* (Gen. 1:1); *beginning* referring to the Torah, as in the verse, *The Lord made me [the Torah] as the beginning of His way* (Prov. 8:22).[1]

For our Sages, Torah pre-existed creation. It emanated from the wisdom of God, who then consulted with it to construct a perfect universe. This Torah, which served as a blueprint to God, was given to humanity at Sinai.[2] Through the study of the drawing, one could acquire knowledge of the mystery and purpose of the universe. It was a particular kind of undertaking, which sought to comprehend the plain and metaphysical meanings of the design. Through this process, two vital truths could be discerned. One was the divine intention for humanity, with a particular emphasis on Israel. Second, Torah comprised the essential truths of human nature, God, and the universe. Torah study could unlock this mystery of God and thereby render the creation of the universe an act of rationality. It thus became the religious act *par excellence*.

These concepts of divine intention and rationality find support in the following mishnah: "These are the things that have no

---

1. *Midrash Rabbah: Genesis Volume I*, trans. H. Freedman (New York: Soncino Press, 1983), p. 1.
2. Ibid.

measure: the four corners of the field, the bringing of the first fruits to the Holy Temple, righteous acts, and the study of Torah."[3, 4]

This beautiful paragraph has a design of its own, for it blends humanity with the divine. "The four corners of the field" is a reference to the *mitzvah* of leaving a portion of your sustenance for the poor and homeless. What constitutes a "corner" is determined by each owner of land. God commands us to care for one another. The bringing of the first fruits is an act that demonstrates on the human level the love for God by stressing spirituality as a priority over the material so that the use of the latter may be directed toward the former. Righteous acts are the creative expression of one's humanity and religiosity in the myriad of life's opportunities. And despite these wonderful imperatives which have no limitation—that is to say, they parallel the infinity of God and the universe—there is more to life than these forms of altruistic human enterprise. Humanity must also pursue an understanding of God through the study of Torah. Thus, study of Torah, righteousness, spirituality, and sensitivity to the plight of others are bound together.

When this line of thought is carried to its logical end, one could conclude that the ascetic life lends itself to an experience of God and is to be preferred to the material. But this mishnah has another paragraph, which gently returns humanity from its spiritual quest for fulfillment through Torah study to the world of human endeavor: "These are the things of which a person partakes of their fruit in this world while capital is stored for him in the world to come. Honoring one's parents, righteous acts, and bringing peace to humanity; but the study of Torah is the equivalent to them all."[5]

Rabbeinu Shimshon from Chartres, France, a thirteenth-century Tosafist, citing a Baraita passage from the Yerushalmi *Peah* found at 4(a), wrote the following commentary to the phrase, "but the study of the Torah is the equivalent to them all": "All of those things which you delight in are not equal in value to it [Torah]

---

3. *Mishnah Peah* 1:1.
4. Ibid.
5. Ibid.

(Proverbs 3:16) and all things that are admired [by people] are not equal to it [Torah]. These [things admired by people] are the precious stones and jewels [material]. But 'I (God) delight in these' [words of Torah] (Jeremiah 9:23)."[6, 7]

The divine intent and its execution in the real world are through the vessel of Torah. Thus, Torah is more valuable to humanity than any material object of desire, for it brings God into the real. But there is an exclusive metaphysical dimension to this comment in the Talmud Yerushalmi which exists separate and apart from the divine intention with regard to the physical. Humanity, through Torah study, temporarily removes itself from the material and enters the realm of God, the paramount reality. Just as God considers it a source of joy and delight, humanity may experience this spiritual vivacity through Torah. Torah study becomes a meeting place, a common ground for both humanity and God to interact.

This teaching is derived from a passage from the Book of Proverbs:

> Riches and honor belong to me [Torah], enduring wealth and success. My fruit is better than gold and my produce better than choice silver. I walk on the way of righteousness, on the paths of justice. I will endow those who love me with substance; I will fill their treasures. The Lord created me at the beginning of His course as the first of His works of old. . . . I was with Him as a confidant, a source of delight every day, rejoicing before Him at all times, rejoicing in His inhabited world, finding delight with mankind. (Proverbs 8:18, et. seq.).[8]

---

6. Ibid., 2b.

7. The full citation from the Jeremiah passage alluded to by Rabbi Shimshon (who is citing the Baraita in the Talmud *Yerushalmi Peah*) reads, "For I the Lord act with kindness, justice, and equity in the world; For in these I delight [*Tanakh*, p. 790.] The *p'shat* of the text appears to be that God delights in acts of kindness, justice, and equity. The *d'rash*, however, is that the word "these" refers to the words of Torah, based on the verb "delight," which also appears in Proverbs citation. Thus the verb and object "delighting in these," instead of being read as referring to the preceding qualities of kindness, justice, and equity, is understood by our Sages as referring to the Proverbs passage, which alludes to the Torah.

8. *Tanakh: The Holy Scriptures—The New JPS Translation According to the Traditional Hebrew Text* (Philadelphia: Jewish Publication Society, 1988), p. 1298.

Once again, spirituality as expressed through the teachings of Torah transcends the physical. Because Torah was there with God as
the blueprint for the creation of the universe, a confidant, a source
of delight for God, its treasures and substances are better than gold
or silver. However, this metaphysical world is not actualized
through the abstract temporal removal of self from the material.
On the contrary, the fulfillment of humanity's pursuit of spirituality is through involvement in the tangible because Torah exists for
the sake of a righteous and just world. It urges humanity to accept
it as the guide for the messianic fulfillment of creation.

This bond between Torah study and its function in civilization is inseparable. A mishnah from *Kiddushin* states: "Anyone who
is learned in Scripture, Mishnah, and human interaction will not
be quick to commit a transgression as it is stated: 'and a threefold
cord will not quickly be broken' (Ecclesiastes 4:12).[9] But all not
engaged in the [learning of] Scripture, Mishnah, or human interaction, are uncivilized."[10]

This mishnah stresses "learning" of divine law as foundational
to civilization. It precedes the human enterprise. One could con-
strue that this mishnah prefers the pursuit of knowledge as a virtue in and of itself. Indeed, many do pursue the metaphysical
through an ascetic lifestyle. The scholar who studies the divine
word endlessly may become indifferent to the realities of the
struggle for existence and fulfillment.

The Talmud, in its discussion of this mishnah, reacts to this tension between the acquisition of knowledge and human circumstance
in relation to the essence of Torah study. If the function of Torah is
to acquire knowledge of God's delight and desire, then knowledge
has priority over the human enterprise. However, if the Torah's primary purpose is to instruct humankind on how to live in the material world, then the existential takes precedence over the quest for
the divine in the abstract. The Gemara resolves this dilemma:

---

9. The "threefold cord" is Scripture, Mishnah, and human interaction.
(Scripture and Mishnah comprise a significant part of the Torah that was given
at Sinai.)

10. *Kiddushin* 40b.

It once happened that Rabbi Tarphon and the Elders of the community were dining at the house of Nithza's in Lydda when this question was asked of them. "Is the pursuit of knowledge greater than the pursuit of living?" Rabbi Tarphon responded, "Human enterprise is greater." Rabbi Akiva answered, "Learning is greater." All of them answered, "The acquisition of knowledge is greater because it enriches human action."[11]

The Talmud answers the dichotomy between knowledge and the pursuit of living by emphasizing the "this-world" application of Torah. Its study is not an esoteric exercise. Instead, contemplation of the divine will is a part of living. When all the rabbis responded "The acquisition of knowledge is greater because it enriches human action," the Gemara was emphasizing the synergistic relationship between the pursuit of living and Torah scholarship, for the latter leads to the ultimate fulfillment of humanity as the expression of the divine intention.

In summary, Torah pre-existed the creation of the universe. As such, its claim upon humankind should be of a higher priority than other human pursuits. Torah becomes the perfect lens which allows for the light of the divine imperative to be refracted onto life's stage. This light, observed through the lens of Torah, empowers a person to witness the divine in the world and thereby fulfill the joy of creation.

The Definition of Torah

The rabbinic definition of Torah embraces two elements. One may be termed "spiritual–material." The Written Law consisting of the Pentateuch and the Oral Law as embodied in the Mishnah, each given by God to Moses at Sinai, are real. We can see them, touch them, and read them. But there is an added dimension to Sinai. God explained the essences of these "Torahs" to Moses and at the same time made it an imperative for humanity to search for and to amplify these principles. In other words, humanity should use the written

---

11. Ibid.

words as a path that would lead to an encounter with the Divine. One could designate this component of Torah as "spiritual–God."

The Sinaitic event is the basis for the binding nature of Torah. It is axiomatic to the rabbis that the Written Torah was given at Sinai. But the Oral Torah is problematic for it seems speculative. Its existence is derived from the exegesis of scriptural passages as recorded in two works: the *Sifra* (a midrashic text on the Book of Leviticus) and the *Sifre* (a collection of *midrashim* on the Book of Deuteronomy), thought to be both compiled near the end of the third century.

The *Sifre* cites Deuteronomy 33:10 as its scriptural proof for the existence of this Oral Law that emanated from Sinai. יורו משפטיך ליעקב ותורתך לישראל ישימו קטורה באפך וכליל על-מזבחך: —"And they shall teach Jacob your laws and your Torahs [read by the Sifre as a plural] to Israel; and they shall put incense before your nostrils and the whole burnt-offering upon the altar."[12] The *Sifre* states: "'*And your Torahs to Israel*': To teach that two Torahs were given to Israel, one which was oral and the other which was written. Agnitum the Gamon asked Rabban Gamliel, 'How many Torahs were given to Israel?' He [Rabban Gamliel] replied, 'two, one written and the other oral.'"[13] The history of rabbinic literature has recognized the close, interdependent relationship between the Written and Oral Law. Both originated at Sinai. The proof for the existence of the latter is derived from the former. Thus, in response to the question by the world, represented by Agnitum the Gamon, as to what is Torah, Rabban Gamliel, the leading authority of the Jewish people living under Roman rule during the second half of the first century, answered with a definition that included both forms of revelation.

The *Sifra* expands the Sinaitic event to include God's amplification of the Torah through Midrash and, as a corollary, extends this activity as an imperative upon humanity. It makes this finding on the basis of Leviticus 26:46: אלא החקים והמשפטים והתורת אשר

---

12. The Hebrew ותורתך could be read as a plural, "your Torahs," or as a singular, "your Torah," because of the absence of the vowels.

13. *Sifre debe-rav*, p. 155.

"These are the laws,[14] rules, נתן ה" בינו ובין בני ישראל בהר סיני ביד-משה: and instructions [the word *torah* in the Hebrew text is in the plural—*hatorot*] that the Lord established, through Moses on Mt. Sinai, between Himself and the Israelite people."[15]

The *Sifra* then begins: "'These are the laws, rules, and instructions: The term 'these laws' refers to the *midrashim*. The rules refer to actual *dinim* [defined as laws that include the hermeneutical rules for the exegetical derivation of law].[16] And the term *hatorot* [since it is in the plural] teaches that two Torahs were given to Israel, one written and one oral."[17] Thus the meaning of Torah encompassed an understanding of law that went far beyond the written text. All the tools were given at Sinai to understand and fulfill the precepts of Torah on the human level. Midrash allowed for the continual expansion and derivation of the law in relation to the infinite wisdom of God. True understanding of both the Written and Oral Laws and their interdependent relationship requires knowledge of Midrash. But there was another component as well that enabled humanity to assist in the amplification of Torah—the hermeneutic rules for the derivation of divine law in the context of each era and social setting. These rules provided the methodology for two activities. One was to derive law that was considered implicit in the sacred texts. The other was to measure human law against the divine instruction of Torah. Thus, both the divine word and the methodology for its implementation in the world were all part of the Sinaitic event.

---

14. The term חוק may be translated as law, rule, custom; assigned share, or mark. The feminine form חקה may be defined as firmly established, distinctive usage, religious observance. In many contexts, this term is used to indicate a divine rule that has no reason (Marcus Jastrow, *Dictionary of the Targumum, Talmud Babli, Yerushalmi, and Midrashic Literature* [New York: The Judaica Press, Inc., 1985], p. 438). Thus, it might be considered a category of divine law that is to be observed solely on faith as a distinct sign of a people. In the context of this midrash from *Sifra*, it refer to those *midrashim* given by God at Sinai that derive *halakhah* (Jewish norms) from the Written Torah (*midrash halakhah*).

15. *Tanakh*, p. 200.

16. Jastrow, *Dictionary*, p. 301.

17. *Sifra Torat Kohanim*, p. 172.

You will recall that Torah was the opportunity to experience the rationality of the universe and the reality of God. The Talmud blends this concept as well into its definition of Torah.[18]

> Hezekiah states [that the term "learned"] means in *halakhot* [pl. of *halakhah*]. Rabbi Yochanan states [that to be "learned" means schooled] in Torah.[19]
>
> An objection is raised. Which is Mishnah? Rabbi Meier states it is *halakhot*. Rabbi Judah states it is Midrash.
>
> What is meant by Torah—the deep, penetrating study [that is, Midrash] of Torah.[20]

The talmudic dialectic is struggling to answer the question, what constitutes the true learning of Torah? It begins with a very simple understanding. If one knows the *halakhot*, the laws that were transmitted by God to Moses at Sinai, which includes both the Written and Oral, then such a person is regarded as "learned" within the Jewish community.[21, 22] Rabbi Hezekiah's construction accepts factual knowledge of the law as sufficient and would not require a theoretical understanding of its formulation. Rabbi Yochanan's answer is that one must be schooled simply in "Torah," though the term is not defined. It implies both the Written and Oral Torah, for in the next paragraph the Talmud seeks to determine the essence of the Mishnah.

---

18. The Gemara is analyzing a mishnah that provides for conditions that effectuate a betrothal. The general rule of the Mishnah is that if one makes a material false representation that induces consent, such betrothal is ineffective. The case in the Gemara regards a person who represents to a prospective bride that he is learned. The Gemara is evaluating the level of knowledge to which this term applies.

19. The brackets were added by this editor for syntactical purposes. A literal translation would omit the terms enclosed within them, thus confusing the reader.

20. *The Babylonian Talmud: Kiddushin*, trans. Rabbi Dr. H. Freedman, ed. Rabbi Dr. I. Epstein (New York: Traditional Press, n.d.), 49a.

21. *Kiddushin* 49a; see Rashi.

22. *Kiddushin* 48a; see Rashi.

In this regard, Rabbi Meier states that it is sufficient to know the *halakhot*—that is, to know the laws, regardless of their basis in Scripture. This position is consistent with Rabbi Yochanan's. However Rabbi Judah, the editor of the Mishnah, argues that the term "Midrash" includes both the written source from which the Oral Law is derived and the means of its derivation. Rashi's commentary clarifies Rabbi Judah's answer: "*Midrash*: This refers to the *Sifra* and *Sifre*, for they contain the laws that are derived from their biblical sources."[23] With this response, the Talmud deepens the idea of "learning" Torah as originally raised by Rabbi Yochanan. It is to comprehend the interdependent relationship between the Oral and Written Law. The former is the derivation of the latter, and thus "learning" Torah is more than mere recitation of its laws. "Learning" is to apprehend the Oral and Written as an undivided whole, rather than separate and distinct.

This process is analogous to the baking of a cake. One can understand the separate ingredients; the sugar, flour, and eggs. But the purpose is to make a cake through the combination of the various ingredients, which are then combined to make the whole. Learning is the understanding of the whole and how each unit operates to create it.

The Talmud, by answering the question, "What is Torah?" as "Midrash Torah," suggests that true learning is a transcendent process. Torah requires the deep penetrating study and elaboration of the sacred texts. The human intellect is capable of grasping Torah as the ultimate divine expression of the rationality of the universe and the purpose of human existence. By defining Torah as "Midrash Torah," the Talmud urges us to explore the Torah in order to uncover these truths and to expound them. The "real" Torah is not only the literal reading of the text. Instead, it exists in the spiritual and metaphysical dimensions, through metaphor and homiletic analysis. The Torah can thus be revealed only through serious study.

Though he lived five hundred years after the final redaction of the Talmud, Moses Maimonides (1135–1204), in his *Introduc-*

---

23. *Kiddushin* 49a. Rashi on תורה.

tion to the Mishneh Torah, incorporates this understanding of Torah by stressing that Sinai required humanity to vivify the Torah in all of its diverse aspects through this *mitzvah* of amplification.[24]

> All the commandments and their explanations were given to Moses at Mount Sinai, for it is said: "And I [God] will give to you the tablets of stone [the Decalogue], the Torah and the *mitzvah*" (Exodus 24:12). The "Torah" is the written law [the Pentateuch]. The term *mitzvah* refers to its explication. And He [God] commanded us to adhere to the law according to the *mitzvah*—that is, interpretation. And this *mitzvah* is referred to as the Oral Law.[25]

This *mitzvah* of interpretation upon which Maimonides centers the Sinaitic revelation consists of two concepts. The first is intellectual engagement with the text. Commandments require interpretation within the context and framework of a community. But there is an added dimension. The Oral Law must be understood as being entwined with Scripture. It is a unique form of pentateuchal expression and hence an expansion of the written text. Thus, the principal theme that runs through the event at Sinai was the duty to understand and to amplify the Written and Oral Traditions and to see both as an undivided entity.[26]

In summary, there exists an inner dynamic within Torah that includes both divine and human aspects. This vibrancy is reflected in the duty both to explore deeply and to amplify its teachings through the midrashic and interpretive enterprises. True knowledge of Torah implicitly accepts the Oral Torah as interdependent with Scripture. Yet, the literary genre of Midrash is devoted to providing coherency to both traditions which radiated from Sinai. When coupled with the human imperative of amplification asked

---

24. Moses Maimonides lived centuries after the talmudic period. As he is a scholar of this genre, however, his description of the sinaitic event is useful to the rabbinic understanding of revelation.

25. Moses Maimonides, *Mishneh Torah*, p. 3.

26. Maimonides may be including *midrash halakhah* as well in the term *mitzvah*. This is evidenced by the use of the Hebrew word פרושׁיה.

by the Talmud, it addresses the question מאי תורה—"What is the meaning of Torah?"

The Chain of Tradition: The Oral Law and Its Embodiment in the Mishnah

There is an inherent difficulty with the authenticity and accuracy of the Oral Law as redacted in the Mishnah. One could argue that it was not transmitted at Sinai, but instead arose subsequent to this seminal event. Even if it is assumed it to be a part of revelation, the claim of accuracy of its oral transmission over a millennia is legitmately subject to skepticism.

The Talmud *Avot* addresses this second concern by providing a historic chain through which each succeeding generation from the time of Moses to Rabbi Yochanan ben Zakkai and his disciples (70 C.E. to 100 C.E.) received the Oral Law that had originated at Sinai.

Moses received the Torah from Sinai and passed the tradition to Joshua, who then transmitted it to the elders. From the elders, [it was transmitted] to the prophets. The prophets then passed it on to the men of the Great Assembly . . . the last survivor of whom was Shimon the Righteous [1:1]. . . . Antigonous, leader of Socho, received the tradition from Shimon the Righteous [1:2]. . . . Yose ben Yoezer (200 B.C.E.), leader of Tzredah, and Yose ben Yochanan, leader of Jerusalem, accepted the tradition from him [1:3]. . . . Yehoshua ben Perachyah and Nittai of Arbel received the tradition from them [Yose ben Yoezer and Yose ben Yochanan] [1:6]. . . . Yehudah ben Tabbai and Shimon ben Shatach received the tradition from them [1:7]. . . . Shemayah and Avtalyon accepted the tradition from them [Yehudah ben Tabbai and Shimon ben Shatach] [1:10]. . . . Hillel and Shammai learned the tradition from them [1:12]. . . . Rabbi Yochanan ben Zakkai accepted the tradition from Hillel and Shammai [2:8]. Rabbi Yochanan ben Zakkai had five disciples. They were Eliezer ben Hyrkanos, Rabbi Yehoshua ben Chanania, Rabbi Yose the Kohen, Rabbi Shimon ben Nesanel, and Rabbi Elazar ben Arach.[27]

---

27. *Avot* 3b–7b.

The chain of tradition recorded in these chapters established the authentic nature of the Oral Law over generations of time beginning at Sinai. It records a teaching by Rabban Gamliel, the grandson of Hillel, who lived shortly before the Second Temple was destroyed. In chapter 2 of *Avot*, Rabbi Judah HaNasi, the redactor of the Oral Law, is described as a descendent of Hillel and the great grandson of Rabban Gamliel.[28] This שלשלת הקבלה (*shalshelet hakabbalah*—"chain of tradition") is grounded principally on learning and accepting the oral teaching from one's predecessor. Thus lineage is an added dimension that strengthens the authenticity of the transmission of the Oral Law from Sinai to the time of its editor, Rabbi Judah HaNasi.

The Embodiment of the Oral Law into the Mishnah

The rabbinic perspective on the history of the redaction of the Oral Torah into the Mishnah is reflected in two sources. One is the famous letter by Sherira HaGaon to the Kairouan Jewish community. The other is by Maimonides, who addressed this topic in the Introduction of his *Mishneh Torah*.

In 987 C.E., Sherira HaGaon, the head of the Babylonian academy, received a letter of inquiry from the Jewish community of Kairouan. One of the questions raised was the gulf between Torah and Mishnah. Another was the process through which the Mishnah became a written document. This inspired him to respond in depth. His answer to these inquiries was that prior to the redaction of the Mishnah, there was no homogenous formulation of the *halakhah*. Concerned that the teaching might be lost, "Rabbi" (the traditional reference to Rabbi Judah HaNasi) took up the project of redacting the Oral Torah. Sherira HaGaon regarded the anonymous teachings (those Mishnahs which simply state the law as opposed to those that contain such lanaguage as "Shammai stated" or "accord-

---

28. For a detailed analysis of the historical data of these figures, see Hermann L. Strack and Gunter Stemberger, *Introduction to the Talmud and Midrash*, trans. Markus Bockmuehl (Minneapolis: Fortress Press, 1992), pp. 69–91.

ing to the words of the Hillel") in the Mishnah to be those of Rabbi Meier, whose rulings were based on those of Rabbi Akiva, who, in turn, received the tradition from his teachers.[29] The necessity for redaction grew out of the conflict between the disciples of Hillel and Shammai over the *halakhah*, which had to be resolved out of the concern for uniformity, particularly in the post-Temple era.[30]

In the introduction to his classic work the *Mishneh Torah*, Maimonides asserts that the primary concern that led to the redaction of the Oral Torah was the fear of its being lost because of changing social and political circumstances. Up to the time of Rabbi Judah HaNasi, the Oral Torah was not written down. Each scholar, however, would write private notes from which the *halakhah* was taught. These notes, consisting in part of hermeneutical rules for the derivation of Oral Law from Scripture, provided the nexus between the Written and Oral Torahs. Concerned that these teachings would be lost, Rabbi Judah HaNasi redacted this tradition and taught the rabbis in public. Maimonides regarded this step as a revolutionary one necessitated by the decrease in the number of students in the rabbinic academies of Palestine, external pressures, and persecutions that resulted in the Jewish Diaspora. Unlike Sherira HaGaon, who attributed the redaction to rabbinic conflicts in the understanding and interpretation of the Oral Torah, Maimonides argued that changes in the Jewish social and political situations necessitated this radical innovation.[31]

In conclusion, the redaction of the Oral Torah by Rabbi Judah HaNasi was justified by the rabbinic communities on two different bases. One was that the continued accuracy of transmission from Sinai to the tannaitic period of Rabbi Judah HaNasi (200 C.E.) was threatened by internal disputes over its meaning. The

---

29. Rabbi Meier was the disciple of Rabbi Akiva. Akiva belongs to the second generation of Tannaim (circa 90–130), whereas Rabbi Meier's prominence began in the third generation of Tannaim (circa 130–160.) Strack and Stemberger, *Introduction*, pp. 79–84.

30. Ibid., p. 139.

31. Moses Maimonides, *Commentary on Pirkey Avoth*, trans. Paul Forcheimer (Jerusalem: Feldheim Publishers, 1974), p. 18.

Mishnah's authenticity rested upon demonstrating that each generation from the time of Moses through the post–Second Temple era had received the Oral Law and had understood its meaning and application. Both Sherira HaGaon and Maimonides acknowledge the conflicts that would invariably arise because of the inherent difficulties of learning law only through oral instruction. Nevertheless, through such literary works as *The Talmud: Mesekhet Avot* and *Seder Tanaaim v'Amoraim*, a detailed chain of authority is established to the satisfaction of the rabbinic community of the tannaitic period, which addresses the problem of inheriting a verbal tradition of at least fifteen hundred years.

The second concern was to justify the necessity for the redaction of the Mishnah in 200 C.E. Here is where the two scholars depart. For Sherira Gaon, the need for reducing it to writing arose from the conflicts that begin to appear from the time of Hillel and Shammai as to what was in fact the law. The need for clarity as to the rules and regulations of a community is a precondition for its continued existence.

Maimonides, however, argues that the Oral Torah was in danger of being altogether lost because of the drastic changes in the Jewish political and social structure that followed the destruction of the Second Temple, resulting in increased persecution and dispersion of the Jewish people. The Jewish people became physically fragmented from one another and needed a cohesive element to retain their identity as a people. These factors compelled the editors to redact the Oral Law of Sinai to writing, and this work became known as the Mishnah.

SUMMARY

Torah study, in the rabbinic tradition, is a meeting ground between God and humanity. If humankind desires to know that which God "delights in" and thus effectuate the latter's design for the universe in the everyday world of human existence, then Torah study is imperative. Four aspects of Torah were given at Sinai. The texts to be studied are comprised of both the Written Law (as embodied in Five

Books of Moses—the Pentateuch) and the Oral Law (as stated in the Mishnah). It includes Midrash, the deep penetrating study of the Torah, which allows the student to enter into the realm of spirituality and metaphysics and serves to reveal the "true" intent of God. It facilitates the awareness that the Written and Oral Torahs are one holistic work. The rules of hermeneutics—that is, the methodology for deriving the divine law through logic and reason—were also given at Sinai. Finally, and perhaps most important, the *mitzvah* to amplify the Torah in each succeeding generation, which would bring forward earlier teachings into the present, was told by God to Moses at Sinai. This, in significant part, was the framework from which the authors of the Talmud perceived their task.

4

The Historical Approach: Towards an Understanding of the Contemporary and Antecedent Literary Genres of the Talmud: Scripture, Midrash, Mishnah, Tosefta, and Baraitot

The historical method is principally concerned with fixing a period for the redaction of the literary antecedents that form the foundation of the Talmud Bavli and with analyzing their structures. These works include Scripture, Midrash, Mishnah, Tosefta, and Baraitot. In this section, we will provide an overview of their development and nature according to scholars engaged in these enterprises.

SCRIPTURE

The term "Scripture" is defined as the Pentateuch—that is, the Five Books of Moses—and includes the Books of the Prophets and Writings (for example, Ecclesiastes, Chronicles). It is the core of the biblical canon for all Jews. During the early Persian period (538

B.C.E. to 428 B.C.E.), a book referred to as the "Torah of Moses" emerged from the Jewish community. While arguably the product of generations of writings, editorial activity ceased at the time of Ezra (circa 428 B.C.E.).[1] When the Jewish people were allowed to return to Israel from their exile in Babylonia in the year 458 B.C.E., Ezra was charged with the task of reconstituting the Jewish community of Israel. Described as a scribal expert in the teaching of the law of Moses, Ezra was given the title "scribe of the law of the God of heaven" (Ezra 7:12).[2] Within the framework of the political stability provided by Nehemiah, who was appointed by Cyrus of Persia to oversee the return to Israel of the Jewish people from their exile in Babylonia, Ezra's task was to make Torah the organizing principle of the Jewish community during the early Second Temple period (428 B.C.E. to 70 C.E.).[3]

A reference is made in the Book of Nehemiah to a document that historians consider to be the "Torah scroll."

When the seventh month arrived, the entire people assembled as one man in the square . . . and they asked Ezra the scribe to bring the scroll of the Teaching of Moses with which the Lord had charged Israel. On the first day of the seventh month, Ezra the priest brought the Teaching before the congregation. . . . He read from it . . . from the first light until midday, to the men and the women and those who could understand; the ears of all the people were given to the scroll of the Teaching. . . . Ezra opened the scroll in the sight of all the people . . . ; as he opened it, all the people stood up. Ezra blessed the Lord, the great God, and all the people answered, "Amen, Amen," with hands upraised. . . . [Certain ministering officials] and the Levites explained the Teaching to the people, while the people stood in their places. They read from the scroll of the Teaching of

---

1. Shaye J. D. Cohen, *From the Maccabees to the Mishnah* (Philadelphia: Westminster Press, 1987), p. 183.

2. There is much debate over the exact time Ezra returned. The range is from 458 B.C.E. to 398 B.C.E. John Bright, in *A History of Israel*, 3d ed. (Philadelphia: Westminster Press, 1981), suggests 428 B.C.E., which corresponds to the rule of Nehemiah, p. 379.

3. Bright, *A History of Israel*, p. 390.

God, translating it and giving the sense; so they [the nation] understood the reading (Nehemiah 8:1–8).[4]

Such noted scholars as Julius Wellhausen, W. F. Albright, and John Bright believe it probable that the completed Pentateuch was in Ezra's possession and that, through his efforts, it became the core document through which faith and practice would be centered during the Second Temple period.[5, 6, 7]

Ezra's reading of the scroll is regarded by many as a watershed in the history of the Jewish people. Robert M. Seltzer writes, "Many modern historians feel that it was at this moment when the Torah book, the Pentateuch in close to its final form, became the unchallenged norm of Israel's religion and when Judaism took its single most important step to becoming a religion of Scripture, indeed, the first scriptural religion."[8] The Talmud's description of the importance of Ezra's work parallels the significance that historians have attributed to the completion of the Written Torah by the time of Ezra.

It is taught in a baraita: Rabbi Yose said that it was fitting that Ezra transmitted the Torah to Israel, for Moses foreshadowed him. Scripture states "and Moses went up to God" (Exodus 18). The Book of Ezra provides "and Ezra went up from Babylonia" (Ezra 7). What was brought up? Just as Scripture refers in the [Exodus] passage to Torah, here also [in Ezra] the verse alludes to Torah.

[There is another parallel between Moses and Ezra]. With regard to Moses, Scripture states, "and the Lord commanded me to teach you the *hukim* [laws which have no apparent rationale— for example, the law of the red heifer] and the *mishpatim* [those statutes which human reason can comprehend—for example, treating the poor fairly] (Deuteronomy 4). With regard to Ezra, the Bible

---

4. *Tanakh*, p. 1519.

5. Bright, *A History of Israel*, p. 390.

6. Julius Wellhausen, *Geschichte Israels* (Berlin: G. Reimer, 1878), p. 421.

7. W. F. Albright, *The Biblical Period from Abraham to Ezra* (New York: Harper Torchbook, 1963), p. 94f.

8. Seltzer, *Jewish People, Jewish Thought*, p. 130.

states that Ezra had prepared his heart to *drash* [to explore deeply, to investigate] the Torah of God and to do and teach Israel its *hok* [singular of *hukim*] and *mishpat* [singular of *mishpatim*].[9]

This passage from the Talmud *Sanhedrin* establishes the centrality of Scripture for the Jewish people at the time of Ezra by comparing his teaching to the Revelation at Sinai. Ezra brought the same Torah when he went up to Israel from Babylonia that Moses had received when he ascended Sinai. Furthermore, Ezra is compared to Moses as the appropriate lawgiver. This allusion to Moses is particularly significant in light of one of the concluding verses of the Written Torah, "Never again did there arise in Israel a prophet like Moses whom the Lord singled out face-to-face."[10]

The Baraita, while not equating Ezra to Moses, nevertheless draws an analogy between the rabbinic task of studying and teaching and the prophecy of Moses. Ezra, according to the Talmud, prepares himself in the rabbinic tradition of intense study in order to teach the divine will as expressed in the written Torah. The Hebrew term *lidrosh* (the infinitive of *drash*, that is, to explore deeply, to investigate), ascribed to Ezra, connects his task to Sinai and thereby lays a foundation for further amplification of Scripture in the Second Temple era through a new literary genre, Midrash.[11]

Thus, both the historical and rabbinic approaches acknowledge the importance of the Pentateuch as the central document through which subsequent generations of Jews would define their community and their sense of historic mission. It is for these reasons that the Pentateuch plays the foundational role in the construction of all subsequent rabbinic literature, including the talmudic dialectic.

---

9. *Sanhedrin* 21b. The terms *hukim, mishpatim,* and *drash* are not defined in the passage, nor does Rashi comment on them. According to the *Sifra* passage, *hukim* referred to *midrash halakhah*, whereas *mishpatim* referred to the rules of hermeneutics.

10. *Tanakh*, p. 334.

11. See *Sanhedrin* at 22a for the problem of transmission from Moses to Ezra.

MIDRASH

The statement in the Baraita that Ezra prepared himself through study to teach the divine word of Torah corresponds with the view of many historians that the Jews of the Second Temple period (428 B.C.E. through 70 C.E.) saw themselves living in an era in which God no longer spoke to them directly. With a written text, the creative spirit was directed towards its explication and produced new literary forms.[12]

One such genre is Midrash. The term is derived from the verb *drash*, which is actually found in the Ezra passage quoted above (7:10). It refers to the study of God's law. Midrash, then, may be seen as a type of literature, oral or written, that stands in direct relationship to a fixed canonical text and is considered to be the authoritative and revealed word of God.[13] Jacob Z. Lauterbach, in his classic work, *Mekilta de-Rabbi Ishmael* (a translation of a collection of third-century *midrashim*), defines Midrash as follows: "[the] study of the Torah, requiring a thorough investigation of its contents, a correct interpretation of the meaning of its words and a deeper penetration into the spirit and sense of its dicta with all their implications, is designated by the term *Midrash* or in its fuller form *Midrash Torah*."[14]

Since the entire Torah was considered to be the word of God, every word, phrase, and sentence contained divine wisdom and instruction. Lauterbach theorizes that the legal segments of the Pentateuch may have been pursued more because of the need for normative standards to guide the Jews of the Second Temple period. The study of the legal portions of the Torah was referred to as *midrash halakhah*.[15]

---

12. Cohen, *From the Maccabees to the Mishnah*, pp. 193–194.
13. Strack and Stemberger, *Introduction*, p. 255.
14. *Mekilta de-Rabbi Ishmael*, trans. Jacob Z. Lauterbach, vol. 1 (Philadelphia: The Jewish Publication Society, 1933), p. xv.
15. Ibid.

Origin and Development of *Midrash Halakhah*

The law embodied in the Pentateuch was generally looked upon as the rule of Israel's life during the Second Temple period. However, with this Written Law (the *torah sh'bichtav*) there developed an Oral Law (the *torah sh'baal peh*). This latter consisted of religious and national customs that underwent permutations and revisions based on changing times and circumstances. The authority for such changes rested in the *sophrim* (scribes such as Ezra) and the *Sanhedrin*, the authorized religious and legal court of Israel during this time.[16]

Moses Mielziner, in his work *Introduction to the Talmud*, advances the theory that *midrash halakhah* developed as a Pharisaic response to the challenge of the Sadducees during the Second Temple period. The latter, a minority religious sect, believed that any law not founded on the Written Torah should be rejected.[17] This view presented a serious challenge to the Pharisees, who had adopted and developed the Oral Law without an express connection to the Pentateuch. Because of the Sadducean threat, some historians theorize that the Pharisees developed this literary genre to demonstrate the Oral Law as implicit in Scripture.

David Weisse Halivni, in his work *Midrash, Mishnah, and Gemara*, disputes Mielziner's account, which presupposes an Oral Law's having developed without reference to Scripture. Instead, he argues that Midrash grew out of the natural biblical predilection for justified law. The Pentateuch in most instances will assert a reason or basis for its pronouncements. For example, Exodus 22:20 states, "And a stranger shalt thou not wrong, neither shalt thou oppress him; for ye were strangers in the land of Egypt."[18] Under this statute, the phrase "and a stranger shalt thou not wrong, neither shalt thou oppress him" is apodictic. Up to this point, no reason is given for the rule. The clause "for ye were strangers in the

---

16. Moses Mielziner, *An Introduction to the Talmud* (New York: Bloch Publishing Company, 1968), pp. 120–121.

17. Ibid., p. 121.

18. *Tanakh*, p. 119.

land of Egypt" is vindicatory. The rationale for treating the stranger justly is Israel's historical experience as a people who were once oppressed. Halivni concludes, on the basis of countless such expressions found in the Bible, that an essential aspect of the Jewish experience from the commencement of the Second Temple period in 428 B.C.E. up to the mishnaic period (70 C.E. to 200 C.E.) was this tendency toward justified law. Midrash was a literary form that allowed this core value to be creatively expressed.[19]

In support of Halivni, midrashic exegesis of earlier scriptural texts are already contained within the Bible (for example, Chronicles is considered by many to be a midrashic work on the books of Samuel and Kings).[20] Halivni contends that Midrash already existed in the second century B.C.E. and thus precedes the mishnaic form. He bases this assertion on *realia* from this period, which reflect conditions that correspond to descriptions in later-redacted midrashic literature and *mishnayot*. The Temple Scroll, which also dates from this period, supports the conclusion that proto-rabbinic *drashot* existed by this period.[21] Thus, an extended prehistory of the Midrash before the rabbinic period (100 B.C.E. through 427 C.E.) cannot be denied, given the above and the existence of such documents as the Targum (an early Aramaic translation of Scripture with midrashic overtones) and the Pesher texts of the Dead Sea Scrolls.[22]

Nature of Midrash

As mentioned above, the Pentateuch may be artificially divided into two areas. One is narrative. The Book of Genesis is a good illustration, for it essentially recounts creation and the patriarchal development of Judaism through the migration into Egypt. *Midrashim* that creatively enhance the Biblical narrative are referred to as *midrash aggadah*.

---

19. David Weiss Halivni, *Midrash, Mishnah, and Gemara: The Jewish Predilection for Justified Law* (Cambridge: Harvard University Press, 1986), p. 4.
20. Strack, and Stemberger, *Introduction*, p. 257.
21. Halivni, *Midrash, Mishnah, and Gemara*, p. 34.
22. Strack and Stemberger, *Introduction*, p. 258.

The other area of midrashic activity concerns the legal portions of the Pentateuch and is referred to as *midrash halakhah*. We are principally concerned with the development of this form, since the talmudic portion of this book (chapters 6 and 7) focuses on the imposition of toraitic and rabbinic oaths.

Midrash halakhah is technically defined as exegetical *midrashim* on the legal portions of the Pentateuch from Exodus through Deuteronomy.[23] Modern scholarship characterizes *midrash halakhah* as fundamentally concerned with deriving or basing law on a scriptural passage.[24, 25] This description is supported by its redacted structure, in which a phrase or a verse is first cited and then followed by its explication.[26]

Halivni divides *midreshei halakhah* (plural for *midrash halakhah*) into two distinct forms, simple and complex. When nothing beyond the text is necessary to obtain the *drashah* (the understanding of the text), the result is a simple *midrash*. In contrast, where a specific hermeneutic device is required (such as a *kal v'chomer*— that is, an *a fortiori* inference—or *gezerah sheva*, a verbal analogy) (see chapter 5), then it is a complex *midrash*. Hillel (30 B.C.E.—20 C.E.) is considered to have developed these analytical tools to derive law from Scripture or to provide scriptural support for an already existing practice. Simple *midrash* preceded complex *midrash*.[27]

Though generally Mishnah does not cite Scripture as support for its law, there are such references in a minority of *mishnayot* (plural for Mishnah). This form, which Halivni terms *mishnaic midrash*, begins with a law and then proceeds to the scriptural verse that supports it. It is recognized by the formula "as it says [in Scripture]." In contrast, *midreshei halakhah* is characterized by such phrases as "it comes to teach" or "it declares."[28] Simple Midrash

23. Ibid., p. 269.

24. *Encyclopaedia Judaica*, s.v. "*Midreshei Halakhah*" (Jerusalem: Keter Publishing House, 1972).

25. Compare to the rabbinic view, which sees *midrash halakhah* as part of the Sinaitic event.

26. *Mekilta De-Rabbi Ishmael*, trans. Lauterbach, 1:xv.

27. Halivni, *Midrash, Mishnah, and Gemara*, p. 34.

28. Ibid.

may be either mishnaic or *midreshei halakhah* and is believed to have existed as early as the second century B.C.E.

Modern scholars have examined the redacted halakhic *midrashim* collected in four major works: *Mekilta of Rabbi Ishmael* on Exodus, *Sifra* on Leviticus, *Sifre* on Numbers, and *Sifre* on Deuteronomy. D. Hoffman has divided these works of *midrash halakhah* into type A and type B. Type A *midrashim* consists of the *Mekilta* and the *Sifre* on Numbers. Type B is comprised of the *Sifra* on Leviticus and the *Sifre* on Deuteronomy. Type A is thought to have originated in the school of Rabbi Ishmael, a rabbi from the tanaitic period—(circa 90–130 C.E.). These works are characterized by extensive use of hermeneutical rules and principles. These *midrashim* are quoted in both Talmuds in the name of Rabbi Ishmael. Third, the tannaitic authority often cited in these works was a known pupil of Rabbi Ishmael (130–160).

Type B *midrashim* are thought to have been developed by the school of Rabbi Akiva (90–130). They are characterized by the use of other rules attributed to Akiva, such as "general to detail" and "detail to general" and "inclusive–exclusive" (see chapter 5).[29]

In practical terms however, one should not regard the demarcation between Akiva and Ishmael as factual. Instead, as Albeck suggests, the differences between these two groups of *midrashim* are actually the work of later redactors who were familiar with both schools. Each of these works included a good deal of material of the other. Thus, as Strack concludes, the nomenclature is purely pragmatic and not historic.[30]

Both types were foundational in the development of the Talmud. The reader will recall that the *sugya* is concerned with determining whether the defendant, after completely denying the plaintiff's claim and then being confronted by witnesses testifying conclusively that he owes part of it, should be permitted to take an oath on the disputed remainder.[31] The dialectic emerges in part

---

29. *Encyclopaedia Judaica*, p. 1522.
30. Strack and Stemberger, *Introduction*, p. 272.
31. The reader may refer to chapter 1, which details the talmudic passage on which this book will focus.

because of two scriptural passages and their midrashic explication. The rule of law that allows the defendant to testify concerning a disputed remainder where the defendant *confesses* to a portion of the plaintiff's claim, is based on the *Mekilta's* (type A Midrash) explication of a scriptural passage. However, the rule that prohibits a defendant from testifying concerning any portion of a claim established by the testimony of witnesses is derived from the *Sifre* on Deuteronomy (type B Midrash). There does appear a certain equivalency between the two concepts in that both an admission and the testimony of two witnesses are conclusive as to the substantive issue to which each pertains. In the former, the plaintiff is permitted to testify concerning the remainder. Since there is a remainder in the Baraita, one could argue that the defendant there be allowed to take an oath as well. We will see, however, that each rule is based on certain assumptions which the dialectic will analyze in determining whether the defendant in the Baraita be permitted to take an oath. The point here is that the dialectic emerges in significant part because the two *midrashim* are analyzing different scriptural passages which, when appropriately applied to the Baraita, yields contrasting results.

  I have provided a general overview as to the dating and nature of Midrash as it developed initially from the post-biblical period up to the tannaitic period. The *midrashim* that comprise the most significant components of this work are taken from three sources: *Mekilta de Rabbi Ishmael, Sifra* on Leviticus, and the *Sifre* on Deuteronomy. The next three sections are devoted to a specific examination as to the redactional history and nature of these works.

Mekilta de-Rabbi Ishmael

The term *mekilta* is an Aramaic word that signifies the derivation of *halakhah* from Scripture according to certain rules. Specifically, the *Mekilta* is a commentary on Exodus 12, 23:19; 31:12–17; and 35:1–3. Its principal concerns are the legal narratives of the second book of the Pentateuch.[32]

---

32. Strack and Stemberger, *Introduction*, pp. 275–276.

During the Roman occupation, Rabbi Ishmael (circa. 110–135) was made a captive and brought to Rome, where he was later redeemed. Upon his return to Palestine, he became a member of the *Sanhedrin*. He is credited with having expanded the seven hermeneutical rules of Hillel to thirteen (see chapter 5).[33] The incorporation of these rules into the daily liturgy of the traditional prayer book supports the theory that the study of *midrash halakhah* is part of "torah study," and thus constitutes a religious act.[34]

Jacob Lauterbach and Jacob Neusner both believe the work to have been edited between 135 and 150 C.E. Indeed, Lauterbach considers it to be the oldest tannaitic exposition. The *Mekilta* reflects the point of view of the older *halakhah*, though it underwent considerable changes.[35] Some of the material contained is from the school of Rabbi Akiva. The rabbis who are cited in it, the form of the individual traditions, and the historical allusions suggest a final compilation in the second half of the third century.[36]

Sifra

This work is also known as the *Torat Kohanim* (the law of the priests). The style is generally more argumentative than that of the *Mekilta* and its essential parts are ascribed to Rabbi Yehudah bar Ilai (135 C.E. to 170 C.E.), a disciple of Rabbi Akiva.[37] This midrashic collection originated in the middle of the second century, but additions were made later by Abba Areca (also known as Rav; 220 C.E. to 250 C.E.) and is therefore called *Siphra debe Rav*.[38]

This attribution is subject to debate among both traditional and modern scholars. Maimonides, in his introduction to the *Mishneh Torah*, states that Rav (a first generation Amora who

---

33. Mielziner, *Introduction to the Talmud*, p. 29.
34. *Siddur Rinnat Yisrael: Ashkenaz Diaspora Version*, ed. and annotated by Shlomo Tal (Jerusalem: Moreshet Publishing Company, 1982), pp. 38–39.
35. *Mekilta de-Rabbi Ishmael*, trans. Lauterbach, 1:23.
36. Strack and Stemberger, *Introduction*, p. 279.
37. *Sanhedrin*, 86a.
38. Mielziner, *Introduction to the Talmud*, p. 19.

learned in Palestine, but then emigrated to Babylonia where he established a school in Sura) composed the *Sifra* and *Sifre* in order to explain and make known "the foundations of the Mishnah." The modern scholar A. Weiss also supports this view that Rav was the author of the work.[39]

The challenge to this theory stems from the fact that Rav often appears unaware of or even contradicts the solution of a problem found in the *Sifra*. For these reasons, D. Hoffman and Albeck regard Rabbi Hiya (the author of the Baraita cited in our passage, who lived during the transition period between the Tannaim and Amoraim, 200 C.E. to 220 C.E.) to be its author. However, H. Strack considers that the work was originally authored by Rabbi Yehudah, but that its final redactor was Rabbi Hiya. While this may be an oversimplification, its numerous literary references to the Mishnah do provide a factual basis that the work may have been originally authored by Rabbi Yehudah HaNasi.[40]

The *Sifra's* emphasis on connecting Mishnah to Scripture—unlike that of the *Mekilta*, which emphasized the derivation of *halakhah* from Scripture—is commented on by Jacob Neusner.

> The pronounced tendency of the *Sifra* is to insist that the Mishnah's laws—commonly cited verbatim—not only derive from Scripture . . . but can only derive from Scripture and cannot be based upon reason. *Sifra* turns out to be a massive, integrated, and coherent critique of the Mishnah, insisting that the Mishnah's laws are true only because the Mishnah's laws derive from the written Torah. . . . *Sifra's* polemic is pointed and explicit.[41]

Neusner's literary analysis of the *Sifra* suggests that its authors recognized the potential challenge to the Mishnah due to its absence of scriptural references. Unlike the *Mekilta*, which is explicit in deriving *halakhah* from Scripture, the *Sifra* is a work that attempts

---

39. Strack and Stemberger, *Introduction*, p. 286.

40. Ibid., p. 287.

41. Jacob Neusner, "Method and Substance in the History of Judaic Ideas, an Exercise," in *Jews, Greeks, and Christians*, ed. R. Hamerton-Kelly and R. Scroggs (Leiden: Brill, 1976), p. 94.

to provide the foundational support of the Pentateuch for the Mishnah. Thus, each work recognizes the central importance that *halakhah*, whether embodied in a *Midrash* or *Mishnah*, must be at a minimum congruent with Scripture.

Sifre

The *Sifre* comprises traditional interpretations consisting of the Books of Numbers and Deuteronomy. Its contents and structure are the exegetical midrashim on Deuteronomy 1:1–30; 3:23–29; 6:4–9; 11:10–26; 31:14–32; and 34.[42] The *Sifre* on Deuteronomy is generally brief and in this regard bears a resemblance to the *Mekilta*.[43]

There appears to be a difference of opinion regarding its attribution. In one section of the Talmud, the work is ascribed to Rabbi Simon b. Jochai, a disciple of Rabbi Akiva. However, at *Sanhedrin* 86(a), the anonymous portions of the *Sifre* are attributed to Rabbi Simeon, a Shammaite. On this basis, the noted scholar Louis Finkelstein argues that this work was later emended by Akiva to reflect the opinions of Hillel. In its present form, it appears to be a combination of both A and B types of *midrashim*, though most scholars assign it to the type B category.[44] The final redaction is considered to have been completed in the late third century.[45]

The rule pertaining to the conclusiveness of the testimony of witnesses, one of the major issues involved in the Talmud's discussion (see chapter 6) is taken from the *Sifre*.

MISHNAH

According to Rabbi Adin Steinsaltz, the Talmud's essential task is the explication and expansion of the Mishnah. It accepts the Mishnah as incontrovertible.[46] The term *Mishnah* designates the

---

42. Strack and Stemberger, *Introduction*, p. 295.
43. Mielziner, *Introduction to the Talmud*, p. 20.
44. Strack and Stemberger, *Introduction*, p. 296.
45. Ibid., p. 297.
46. Steinsaltz, *The Talmud: A Reference Guide*, p. 3.

"Oral Law" as compiled by Rabbi Judah HaNasi and his colleagues circa 200 C.E.

The structure of the Talmud supports Steinsaltz's analysis. Each section of Talmud begins with a Mishnah, followed by a section called the Gemara (literally, "the finishing"). The Gemara discusses the meaning of the key phrases. A mishnah could be analogized to a statute in American law and the Gemara to the interpretation and implementation of the law in various contexts, including a homiletical or metaphoric use. Often, the Gemara will use the Mishnah in an associative manner, discussing a teaching that is only tangentially related to the Mishnah. Nonetheless, the Mishnah provides the basis for the discussion of each *sugya* of the Talmud. For this reason, a detailed discussion is necessary in order for the reader to understand its seminal role in the development of the halakhic process.

In this section, four elements will be considered: (1) the etymology of the term *Mishnah* and its structure; (2) the historical setting that gave rise to the necessity for its redaction; (3) the Mishnah's claim of authority; (4) its nature and relationship to both Scripture and Midrash.

Mishnah Defined

The term *Mishnah* is defined in two contrasting fashions that have implications in terms of its level of authoritativeness within rabbinic literature. Some consider it to be the feminine form of the Hebrew word *mishnah*, meaning second in rank. Under this definition, the Oral Law as reflected in the Mishnah would take a second position to the Written law contained in the Pentateuch. Others consider it to be derived from the Hebrew verb *shanah*, meaning to transmit or teach orally. According to Mielziner, *Mishnah* may be defined as the instruction in the traditional oral teaching in contrast to the term *mikra*, which refers to the laws of the Bible. This reflects a view of Mishnah as independent and thus on an equal footing with its written counterpart.[47]

---

47. Mielziner, *Introduction to the Talmud*, pp. 6–7.

H. L. Strack defines the Hebrew verb *shanah* in a more technical sense. It refers to "repetition" in the sense of learning or teaching of the oral tradition by repeated recitation. It also means "to study."[48] Mishnah is thus given both an analytic and a memorization component. It is analytic in that it stands as an independent source of law. Its structure, however, is designed to facilitate oral transmission.

Historical Setting

Two important events provided the impetus for the redaction of the Mishnah. The first was the destruction of the Second Temple in 70 c.e. The other was the failed Bar Kochba rebellion against the Roman Empire in 135 c.e. In a span of seventy years, Jerusalem suffered devastation. Hundreds of thousands of Jews were killed or enslaved and their property confiscated by the Romans. The country was renamed from Judea (which meant "land of the Jews") to Palestine ("land of the Philistines").[49]

The breakdown of national and religious structures after the destruction, coupled with official restrictions and economic hardships imposed by Roman authority, made life for the Jew one of near despair. Nevertheless, the first post-Temple academy was founded at Yavneh by Rabbi Yochanan ben Zakkai. There, he was authorized by Rome to "teach his pupils" and to "perform the commandments." He reinstituted the Sanhedrin and announced the New Moons and leap years. His religious approach laid a foundation for generations of Jews to follow. One was the elevation of memory to a sacred act by recalling, through ritual, Jerusalem during the Second Temple period. The other was to provide ways of adapting to new circumstances by discarding Temple practices that interfered with the course of a new Jewish life.[50]

---

48. Strack and Stemberger, *Introduction*, p. 123.

49. Cohen, *From the Maccabees to the Mishnah*, p. 215.

50. Shmuel Safrai, "The Era of the Mishnah and Talmud," in *A History of the Jewish People*, ed. H. H. Ben-Sasson, trans. George Weidenfeld and Nicolson Ltd. (Cambridge, MA: Harvard University Press, 1976), p. 320.

Near the end of Rabbi Yochanan's life, the academy was run by Rabban Gamliel, who enjoyed the widespread support of the Jews in both Israel and the Diaspora and of the authorities in Rome. Roman toleration was evidenced by the fact that Rabban Gamliel was given the title and political office of Nasi. The Nasi was the central political office of Palestinian Jewry after the fall of Jerusalem. Its power increased substantially from the second to the end of the fourth century. Through this office, Rabban Gamliel unified the religious leadership and attracted many of the leading Tannaim of the period, including Rabbi Akiva, to study at Yavneh.

These developments led to the development of a *halakhah* that appeared more definitive than in the Temple period. The necessity for uniformity, given the social and political climate of Roman rule, led the rabbinic leadership to establish the rulings of Hillel as the authority for *halakhah*. This was a significant development because of the continuing debates between the schools of Hillel and Shammai, on the majority of religious practices.[51]

After the devastating loss to the Romans in the Bar Kochba revolt (135 C.E.), the center for Jewish learning and leadership shifted to the Galilee. Rabbi Meier became one of the leading authorities following the martyrdom of Rabbi Akiva and was the teacher of Rabbi Judah HaNasi. Because Rabbi Judah was the grandson of the Nasi (Rabban Simeon ben Gamliel), and the great-grandson of Rabban Gamliel, he possessed a strong background in the varying trends of this oral tradition and of the political and social climate of the Jewish people living both in Israel and in the Diaspora. Thus, he was eminently qualified to edit the redaction of this anthology of Jewish law.[52]

The historical factors that influenced the redaction of the Oral Law may be summarized as follows. The political climate of Roman rule, coupled with the social instability of Jewish life in Israel, made the continuity of rabbinic scholarship difficult. It became onerous to maintain this tradition of oral transmission, and confusion over both its meaning and application resulted. The

---

51. Ibid., p. 324.
52. Ibid., p. 341.

advantages of reducing this tradition to writing would be to protect and preserve it in light of an increasingly unstable and hostile political climate. It would simplify its transmission because no longer would memorization be a prerequisite to its study and usage. Preservation and accessibility to this tradition were paramount. For these reasons, scholars such as David Halivni, David Kraemer, and Jacob Neusner assert that the predominant literary form of the Mishnah, essentially apodictic without an explicit foundational basis in Scripture, was dictated in significant part by the social conditions of the era.

The Nature of the Mishnah

The Mishnah in its present form could not have been the sole work of its redactor, Rabbi Judah HaNasi. Numerous additions were made over time, and there are teachers mentioned who lived after Rabbi Judah HaNasi. Thus, the term "redactor" must be broadly understood to mean that Rabbi Judah HaNasi was the main figure under whose authority the Mishnah essentially took shape.[53]

While the express purpose of the Mishnah is the written redaction of the Oral Law, it often records minority opinions and cites majority opinions with which its editor disagrees.[54] Thus, its essential nature becomes an issue. There are three divergent views in this regard.

Albeck considers the Mishnah an academic exercise. Its purpose was not to organize halakhic decisions for "practical applications." Instead, Albeck assumes that the redactor made no changes or cuts in the material before him, but wrote the Mishnah in the form in which he had received it.[55] This would correspond to the notion of transmission from Sinai and the necessity for its preservation in the most pristine form possible. Intelligibility and readability were not its principal concerns. Instead, the preservation of God's word as expressed at Sinai was its organizing principle.

---

53. Strack and Stemberger, *Introduction*, pp. 149–150.
54. *Eruvin* 38b.
55. Strack and Stemberger, *Introduction*, p. 151.

The most widespread view, as expressed by J. N. Epstein, is that the Mishnah is a legal canon in which the anonymous decisions respectively represent the current state of halakhic understanding. Rabbi Judah edited the existing *halakhot* and combined various sources, but preferred the majority opinion to his own. Thus, the Mishnah was created through consensus. This would account for Rabbi Judah's divergent opinion, which is sometimes cited in either the Mishnah or the Talmud. It also renders it more plausible to regard the Mishnah as a group project, consistent with the established academies in the Galilee and Yavneh, with Rabbi Judah HaNasi as the overseer of the work. Furthermore, the Mishnah does not show any evidence of a personal style. There is evidence that the Amoraim (the rabbis who lived in the period which followed the Tannaim, circa 250–427) regarded the Mishnah as an internally consistent legal code.[56]

The Mishnah is regarded by some as a collection of sources that included laws that were no longer valid (for example, the laws pertaining to purification and Temple ritual). Its being such a collection would account for the internal contradictions and anonymous decisions that would, by necessity, diverge from the Rabbi Judah's view.[57]

As to its style, the essential difference between Mishnah and Midrash is the Mishnah's lack of explicit citation to Scripture. It is on this basis many scholars conclude that the Mishnah is self-authoritative. The Mishnah had, as its first priority, to provide the essential basic definitions of the early rabbinic community. To this end, the Mishnah created a crisis because in response to change, it never justified its response. For this reason, Jacob Neusner considers this form to be inherently lacking.[58]

A selection from a mishnah of our *sugya* illustrates this feature:

> Two men are holding onto a garment. This one claims "I found it" and the other claims "I found it." This one claims "all of it is

---

56. Ibid., p. 152.
57. Ibid., p. 154.
58. Kraemer, *Mind of the Talmud*, p. 117.

mine" and the other claims "all of it is mine." This one swears that he owns less than a one-half interest in it and the other one swears that he does not own less than a one-half interest in it and they divide it.[59]

Several items illustrate the varying views that describe the nature of this work. First, there is no citation to any scriptural passage. Second, the terseness and abbreviated nature of the language is evidence that the work may have been the subject of memorization and then oral transmission. Certain terms that would render the work more intelligible without resort to commentary would include the contextual setting. Under what circumstances did the men come upon the garment? Where is the claim being presented (presumably in a rabbinic court)? The text itself does not make explicit the nature of the oath (what is the formula for swearing), nor does it state the precise manner in which the garment is to be divided. Is the item to be cut in half or sold and then the proceeds divided? For these reasons, many scholars argue that the style suggests a work that was subject to memorization and intended for a select audience because it omits important elements that would be known only to a limited community, such as rabbinic scholars.

An example of minority opinions recorded in a *mishnah* cited in the *sugya* of our Gemara:

. . . One witness said, he ate [of the forbidden fat pertaining to an offering]. And he responds, I did not eat [of it]. He is exempt [from bringing a guilt-offering]. Two said [presumably witnesses], he ate [of the forbidden fat]. And he replied: "I did not eat [of it]." Rabbi Meier would obligate him [to bring an offering]. Rabbi Meier stated: "If two [witnesses, through their testimony] have the power to impose the stringent penalty of death [in an appropriate case], how much the more so should they [through their testimony in this case] compel him to undertake the less stringent penalty of an offering?" They [the Sages] responded [to R. Meier in an effort to refute his rationale], what if he wishes to state: "I did it deliberately."[60]

---

59. *Bava Metziah*, 2b.
60. *Bava Metziah*, 3b.

[Comment: The response by the sages is rhetorical. The defendant could state, "I ate the fat deliberately." If so, then he is exempt from the guilt-offering since such an offering in the Temple, before God, requires sincerity on the part of the one who sacrifices. Thus, the defendant, by saying I did not eat of the fat, is believed, for there is nothing gained by swearing falsely.]

Once again, the terseness of the style is illustrated by the number of parenthetical expressions added by the author of this book in order to facilitate the reader's basic understanding of the text. The important statement by the Sages, "what if he did it deliberately," which ends this *mishnah*, presumes the reader to know that the sin-offering requires an admission before God of guilt. The theory that the Mishnah was essentially an oral tradition that contained mnemonic devices to facilitate memorization is illustrated by this abbreviated literary style.

However, this *mishnah* points to two additional features of Rabbi Judah's enterprise. First, the minority opinion of Rabbi Meier is recorded. Explicitly, the Mishnah acknowledges a conflict in the transmission process such that there is, at least in some instances, a debate as to what the law actually is. Rabbi Meier states that the defendant is obligated to bring an offering when two witnesses testify against him. On the other hand, the Sages state he is not liable for such an offering, at least where he states in response that he committed the transgression deliberately. Finally, Rabbi Meier derives his ruling based on a hermeneutic principle of *kal v'chomer*, an *a fortiori* inference. Unlike the first *mishnah*, the ruling of Rabbi Meier is vindicatory (that is, based on the reasoning of an *a fortiori* inference).[61] If the power of testimony can compel a court to invoke the death penalty, then how much the more so should the testimony of two witnesses be sufficient to compel the defendant to bring a guilt-offering. The majority dispute Rabbi Meier's reasoning by stating, what if he responded that he did it deliberately. Albeck comments: "'I did it deliberately':—He would be exempt

---

61. For a more thorough treatment of the hermeneutic rule of *kal v'chomer*, see chapter 3.

from bringing an offering. And since he would be able to exempt himself from this type of claim [by saying he did it deliberately], even when he says 'I ate it' [despite the testimony of two witnesses who deny that he ate the fat[62]], he is believed."[63]

This *mishnah* is an example of those type of *mishnayot* (plural for *mishnah*) which attempt to justify their opinion either through Scripture, reason, or other *mishnayot* that are analogous to them. It would fit the category of a complex *mishnaic midrash* because of its use of a hermeneutical principle, in this case a *kal v'chomer*. Furthermore, knowledge of Scripture is a prerequisite to the understanding of this *mishnah*, since the former details the nature of guilt-offerings and the circumstances under which they are required. Thus, the opinion represented by many scholars, such as Dr. Ben Zion Wacholder and Dr. Eugene Mihaly of the Hebrew Union College—Jewish Institute of Religion, that Scripture is implicit in Mishnah (one could argue, even explicit in this case) is evidenced by this illustration.

EVIDENCE THAT THE MISHNAH WAS AN EDITED VERSION OF THE ORAL LAW

Throughout the sections that follow, on the Tosefta and the Baraitot, it has been assumed that the Mishnah is a redacted work. The term "redacted" carries with it the notion that certain parts of the original work may not have been included. The origin of these works and their intended purpose is the subject of much scholarly research, though no definitive conclusions may be drawn.

Tosefta

Literally, the term *tosefta* means "addition" or "supplement," in the sense of an additional halakhic teaching that relates to the

---

62. The testimony of two witnesses under toraitic law renders the matter conclusive.

63. *The Mishnah: Seder Kodashim,* commentary by Hanoch Albeck (Tel Aviv: Dvir Publishing House, 1988), p. 254. Translation of comment by Albeck provided by author.

Mishnah.[64] According to Mielziner, it consists of earlier compila-
tions of *halakhah* made by Rabbi Akiva, Rabbi Meier, and Rabbi
Nehemiah which, for whatever the reason, were not included in
the Mishnah. It also includes additions by one of Rabbi Judah
HaNasi's disciples, such as Rabbi Hiya.[65]

Strack asserts that the common features between the Tosefta
and Mishnah indicate that the works were contemporaneous, with
a final redaction occurring in the late third or fourth century in
Palestine.[66]

The Tosefta was considered of inferior authority and thus non-
halakhic by the final editors of the Mishnah. This view has been
maintained throughout subsequent generations of rabbinic scholars. Alfasi, an eleventh-century Spanish codifier of talmudic law,
holds to this opinion as well.[67]

Baraitot

As previously discussed, a baraita is a law extraneous to the
Mishnah. It is distinguished in the Talmud by the phrase *tanyah*
and is subordinate to the *mishnah* to which it is often juxtaposed.
Often, these Baraitot seem to conflict with either other Baraitot or
the authorized Mishnah.[68] The task of the authors of the Talmud
in many instances is to harmonize Baraitot with the *mishnah* it is
discussing. Because of the fragmentary nature of these statements,
the dating of their origin by scholars is considered speculative.

SUMMARY

The historical approach recognizes the inherent difficulty in deriving
an accurate dating of the sources that comprise the Talmud. Clearly,

---

64. Strack and Stemberger, *Introduction*, p. 168.
65. Mielziner, *Introduction to the Talmud*, p. 17.
66. Strack and Stemberger, *Introduction*, p. 176.
67. Ibid., p. 175.
68. Mielziner, *Introduction to the Talmud*, pp. 20–21.

such approaches cannot substantiate the rabbinic claim of Sinaitic authority for either the Written or Oral Law. However, certain tentative conclusions may be drawn. First, the return of the Jews from the first exile in 458 B.C.E. was accompanied by the adoption of the Mosaic Law. This Written Law became the central document through which the postbiblical Jewish society in Israel would define itself.

Second, accompanying the return of the Written Law, two new literary genres arose. One was Midrash, which addressed the necessity to explicate the Pentateuchal Law. But certain laws or customs, some of which may have predated the return from exile, were independent of Scripture or, at best, made no attempt to justify their authority through a written text. This form became known as the Mishnah. Halivni suggests that Midrash predated the mishnaic form because of the Jewish predilection for justified law as evidenced in the written Torah, while other scholars remain uncommitted. In any event, most agree that the redaction of these midrashim was completed by the middle to the end of the third century. However, both historians and traditionalists would concur that the Mishnah was redacted in 200 C.E. under the supervision of Rabbi Judah HaNasi. Both groups would further submit that exigent social and political circumstances necessitated the shift in the mode of transmission from a verbal to a documentary form.

Regardless of the approach, the Talmud's antecedent sources consist of Scripture, Mishnah, Midrash, Baraitot, and Tosefta. These form the building blocks of the talmudic dialectic that is the methodology for discerning the divine will. Given the authoritativeness of Scripture in the rabbinic model and the theory of unity between it and the Oral Law, knowledge of the former, which would include its midrashic explication, would be a prerequisite toward an understanding of the Talmud's treatment of a *mishnah*. Thus, in order to understand the rabbinic treatment of the legal narratives of Scripture, one must possess the knowledge of the methodology they utilized to derive *halakhah* from it and/or to provide a scriptural underpinning to the mishnaic enterprise. With this in mind, we now turn our attention to one of the basic methodological features of this process, the rules of hermeneutics that establish the parameters of these endeavors.

5

The Hermeneutics
of the Talmud

INTRODUCTION

Our task now is to examine the rules of logic upon which the Torah is expounded. These rules constitute the modes through which both the Midrash and the Talmud speak. Through these *midot* (principles of interpretations; literally, measures) laws are derived and talmudic arguments formulated, thus preventing capricious explanations of the biblical text. These rules are technical and require a level of mastery in order to appreciate the Gemara. In rabbinic Hebrew, these rules are referred to as המדות שהתורה נדרשת בהן, "the principles through which the Torah is expounded."[1]

    Three sets of hermeneutic rules are attributed to different sources. The first was ascribed to Hillel (30 B.C.E.–20 C.E.) and consisted of seven rules.[2] Rabbi Ishmael (circa 120) expanded these rules to thirteen.[3] Since Torah study was considered a religious act, Rabbi Ishmael's principles of hermeneutics became part of the tra-

---

1. *Sifra*, p. 3.
2. *Tosefta Sanhedrin*, Zuckermandel edition, pp. 7–11.
3. *Sifra*, pp. 3–6.

ditional daily liturgy beginning in the ninth century. Finally, Rabbi Eliezer ben Yose the Galilean (circa 170) expounded thirty-two such rules, which included those developed by Hillel and Ishmael.[4] The latter are chiefly aggadic and their redaction is considered to be post-talmudic.[5]

Four of the thirteen rules of Rabbi Ishmael apply here. Each of these rules is utilized in either the *sugya* (chapter 6) and/or the midrashic sources contained in the scriptural foundation (chapter 7). These rules are:

1. **Kal V'Chomer** (קל וחומר): an argument from a minor premise (*kal*) to a major premise (*homer*). It is commonly referred to as an *a fortiori* inference.
2. **Binyan Av Mishnei Ketuvim** (בנין אב משני כתובים): a construction—בנין—of a scriptural passage or rule drawn from two separate sources, which then serves as an underpinning upon which a third ruling will be based.
3. **Gezera Shavah** (גזרה שוה): a comparison of similar expressions: If the same word occurs in two Pentateuchal passages, then its construction and usage in one should be applied to the other.
4. **K'lal u'phrat ukhlal i attah dan ella ke-ein ha-perat** (כלל ופרט וכלל אי אתה דן כעין הפרט): Literally, it means "general, particular, general—you can only rule like that of the particular." Where a general rule is first stated, then followed by a series of specific illustrations, concluding with a restatement of the general, then the general rule may be applied only to an item that shares the common characteristic of the specific articles contained in the passage.[6]

---

4. Strack and Stemberger, *Introduction*, pp. 19–25; Aryeh Carmell, *Aiding Talmud Study*, 5th ed. (Jerusalem: Feldheim Publishers, 1988), p. 89 (attached appendix titled "Order of the Tannaim and Amoraim").

5. *Encyclopaedia Judaica*, pp. 367–368.

6. Ibid., pp. 368–369.

ORIGIN AND DEVELOPMENT

The earliest mention of hermeneutical rules is a baraita cited in the introduction to the *Sifra*.[7] However, the Talmud *Pesachim* (which treats the subject of Passover) and the *Tosefta Sanhedrin* (concerned with judicial topics) record incidences in which only three of these rules are attributed to Hillel.[8] These were not actually invented by Hillel but constituted a collation of the main types of argumentation used during the early tannaitic period (10 C.E.–90 C.E.).

The Sadducees, a Jewish sect that existed during the Second Temple period, rejected this "science" of Biblical hermeneutics. Instead, they preferred a more literal construction of Scripture. Judah Hadasi, an eleventh-century Karaite author,[9] argued that these principles of logic were borrowed from Hellenistic sources and therefore an inappropriate mode for deriving law from Scripture.[10] However, from a historical perspective, there does not appear to be a direct adoption of these rules from the Greek world, even though there may be some correlation between Hellenistic and rabbinic rules of logical construction.[11]

These rules, though difficult to understand, serve an important function. They provide a common ground upon which to interpret Scripture and thereby fulfill the commandment to explore, to discover, and to amplify the various layers of the divine plan.

---

7. *Sifra*, p. 3.

8. *Pesachim* 66a. The Talmud relates an incident involving Hillel's explication of the rule that permits the slaughtering of the paschal offering on Shabbat. He derives this rule through one of the principles known as a *gezarah shava*, a verbal analogy. (See topic heading "*gezerah shava*" in this chapter.) The Tosefta states that two additional rules are ascribed to Hillel. These are the *kal v'chomer*, an argument from analogy, and *heqesh*, an argument of equivalency pertaining to two topics and not utilized in the *sugya*.

9. The Karaites were a religious sect that began in the middle of the eighth century. Like the Sadducees, whom they considered their predecessors, they rejected the pharisaic claim of the "Oral Torah." See Seltzer, *Jewish People, Jewish Thought*, p. 341.

10. *Encyclopaedia Judaica*, p. 367.

11. Strack and Stemberger, *Introduction*, p. 20.

Without an agreed-upon methodology, the scholarly communities of the tannaitic, amoraic, and saboraic periods (100 B.C.E. to 600 C.E.), could not have developed *halakhah* in an orderly and discernable fashion. The Bible would have become the written equivalent of the biblical phrase *tohu vavohu* (darkness and void, used to describe the moment immediately after the creation of earth) for it would be relativistic instead of seeking the universal through a disciplined study. Arguably, divine insight into earthly affairs would be left to mysticism. The hermeneutic rules of construction, while justified through Scripture, are a uniquely human invention, a function of human rationalism.

KAL V'CHOMER (KV): AN A FORTIORI INFERENCE

A KV is a type of analogy usually formulated as a syllogism. The Hebrew word *kal* means "light in weight." From a legal point of view, the *kal* portion of the syllogism is regarded as being less significant. The word *chomer* means heavy and connotes a matter of great weight or importance.

The rationale of the KV rests on the assumption that laws operate in proportion to the seriousness of the case. In matters that reflect underlying values considered less significant to the community, a lenient rule is applied. However, where the act under consideration is regarded as a greater threat to society, at a minimum the same penalty should apply, though usually a greater stringency will be invoked. For example, assume two persons A and C. A *accidentally* strikes B and causes B harm. C *intentionally* strikes D in precisely the same manner in which A struck B, causing D the identical injuries that B suffered. Even though their acts are identical, we would expect A to be treated more leniently under the law than C because the latter's act was intentional. In talmudic language, the KV might be phrased as follows: "A, who accidentally struck B, suffered the penalty of having to pay damages in the amount of one hundred dollars, then how much the more so should C, who intentionally struck D, pay at least one hundred dollars." C receives, at the minimum, the same penalty as A, but more likely will suffer a harsher penalty because the severity of the law increases in relation to acts that increase the danger to a community. This rationale underlies the KV, with one modification. If a legal stringency is applied to a matter of minor importance (the *kal*), then in a related matter of major import (*chomer*), at the minimum, the same penalty should apply. The rule operates in reverse as well. If the law is lenient in a significant matter, then one may conclude the same leniency at a minimum will apply in a similar case that is of lesser importance.[12]

An Illustration of the KV from Scripture: the Story of Miriam

A story is told in the Book of Numbers in which Aaron and his sister Miriam speak against Moses to the Israelites because the latter had married a Cushite woman. Their argument is a pretext to challenge Moses' leadership: "Has the Lord spoken only through Moses? Has He not spoken through us as well?" (Numbers 12:2).[13] God became enraged, as it were, at this outburst and suddenly appeared as a pillar of cloud at the Tent of Meeting. There, the Almighty confronts them: "Hear these My words. When a prophet of the Lord arises among you, I make Myself known to him in a vision, I speak with him in a dream. Not so with My servant Moses; he is trusted throughout My household. With him I speak mouth to mouth and not in riddles, and he beholds the likeness of the Lord" (Numbers 12:6–8).[14] Immediately, the pillar withdrew from the Tent. Aaron turned to his sister, who had suddenly developed leprosy. Aaron repented and pleaded with Moses that she should not die with half her flesh eaten away. Moses cried out for God to heal her. God replied: "If her father spat in her face, would she not bear her shame for seven days? Let her be shut out of camp for seven days, and then let her be readmitted" (Numbers 12:14).[15] This is the biblical

---

12. Mielziner, *Introduction to the Talmud*, p. 131.
13. *Tanakh*, p. 227.
14. Ibid.
15. Ibid.

derivation for the KV. If a father humiliated his daughter (because of her wrongful conduct) in such a way that she would bear shame for seven days, then how much the more so should God humiliate one of his children, who has committed the sin of challenging God's judgment in selecting Moses as God's vessel to Israel, to bear shame for at least seven days.

From this incident, the Talmud derives a basic principle of the KV which limits its effect and serves as an additional tool for understanding its operation. The Gemara in the tractate *Bava Kamma* provides:

> The principle of *dayo* [a limitation on the KV that the law derived from such an inference cannot go beyond the source from which it is based] is derived from Scripture, for a baraita teaches: "God said to Moses, if in a case where a father justifiably spits before her, surely she would suffer embarrassment for seven days." How much the more so, in the case involving the Divine Presence [which would be a far greater offense] should she suffer embarrassment for [a greater period than] seven days. Nevertheless, it is sufficient for the law to be the same as the law found in the source from which the inference is made.[16]

In this baraita, two principles are shown. First, there must exist a sufficient level of similarity such that the law in one should apply to the other. This is the wrongful conduct of the child against the parent that results in his/her humiliation. Despite the similarity of the two cases, one would normally expect the punishment against Miriam to be more severe because it involves the divine. However, since God "justifies" the necessity for punitive action from the case of the father–daughter relationship, we learn that the punishment cannot exceed that of the original source from which the analogy is made.

An example from our *sugya* will serve to illustrate the KV in the talmudic process. Recall from chapter 1 Rabbi Hiya's rule that would require a defendant to take an oath denying the remainder

---

16. *Bava Kamma* 25a.

of the plaintiff's claim where witnesses have testified to only a part. Rabbi Hiya argues that the foundation for his ruling rests on the principle that the effect of admissions (which results in an oath) does not have any greater impact than the testimony of witnesses. This rule of law, he asserts, is derived from a KV.[17]

The Gemara will then try to formulate in three separate instances this KV. One such instance is as follows: "And what is this KV? If an admission that does not render the defendant obligated [as to the disputed remainder], yet nevertheless requires him to take an oath, then how much the more so should witnesses, who do render him liable for monies, compel him to take an oath on the disputed remainder."[18] In this case, the source of the KV is the rule of law pertaining to a partial admission (ADM). A defendant who admits to a part of the plaintiff's claim is not responsible for monies.[19] Nevertheless, the defendant must take an oath. In the more severe case where witnesses (WS) have obligated the defendant for monies, how much the more so should the same requirement of the oath be imposed be on the disputed remainder.

Moses Mielziner summarizes the application of the KV as containing three elements. The first premise is that case A and case B have a relationship of minor and major importance. Second, A contains a certain restrictive or permissive law. Third, this same

---

17. *Bava Metziah* 3a. An admission to any issue in a lawsuit dispenses with the necessity for any further proof. In this sense, it is considered a "lighter" case. Nevertheless, an oath, which is a stringent condition, is administered against the defendant despite his apparent honesty. But where a defendant has denied a claim in its entirety such that the plaintiff has been forced to produce independent evidence, the former's honesty cannot be presumed. In such a case, at a minimum the same stringency of the oath should be administered on the remainder.

18. In Jewish law, once two witnesses have testified on a particular aspect of a lawsuit, in the absence of two contradictory witnesses, it is considered *res judicata* (a final determination as to that issue) and the defendant is barred from testifying on that part of the litigation.

19. The reader may be confused because an admission does oblige the defendant for the sum to which he admits. The Gemara will challenge the KV on this basis. See chapter 6 at "B. Challenge to KV Number 1."

law is even more applicable to B.[20] When this formulation is applied to the above example, it becomes obvious that the law of ADM is of lesser significance than that of WS in that the former does not oblige the defendant for monies, whereas the latter does. Nevertheless, an ADM also has the stringency of the oath as to a disputed remainder. At the minimum, this demand should be applied to the case of WS who oblige the defendant for monies.

Refutation of the *Kal V'chomer*

A KV is refutable by two means. The most common is to demonstrate that the premise in the antecedent (the A element), which was considered to be of minor importance, is in some other respect of considerable importance. Then, one must show that B is not as important in the same respect. In other words, the respective cases are distinguishable such that the analogy and the inference drawn are unsuitable. In effect, element A, which implies the relationship between the two terms of the syllogism, is a false assumption.

In the above example, the Gemara challenges this KV by using this approach. "Is it possible to maintain that an admission does not oblige the defendant for the payment of monies? Surely, the admission by a litigant is equivalent to the testimony of one hundred witnesses!"[21] According to the challenge, an important distinction between these two rules exists. Once a litigant has admitted to something, he becomes obligated. No further testimony is necessary. Second, Jewish law considers a single admission to be as powerful as countless witnesses. Thus, admissions and witnesses do not stand in a relationship of minor to major importance, and thus no inference may be drawn.[22] The Gemara will then suggest a new KV.

---

20. Mielziner, *Introduction to the Talmud*, p. 130.

21. *Bava Metziah* 4a.

22. If one examines Rabbi Hiya's formulation, it is clear that he does not require that the law of witnesses be of major importance in relation to the law of admissions. Rather, the effect of an admission, in relation to the oath, should not be any more efficacious than that of witnesses. Therefore, the Baraita would hold true if one could even demonstrate a legal equivalency between them. The significance of this formulation in light of the scriptural foundation developed in chapter 7 will be developed more fully in chapter 8.

Another refutation of a KV is to demonstrate that the peculiar law in A cannot be transferred to B for the following reason: There exists a case C that is legally equivalent to B, but the specific law in A does not apply to C. As a result, this same law cannot be utilized in B.[23]

The Importance of Preserving a Refuted KV

One might argue that, given the ease with which the Gemara refutes the first KV formulation, little value is gained from including it within the talmudic dialectic. Since the Talmud's primary purpose is to discern the divine intention, it is confusing to include such material.

In response, the Talmud emphasizes the unique role of humanity in the process of understanding divine law. The rabbinic communities of this period believed that the creation of the universe and its continued existence was an act of rationality. A nexus between God and humanity is intelligence, and, thus, the engagement of the human intellect (not the intellect itself) must be accorded revered status, even if the resulting formulation is refuted. This reverence for the deliberative process is reflected in the following passage from the Talmud *Berakhot* (a tractate dealing with blessings):

> Rabbi Judah said in the name of Samuel: If someone awoke to study before reading the Shema he must bless. . . . Rabbi Huna said: For [the study of] Scripture one must bless, but for Midrash one need not bless. Rabbi Eleazar stated: For Scripture and Midrash, one must bless, but for Mishnah one does not have to bless. Rabbi Yochanan said: even for Mishnah, one must recite a blessing. And Rava said: Even for Talmud, one must bless.[24]

This citation illustrates the development of sacred literature to include that of the Talmud. This *sugya* began with the requirement of reciting a blessing only for the study of Scripture. It con-

---

23. Mielziner, *Introduction to Talmud*, p. 6.
24. *Berakhot* 11b.

cluded with Rava, who held that the talmudic process was a holy endeavor.

Rashi, in a parallel allusion to a midrash, comments: "Even for [the study of] Gemara[25] it is necessary to [recite] a blessing: For it is a principle of the Torah that divine instruction emanates from it [the Gemara]."[26] The phrase "that divine instruction emanates from it" is also found in *Genesis Rabbah*, a collection of *midrashim* on Genesis that scholars date between the eighth and ninth centuries. The Midrash is exploring the meaning of Genesis 22:2, when God first tells Abraham to sacrifice his beloved son Isaac: "And He [God] said, 'Take your son, your favored one, Isaac, whom you love, and go [for your benefit] to the land of Moriah, and offer him there as a burnt offering on one of the heights that I will point out to you.'"[27] The Midrash comments on the phrase, "and go [for your benefit] to the land of Moriah": "Rabbi Hiya Rabbah and Rabbi Yonai: One [rabbi] said, to a place where divine wisdom will emanate from the world."[28] Rashi writes: [The divine instruction went out] from the Sanhedrin that would sit in the Temple courtroom as it says in Scripture 'that the Torah will go forth from Zion.'[29]

---

25. Rashi may be citing a different manuscript than the Vilna edition, for he uses the word *gemara* (גמרא) instead of *talmud* (תלמוד) in his initial reference. It is also possible that Rashi is suggesting that the terms are synonymous. The significance of this latter interpretation is brought out above.

26. The Hebrew is important to establish Rashi's allusion to a midrash from *Genesis Rabbah*.

אף לגמרא צריך לברך: שהוא עיקר התורה שממנו הוראה יוצאה:

27. *Tanakh*, p. 31.

28. *Midrash Rabbah*, p. 224. The identical phrase שהוראה יצאה is found in this midrash as in Rashi's commentary. This suggests that Rashi is equating the writing of the Talmud with the Temple Mount, which was considered the dwelling place of the Almighty from where divine teaching emanated. The term "הוראה" is ambiguous in the rabbinic literature of this period. It can represent Divine Wisdom or human, but inspired, teaching. This latter understanding is reflected by allusion to the Sannhedrin which was empowered to issue *takanot*, halakhic rulings, which were not explicitly derivative of Scripture. In contrast, Mount Moriah symbolizes a direct encounter with the divine for the purpose of demonstrating the submission of the human will to God's directives.

29. *Berakhot* 11b.

The historical institutions of the Temple and the Sanhedrin are linked to the mystical relation between God and Abraham at Mount Moriah. Abraham submits to the divine will wholeheartedly. Yet, *midrashim* on the story of the binding of Isaac reflect an Abraham who examines closely the humanity of what God has called upon him to do. All of this occurred at Mount Moriah. Likewise, this same place was to be identified later in tradition as the site of the Temple and the Sanhedrin, where humanity would again meet with the divine in order to discern God's will, to submit to it, and to integrate it in the world. With the Temple destroyed and the institution of the Sanhedrin dismantled for centuries, the seat of divine wisdom where humanity and the divine would once again encounter one another would be through the Talmud, a symbol of the rational endeavor to discern God's intention.

Rashi comments on the nature of Gemara: "The Gemara's purpose is to establish the rationale of the Mishnah, to harmonize contradictory mishnaic passages, and to determine where a relation [in law through analogy] is defective."[30] Therefore, the process of argumentation, even if refuted through the dialectic, is a sacred task, and each assertion is worthy of consideration. For these reasons, Rava ruled it necessary to recite the following blessing before engaging in talmudic studies: "Blessed are you, Lord our God, king of the universe, who has sanctified us through his commandments and has commanded us to engage in words of Torah."[31] An "engagement in the words of Torah" includes all the various modes of intellectual processes. It involves formulation, analysis, criticism, and often a new assertion of the law. The task is sacred and, therefore, even arguments that are refutable must be recorded and carefully weighed. It is an enterprise worthy of human blessing.

In summary, a KV allows for the engagement of the rational faculty with scriptural and oral legislation. On the basis of analyzing certain passages, relationships between legal circumstances may be established from which inferences may be drawn. However, these

---

30. Ibid.
31. Ibid.

inferences may be challenged by examining the assumptions that provide the basis for the KV syllogism. This examination by the Talmud continues the chain of הוראה (divine instruction), which began with Abraham and God at Mount Moriah, continued with the Sanhedrin, and is now revealed in the pages of the Gemara.

BINYAN AV MISHNEI K'TUVIM

This rule of interpretation is based on induction. Its structure is somewhat complex, and a few readings may be required to understand its operative effect. However, the following syllogism may prove helpful as a foundation for understanding its application in the *sugya*.

1. Case A is analogous to Case B.
2. Therefore, an assertion is made that the law of A should apply to B.
3. An objection is raised regarding the analogy so as to render it nonviable.
4. Case C is introduced, which is similar to A. The same law applies in each case.
5. C is analogous to B.
6. Therefore, since C is analogous to both B and A, the same law should apply to C as well.
7. A challenge is made to the analogy of C to B.
8. This challenge is then minimized by showing that A and C share a common factor that causes the rule to be invoked.
9. B shares this common factor as well. Therefore, the same law of A and C should apply to B as well.[32]

The application of these steps to an example from the passage in *Bava Metziah* will clarify this hermeneutic rule. A, B, and C are defined as follows:

---

32. Steinsaltz, *The Talmud: A Reference Guide*, p. 150.

Case A: The law of partial admission (ADM): If a defendant admits to part of the plaintiff's claim, then an oath is required of him/her on the remainder and the defendant then relieved of further liability.

Case B: Where the testimony of two witnesses establishes partial validity to plaintiff's case, Rabbi Hiya rules that an oath is imposed on the remainder and the defendant then is relieved of liability (WS). (The Gemara attempts to clarify Rabbi Hiya's reasoning, which supports the ruling through this hermeneutic principle of *binyan av mishnei k'etuvim*.)

Case C: The law of one witness (SW): Where one witness testifies to a part of the claim, the defendant is required to take an oath rebutting the witness's testimony. This oath is then rolled over to compel the defendant to swear on the remainder.

Applying these cases to the rule, yields the following:

1. A is analogous to B: In both cases, the partial validity of the plaintiff's claim is established. There is also a disputed balance. One would normally expect that the harsh requirement of an oath would not be dictated, since the defendant has voluntarily admitted to owing a partial. He should be believed without an oath as to the remainder. Nevertheless, an oath is enjoined.
2. The assertion that the law of A should apply to B: How much the more so that Case B, which is more stringent, since the plaintiff has been forced to bring witnesses in light of the defendant's denial, compel the defendant to take an oath.
3. The objection which makes the analogy invalid: The case of ADM is distinguishable from that of WS in that the former is not subject to contradiction. Once an admission is made, no witness may refute it. In the case of WS, the defendant may bring other witnesses to testify on his/her behalf. Therefore, the law of A should not apply to B.

4. C is introduced, which is analogous to A: The plaintiff may bring a single witness, causing the defendant to take an oath on that portion of the claim to which the single witness has testified. Once the defendant takes an oath on that portion, it is "rolled over" to apply to the unsubstantiated segment of the plaintiff's claim. Thus, the oath is applied in both SW and ADM. C is analogous to A.

5. C is analogous to B: Both are subject to the law of contradiction. In B, the defendant may bring witnesses to testify against the plaintiff's. Likewise in C, the defendant may produce other witnesses to contradict the plaintiff's proof. Thus C is similar to B.

6. Since C is analogous to both A and B, the same law should apply to B as well: As shown above, C is similar to A and B. In A and C, an oath is imposed on the remainder, upon which no evidence has been proffered. C is analogous to B in that the defendant can produce other witnesses to contradict the testimony of the plaintiff's witnesses. Since, in C, the defendant is obliged to take an oath, likewise in B, the same requirement should be imposed.

7. The challenge to the analogy between C and B: C is distinguishable from B. The only reason the oath is imposed on the remainder in C is that the defendant must give testimony refuting the single witness. But in B, the defendant is barred from taking an oath and contradicting the testimony of the two witnesses. Thus, no oath may be dictated on the remainder based solely on the analogy of the SW to WS.

8. This challenge is minimized by showing that both A and C share a common factor: Both A and C evolved through a claim and denial by the respective litigants. It is this factor that allows the oath to be imposed on the disputed remainder in these cases.

9. B shares this common factor as well: Case B arises because of a claim and denial. Therefore, an oath should be imposed on the disputed remainder in the case presented in the Baraita.

To summarize: A *binyan av* is similar to an algebraic equation. If A = C (in an important aspect) and B = C (in the same respect), even though A and B may be significantly distinguishable, nevertheless A = B such that the law that applies to both A and C can now be applied to B.

GEZERA SHAVAH

Literally, a *gezera shavah* means "a similar decision." If a word or phrase is found in separate biblical passages and defined in one of them, then its interpretation may be applied in the other verse.[33]

The *gezera shavah* is also used to apply a rule of law found in one scriptural passage to another. If a term is contained in a section of Scripture along with a rule of law, then if the same term is found in a separate passage in which no rule is provided, one may infer the rule's application to this passage as well.[34]

There are restrictions for its use. First, the identical expression must be undefined in at least one of the verses and appear superfluous. Second, no one is permitted to reason from a *gezera shava* on his/her own strength. Rather, a *gezera shavah* must be learned from a rabbinic authority within the chain of tradition.[35]

An example taken from the *Mekilta de-Rabbi Ishmael* illustrates its use. Exodus 22:6–7 provides: "(6) When a man gives money or goods to another for safekeeping, and they are stolen from the man's house—if the thief is caught, he shall pay double; (7) if the thief is not caught, the owner of the house shall depose before 'Elohim' (literally, God) *that he has not laid hands on the other's property*."[36] The phrase "the owner of the house [that is, the bailee] shall depose before 'Elohim'" is ambiguous. The *Mekilta* turns its attention to Exodus 22:9–10: "(9) When a man gives to another an ass, an ox,

---

33. Mielziner, *Introduction to the Talmud*, p. 143.
34. Steinsaltz, *The Talmud: A Reference Guide*, p. 150.
35. Strack and Stemberger, *Introduction*, p. 21.
36. *Tanakh*, p. 119.

a sheep or any other animal to guard, and it dies or is injured or is carried off, with no witnesses about, (10) an oath before God shall decide between the two of them that *he has not laid hands on the other's property*."[37] The phrase "he has not laid hands on the other's property" is found in both sections. Therefore, the law that applies in 22:9–10 pertaining to negligent bailment may be applied to 22:6–7 relating to stolen property. In the former, the individual is brought before "Elohim," which the *Mekilta* interprets to be a court of law. Since the alleged negligent bailee is brought before judges and is made to swear that he has not misappropriated the item, then the bailee in the stolen property case must be brought before a tribunal and swear that he has not made use of the item for his own benefit.[38] Thus, an entire body of law may be transferred from one scenario to another on the basis of an identical expression found in each passage.

K'LAL U'PHRAT UKHLAL

Where a scriptural passage contains a general statement of law, followed by a list of details and then a restatement of general principle, the rule of law applies only to the common element found in the specific items.[39]

A good illustration is taken from the *Mekilta*. Exodus 22:8 provides: "In all charges of misappropriation—pertaining to an ox, an ass, a sheep, a garment, or any other loss whereof one party alleges, 'this is it'—the case of both shall be brought before God: he whom God declares guilty shall pay double to the other."[40] Dissection of each of the phrases will demonstrate how the rule operates:

1. *In all charges of misappropriation*: This is a general statement. If a rule was then stated, it would apply to any item.

---

37. Ibid.

38. *Mekilta de-Rabbi Ishmael*, ed. H. S. Horowitz and I. A. Rabin (Jerusalem, 1970), p. 300.

39. Mielziner, *Introduction to the Talmud*, p. 167.

40. *Tanakh*, p. 119.

2. *Pertaining to an ox, an ass, a sheep, a garment*: These are specific items and thus far the rule would operate to include only these specific articles.
3. *Or any other loss*: This is a general statement indicating once again any item which is alleged to have been misappropriated by another.

The *Mekilta* analyzes the common factor of the specific items because of the general phrase "or any other loss." It notes that each of the items is personal property and capable of being moved. In common law, they are referred to as chattels. Thus, the rule that is subsequently formulated will not apply to real property—that is, land.[41]

This law may be stated as follows. In any matter involving a charge of misappropriation of personal property in which the defendant states, "This is it," and the plaintiff disagrees, the case shall be brought before a court of law. Each will have to take an oath and the court will determine the guilt of the respective parties. If the defendant is found guilty, then he must pay double damages to the plaintiff.[42]

CONCLUSION

Moses L. Mielziner characterizes these rules as artificial because their aim is to provide a methodology which would justify the Oral Law with the Written Law.[43] Rabbi Isaac Unterman argues that these rules evolved as a response to the Sadducees, who undermined the legality of the Oral Torah because its basis in Scripture was not apparent. He concludes that in order to extend Scripture to em-

---

41. Horowitz and Rabin, *Mekilta de-Rabbi Ishmael*, pp. 300–301.

42. As will be shown in chapter 7, the phrase, "this is it" is the scriptural basis for the rule of invoking an oath on the remainder where the defendant admits to a part of the plaintiff's claim. The phrase "this is it" constitutes an admission of at least a minimum level of liability. Since the remainder is in dispute, an oath is mandated based on this passage.

43. Mielziner, *Introduction to the Talmud*, p. 186.

brace the oral tradition, a logical method was employed that established a strong connection between the two in order to meet the Sadducean challenge.[44]

Dr. David Kraemer, in his important work *The Mind of the Talmud: An Intellectual History of the Bavli*, suggests that because divine revelation ceased after Sinai and the prophetic period, knowledge of God's intention could be discerned only through intellectual engagement with the sacred texts. As such, the interpretive enterprise itself was regarded as sacrosanct: "The point that emerges from the 'talmudic' form common to the Yerushalmi and the Bavli is the same: the most important concern may not be truth, but the process by which that truth is approached."[45]

There is an added dimension to the arguments that have been set forth above by these eminent scholars. The rabbis of the tannaitic, amoraic, and saboraic periods were masters of both Scripture and the subsequent literary genres that were based on it. Their area of expertise was the understanding of sacred texts and traditions that they considered an expression of the divine. Consistent methodology for amplification would have been an important factor, for it brought humanity's most distinguishing features—intelligence, reflection, and logic—into the process of discerning the meaning of Sinai. These hermeneutic rules were a concrete expression that just as the act of creation was a purposeful act, its rationality could be understood only through a disciplined system of logic and reason.

Hermeneutics and the talmudic dialectic form were the processes through which the rabbinic communities approached the sacred texts. But these tools, uniquely human but regarded as a blessing from the divine worthy of a daily prayer of thanksgiving, were not the center of the endeavor. A simple analogy might illustrate the difference. Materials, tools, and skill are necessary for the carpenter to build a house.

Applying Dr. Kraemer's analysis, the builder's most important concerns are the building materials and skill, not the finished prod-

---

44. Isaac Unterman, *The Talmud: An Analytical Guide to Its History and Teachings* (New York: Bloch Publishing Company, 1952), p. 106.
45. Kraemer, *Mind of the Talmud*, p. 122.

uct. His theory suggests that the hermeneutic rules and their application might be more valued than the divine truth represented by the sacred texts. Extending the argument one step further, human reason and argumentation would be more important to the rabbinic communities of this period than the sacred literature which they viewed as their mission to comprehend.

True, the structure of the Gemara reflects the importance of the rational faculty of humankind in comprehending the divine. The hermeneutic rules and the talmudic dialectic, the products of the human intellect, were significant tools and building materials, but they were not regarded as the heart of the enterprise. Instead, the utilization of these devices provided a common language and methodology. These instruments, like the tools and materials in the hands of skilled carpenters, allowed the rabbis of the period from 100 B.C.E. to 600 C.E. to engage these texts as a community of scholars.

Most important, the hermeneutic rules established the foundation for cross-generational discussion with the ultimate goal of discerning the divine intention and of implementing it in the world. They were building a home for the divine will on earth.

However, it would take generations, perhaps an eternity, to complete this dwelling place of God on earth. Human understanding of the divine, found in the endless pages of the sacred literature, became God's abode. Therefore, a common methodology would afford them the opportunity for cross-generational dialogue and continuation of this building process. A scholar from the amoraic period (250–425 C.E.) could engage in a dialogue with a rabbi from the tannaitic period (10 C.E.–250 C.E.). Ultimately, in the hands of the Talmud's authors, a rabbi from any one period could debate, argue, or reason with a scholar from another generation, whether earlier or later in time. However, this genius of human creativity was always subordinate to its goal; the building of God's design from the blueprint of Torah into the realities of human existence and growth.

A consistent methodology and common language were the human imperative. With this in mind, we now enter a small section of this still incomplete dwelling place by examining the Baraita of Rabbi Hiya from *Bava Metziah*.

6

The Talmud's Response to the Baraita of Rabbi Hiya

We now turn to an analysis of the Baraita of Rabbi Hiya as engaged by the Gemara in the Talmud *Bava Metziah* 3a–4a. The writing will appear at times legalistic and syllogistic because of the abbreviated nature of the language and the style of the text. Though the translation is not literal, an attempt has been made to capture the "flavor" of a direct reading.[1] A full translation of the Rashi to this text is provided as well.[2]

An aim of the author's commentary is to furnish the necessary antecedent materials which, though cited in the text, are not fully explicated. For example, the authors assume that the reader comprehends the Mishnah under which this topic is presented, for one of their goals is to test whether the Baraita is consistent with the Oral Tradition edited by Rabbi Judah HaNasi. Wherever appropriate, such texts and their analysis will appear as an additional aide in understanding the *sugya*.

---

1. These segments will be delineated by appearing in bold print in order to distinguish the text from the analysis segments of this work. Words enclosed in square brackets were inserted to provide syntax and clarity for the reader. (The outline headings are not part of the actual text of the Gemara. They are to enable the reader to anticipate the nature of the forthcoming argument.)

2. These remarks will appear in italics.

From this process, certain theological issues and their role in the development of the talmudic dialectic will emerge. For example, when one disengages from the text and examines its thematic structure, one of the central concerns is the imposition of an oath. This oath injects the divine element in a legal endeavor to resolve a dispute—a procedure adopted in Anglo-American jurisprudence without hesitation. Yet the Gemara's exhausting analysis suggests that the decision to adopt Rabbi Hiya's rule as part of the corpus of *halakhah* was heavily debated. This fact points to underlying religious themes more fully developed in such antecedent works as Scripture, Mishnah, and Midrash. These are the sources that provided the necessary fuel for the dialectic of the Bavli. These topics will be highlighted and then analyzed in chapter 7.

I. THE RULE AND RATIONALE OF RABBI HIYA

The Baraita of Rabbi Hiya teaches the following. The plaintiff claims that the defendant owes him one hundred dollars, which the defendant completely denies. Witnesses then testify that the defendant owes fifty dollars. In such a case, [in order to be relieved of any further liability,] the defendant pays the fifty dollars [if he cannot produce his own witnesses] and swears [that he does not owe anything] on the remainder. The rationale for this rule is that a defendant's admission should not have any greater effect than the testimony of witnesses and [this principle] is derived by a KV.

Comment: This baraita assumes the reader's familiarity with two scriptural principles. One provides that when two witnesses testify to any matter on behalf of a litigant and the opposing party fails to offer both contrary and independent evidence, those matters are considered concluded and the defendant is barred from testifying.[3] This rule has already been referred to in Chapter 5 and

---

3. See Deuteronomy 19:15. In modern law, this would be referred to as *res judicata*—that is, the matter fully adjudicated. Obviously, the defendant in a modern court may testify regardless of the lack of independent proof in his defense or the number of witnesses a plaintiff may produce.

will be designated by the symbol "WS" (witnesses) throughout this chapter. The other is with regard to admissions. When a litigant admits to a part of the plaintiff's claim, but there is no independent evidence to support the balance, the defendant may take an oath disavowing liability on the remainder. This rule, also already referred to in chapter 5, will be designated by the symbol "ADM" (admissions).

Rabbi Hiya's argument rests on the assumption that ADM and WS either stand in a legally analogous relation of minor to major importance or, at a minimum, are legally equivalent in their impact on litigation. Therefore, the rule in the case of ADM may be applied to the Baraita. Both cases have the effect of conclusively establishing disputed issues. When a defendant admits liability, no further proof is necessary. Likewise, when two witnesses testify on a matter and the defendant lacks contradictory, independent evidence, then their testimony is conclusive. Since ADM permits an oath on a disputed remainder, then under this case, in which witnesses testify and there remains an issue of further liability, Rabbi Hiya argues that an oath should be imposed as well.

The Baraita harmonizes [Aramaic _v'tanah tunah_] with the Mishnah "where two are holding onto a garment and this one states 'I found it,' and so on." And here [in the case of the Mishnah], each is holding [onto a part of the garment] [and] we [the court] are witnesses to the fact that what each is holding onto belongs to him. Yet it is taught [in the Mishnah], each one takes an oath.

Comment: The Gemara begins by drawing a relationship between the Baraita and the Mishnah at the beginning of this tractate. At this juncture, it is important to set forth the relevant section of the Mishnah and Rashi's commentary on it.

Two [litigants who have come before a court] are [literally] holding onto a garment. This one states 'I found it' and this one states 'I found it.' This one claims 'all of it is mine.' And this one claims 'all of it is mine.' This one swears that he does not have less than a one-half interest in the garment and the other swears that he does not have less than a one-half interest. They divide the article [in accordance with their oath] and each acquires a one-half interest in it.[4]

Rashi: *The Mishnah assumes that both have actual possession of a part for if only one had it in his control, then the other would have to furnish independent proof through witnesses in order to acquire any interest in it. The reason is that sworn testimony by a litigant in the absence of any other evidence is legally insufficient to take property that is in the possession of another.[5]*

Comment: We return now to the "Rashi" and explanatory comments of the Gemara on the Baraita of Rabbi Hiya.

Rashi: *The Baraita harmonizes [Aramaic v'tanah tunah] with the Mishnah: And our Tanna supports "me."*

Comment: Rashi's pronominal reference of "me" is ambiguous. Rabbi Steinsaltz reads this expression as referring to Rabbi Hiya. The phrase "*v'tanah tunah*" is a continuation of the Baraita. Another possibility is that it refers to the "Tanna" who is teaching Rabbi Hiya's *baraita* and that the editors of the Gemara are simply recording it. Finally, the phrase *v'tanah tunah* may be the creative hand of the authors of the Gemara to demonstrate the relationship between the Baraita and the Mishnah.

    The Aramaic term *v'tanah tunah* [literally and the author of the Mishnah taught similarly] suggests that the Baraita is of paramount importance to the theoretical nature of the Gemara. It signals to the reader that the Tanna (that is, Rabbi Judah HaNasi) of the Mishnah would accept Rabbi Hiya's ruling as consistent with the Mishnah, which is regarded as the redaction of the Oral Law given at Sinai. In modern legal terminology, it introduces the reader to the principle of *stare decisis*. This axiom provides where the case at issue is, in all significant aspects, factually analogous to a prior

---

4. *Bava Metziah* 2a.
5. Rashi, *Bava Metziah* 2a. This is only a paraphrase of the Rashi.

matter the rule of the prior case should apply to the one before the court.

Rashi: This one states . . . yet it is taught, each one takes an oath: We are witnesses to the fact that each one is holding (onto the garment): This (the fact that each one is seized to part of the claim) is a dispute.

Comment: While Rashi's comment here is somewhat abbreviated, nevertheless he is explicating the analogy between the Baraita and the Mishnah. Like the Baraita, in the Mishnah's case there are witnesses (i.e., the court). As in Rabbi Hiya's case there is a dispute, likewise in the Mishnah there is a controversy.

Rashi: Belongs to him/her: That certainly, each one has possession before us (the rabbinic court) and certainly each one claims all of it while denying the claim of the other for he/she states 'all of it is mine, even that part which is in your hand.' We (the court) are witnesses that each one has possession of a part and we obligate each to take an oath on the remainder of that half that he/she has detained for him or herself.

Comment: Rashi continues with the analogy between the Baraita and the Mishnah. This similarity may be expressed as follows: In the Mishnah, the court acts as a witness because it can see that each party is holding a part while claiming the entire aricle. In such a case, (where there is a dispute with no independent evidence to resolve it), the Mishnah determines that liability and entitlement are resolved through an oath. Likewise, in the case of the Baraita, two witnesses have testified conclusively as to a part of the plaintiff's claim. As in the Mishnah, there is a disputed remainder. The mechanism to settle the dispute should be the oath. Thus, Rabbi Hiya's ruling is, at first reading, consistent with the Mishnah.

In concluding this section, the term *v'tanah tunah* suggests another important point. Why does this teaching of Rabbi Hiya appear as part of the Gemara's analysis to the first Mishnah in *Bava Metziah*? One might argue that this Baraita should have appeared in the tractate *Shavuot*, which is principally concerned with toraitic and rabbinic oaths. This phrase is telling the reader that the locus of this Baraita is appropriate within the context of this Mishnah of *Bava Metziah*, for the latter is principally concerned with claims and denials in litigation that cannot be substantiated by independent proofs. The authors of the Bavli are signaling the reader through this technical term that the real subject matter of the Baraita is the competing demands for justice made by both litigants where there is an absence of independent evidence to determine the truth of the plaintiff's claim or the assertion of innocence by the defendant. This accounts for the Baraita's appearance in this tractate.

II. THE NECESSITY FOR THE KV

What then is the necessity and meaning of the statement that an admission does not have a greater effect than the testimony of witnesses and that this rationale is supported by a KV?[6]

Rashi: What then is the necessity and meaning for the KV: *The Gemara seeks to know the precise derivation of the conclusion reached by Rabbi Hiya, for surely [one might normally think that] an admission does have a greater effect than the testimony of witnesses. Thus it is necessary for the Tanna to derive from a* kal v'chomer *that an admission is not more efficacious than the testimony of witnesses.*

Comment: Rashi is informing the reader as to the number of challenges to the KV formulations that are to follow. Most would think that ADM is more efficacious than WS, particularly since the former is conclusive in litigation, whereas the latter may be contradicted or refuted by other witnesses. Thus, the Gemara will take up the issue of the necessity for the KV.

So that you should not hold that on account of his admission, the Merciful One "forced" [in the sense of it being against his will] an oath upon him, as Rabbah has explained, for he taught:

---

6. *Bava Metziah* 3a.

For what reason does the Torah state that a litigant who admits to part of a claim [brought against him] must take an oath [as to the disputed portion]? There is a presumption that no person is so arrogant before his creditor [as to deny his claim entirely]. The defendant wants to deny the claim entirely, but he cannot deny it because human nature precludes someone from being so arrogant. The debtor needs to confess to all of it, but he cannot. And the reason he does not admit to all of it is that he wants to delay paying him, thinking "when I have the money, then I will pay him." And the Merciful One states, "Force an oath upon him so that he will admit to all of it." But in the case of witnesses, it is not at all possible to argue in this fashion. Thus, he [Rabbi Hiya] teaches us [the Baraita] based on a *kal v'chomer*.

Rashi: For what reason does the Torah state: *For it [the Torah] does not regard this debtor as the legal equivalent of one who has restored a lost article to its rightful owner, who, under toraitic law, is exempt from the oath. The reason is that the debtor [in this case, unlike one who has restored property to a rightful owner] has not denied the claim entirely.*

Comment: Where one restores lost property to an owner, he/she is exempt from taking an oath, despite a claim by the plaintiff that it remains in the possession of the defendant. This is to be distinguished from a bailment, in which A deposits with B an article for safekeeping and A claims that either all or part remains with B or has been misappropriated. In the following chapter, the seriousness of a toraitic oath in these respective contexts is discussed.

Rashi: The debtor needs to confess to all of it: *You [the reader] might wonder, "since he is suspect concerning the money [having admitted to a part and having denied a part], he should be suspect with respect to the oath as well and we should not compel him to take an oath."*[7]

---

7. The principle of מגו [since] is a halakhic form of reasoning similar to a *kal v'chomer*. In this case, since there already is a suspicion on his defense, since he has admitted to a part and having denied a part, it raises a sufficient

[Rashi responds] He is not suspect on the monetary claim because he truly seeks to admit all of it. It simply is a matter that the money is not "in his hand." Thus, he rationalizes, "When I have the money, then I will pay him."

But [with respect to the debtor who has totally denied the claim], it is not possible to reason in the same fashion, for surely he has denied the claim in its entirety. And therefore let us invoke the principle of מיגו [mego—a term that introduces a legal formulation "since . . . then . . ."] that since he is suspect with regard to the monetary claim, he should be suspect with regard to the oath as well.

Comment: In the case of an ADM, the Torah imposes an oath upon the defendant to deny the balance of the claim. The rationale for this rule, provided by Rabbah, is derived from the following. A loans B a certain sum of money (interest free), of which B admits owing only a part. B then swears that he owes nothing on the remainder. The psychological tension in the borrower is evident, for part of him wishes to deny the entire claim. Yet, he is not so arrogant as to repudiate it altogether. Paradoxically, another part of him wants to admit the entire claim, but he lacks sufficient funds. Thus, in order to "buy time," he admits to only a portion. The Torah therefore imposes an oath to relieve the anxiety that results from the half-truth and half-lie of the defendant.

However, this psychological tension, which results in an oath, is absent in the Baraita. There, the defendant denies everything, forcing the plaintiff to produce witnesses. Without an admission, there is no extrinsic evidence of the defendant's desire for honesty sufficient to impose a toraitic oath. Therefore, the case of an ADM is not legally equivalent to the case of WS. For this reason, Rabbi Hiya must provide, through a rule of hermeneutics such as a KV, a basis for requiring an oath on the remainder in the case of WS.

---

degree of doubt as to his credibility. The oath, in the view of the Sages, is a serious act. Thus, the defendant, because he already is under a cloud of suspicion, should be barred from taking the oath.

III. KV NUMBER 1

A. ADM and WS Are Legally Analogous and Stand in a Relation of Minor to Major Importance Because the Former Does Not Require Payment, Whereas the Latter Does

And what is the KV? An admission to a part of a claim does not obligate one for payment of monies [Aramaic, *mamon*]. Nevertheless, it does require him to take an oath as to the remainder. However, WS do oblige the defendant to pay. Thus, if an admission, which does not require payment, nevertheless enjoins the defendant to take an oath, how much the more so should witnesses, who do render a litigant liable for monies, compel an oath as to the remainder.

Rashi: An admission does not obligate the defendant for the payment of monies [with regard to that which he has admitted]: *The Gemara will explain this statement further on.*

Comment: It will be helpful to keep in mind that the stringency under consideration in all the KV formulations in this *sugya* is whether or not to impose the oath.

At first, this syllogism seems to make little sense. Surely, if one admits that he/she owes the plaintiff a certain amount of money, then that person must pay. Rashi is informing us that the Gemara will clarify this formulation.

B. Challenge to KV Number 1: ADM Is Legally More Powerful Than WS

The Gemara rhetorically asks, "Admissions do not obligate one for the payment of monies?" [Citing a baraita from the Tosefta of *Bava Metziah*,] the Gemara asserts, "surely the admission of a litigant is the equivalent of the testimony of one hundred witnesses."

Rashi: The admission of a litigant is the equivalent [of the testimony of] one hundred witnesses: *This statement is found in a Tosefta from the first chapter of* Bava Metziah.

Comment: In the phrase "the admission of a litigant is the equivalent of the testimony of one hundred witnesses," "the equivalent of" is understood in the sense of "like" or "resembles." Imagine one hundred witnesses testifying against a defendant that he/she owes the plaintiff money. Such testimony would be conclusive. Once a litigant admits to the plaintiff's claim, no further proof is required. Even two hundred witnesses would not override his/her admission in open court. Thus, the laws of ADM and WS do not stand in a relation of minor to major importance. Instead, an admission is *more powerful* than the testimony of witnesses [and thus this KV formulation does not support Rabbi Hiya's ruling].

C. Response and KV Number 2: WS Impose the Severe Penalty of Fines Whereas ADM Do Not: Thus They Do Stand in a Relation of Minor to Major Importance

What then is the meaning of the word *mamon* [monies, as formulated in the KV]? [The answer]: It means a fine. The admission of a litigant, even though it does not obligate him/her for a fine, nevertheless imposes an oath [as to the remainder]. How much the more so should the defendant in the case of witnesses, whose [conclusive] testimonies do render the defendant liable for a fine, render him liable to take an oath.

Rashi: This rule [that an admission exempts the defendant from a fine] is derived from Bava Kamma [a different tractate of the Talmud] at 75[a]. Scripture exempts the one who admits the claim brought against him from a fine, [for the statement at Exodus 22:8] ". . . and whom the judges shall condemn, he shall pay double to his neighbor," singles out the one who condemns himself.

Comment: Rashi provides the reader with the talmudic discussion in *Bava Kamma* wherein it is derived from Scripture that one who admits to a claim in open court is exempt from a fine. The language "and whom the judges shall condemn, he/she shall pay double to his/her neighbor" by inference excludes the one who has already admitted liability.

Thus, the challenge to the KV formulation is resolved by defining the term *mamon* (money) as a fine. While both may conclusively determine liability, where the defendant admits to the claim of the plaintiff, no fine is levied on account of the defendant's overt act of honesty in open court. Nevertheless, an oath on any disputed balance is imposed if the defendant wishes to be relieved of further liability. In contrast, where witnesses are required because of the defendant's denial, a fine may be assessed because of the defendant's apparent dishonesty. Since an oath is required in the case of an ADM despite the defendant's truthfulness and the absence of a fine, how much the more so in the case of WS, where the defendant's integrity is in question and a fine charged, should the oath be imposed.

The Gemara will now continue to challenge Rabbi Hiya's assumption that the relationship between ADM and WS is one of minor to major, or at a minimum one of equivalency, by examining the specific characteristics of both ADM and WS and their efficacy with regard to religious obligations.

IV. THE RELATIONSHIP BETWEEN ADMISSIONS AND WITNESSES

A. Challenge: An Admission Charges a Litigant with Greater Religious Obligations Than the Testimony of Witnesses

The distinguishing characteristic between ADM and WS [so as to preclude a KV] is that the former requires a sin offering, whereas the latter does not.

Rashi: An admission does require the bringing of an offering: *For it is written, "And the one who confesses that he/she has sinned, he/she shall bring [his/her guilt offering]" (Leviticus 5:5).*

Comment: Rashi is informing the reader that this argument, raised by the Gemara, is supported in Scripture at Leviticus 5:5. In order to understand the comment, the full citation from Leviticus 5:4–6 is set forth:

Or when a person utters an oath to bad or good purpose—whatever a man may utter in an oath—and, though he has known it, the fact has escaped him, but later he realizes his guilt in any of these matters—when he realizes his guilt in any of these matters, he shall confess that wherein. And he shall bring as his penalty to the Lord, for the sin of which he is guilty, a female from the flock, sheep or goat; and the priest shall make expiation on his behalf of his sin [Leviticus 5:4–6].[8]

The Torah requires two psychological elements in order for an unkept oath to be atoned for: self-acknowledgment and confession. The person must have an inner awareness of his sin. Second, there must be the overt act of confession—that is, an *admission* of the sin. When a person's actions are congruent with his conscience, he is authentic. Only in this ontological state may a person commune with God by means of the sin offering.[9]

This same principle of "realization of guilt" applies where one has failed to properly perform any commandment, even if his/her act or failure to act was unintentional. Even then, Scripture requires that the individual realize the wrongfulness of the act itself and then, to be relieved of this guilt, bring an offering:

If any person from among the populace unwittingly incurs guilt by doing any of the things which by the Lord's commandments ought not to be done, and he realizes his guilt—[28] or the sin of which he is guilty is brought to his knowledge—he shall bring a female goat without blemish as his offering for the sin of which he is guilty [Leviticus 4:27–28].[10]

In both instances, the essential characteristic of an admission is an overt act that reflects the conscious awareness of wrongdoing. Confession and offering are the behaviors that represent contrition for this state of being.

---

8. *Tanakh*, p. 158.
9. *Bava Metziah* 3b (Rashi).
10. *Tanakh*, p. 157.

But when you examine the case of WS, they [through their testimony] do not obligate the defendant to bring an offering!

Rashi: If they [witnesses] have contradicted his denial in court, he does not bring an offering, for it is written in Scripture, "or [the sin of which he is guilty] is brought to his 'knowledge' [Leviticus 4:28]." However, [he does not bring such an offering] where others inform him of his mistake.

Comment: Leviticus 4:27–28 provides: "[27] If any person from among the populace unwittingly incurs guilt by doing any of the things which by the Lord's commandments ought not to be done, *and he realizes his guilt*—[28] or the sin of which he is guilty is brought to his knowledge—he shall bring a female goat without blemish as his offering for the sin of which he is guilty."[11]

Whether one commmits an act intentionally or unintentionally, one must have conscious awareness of his/her wrong. An ADM evidences this state of mind and therefore an additional obligation is imposed. There is no such evidence of contrition in the case of WS and thus no religious liability can be imposed. Thus, the assumption of legal equivalency between an ADM and WS so as to support a KV is refuted. Instead, an ADM does have a more powerful effect than WS, for the former imposes the added requirement of an offering.

B. Response: Rabbi Hiya Relies on a Minority Opinion that Supports This KV

[This challenge that you are making] does not pose a difficulty. Rabbi Hiya relies on the minority opinion of Rabbi Meier as recorded in the following Mishnah:

> Two witnesses stated to an individual that "you [accidentally] ate of the forbidden fat [of an offering]." He denies it. Rabbi Meier would obligate him [to bring an offering], whereas the Sages

---

11. Ibid., p.157.

would exempt him. Rabbi Meier argues that if two witnesses can impose the death penalty by their testimony, then how much the more so should their statements impose the lighter penalty of a guilt offering. The Sages respond, what if he wanted to say, "I did it deliberately."[12]

Rashi: [The witnesses] said to him: "You mistakenly ate the forbidden fat of an offering." He responds, "I did not eat." *[The rule is] that he is exempt from bringing an offering. The reasoning is that [if R. Meier's rule was adopted] it would always be possible for him to admit it and add the words that he did so "deliberately" and thus exempt himself from bringing an offering. Therefore, of what material advantage is it for him to lie?*

Comment: If his response to their testimony was that he knowingly ate of the forbidden fat, then everyone would agree (including Rabbi Meier) that he would be exempt from such an offering. A sin offering means that the individual acknowledges wrongdoing. A response such as "I did it deliberately" in the presence of witnesses is defiant and reflects an inappropriate mental state to perform a religious act. It says, "I didn't do anything wrong, even if the community norm suggests that I did!"

The area of disagreement between Rabbi Meier and the Sages is negligence. If witnesses testify that the defendant actually ate the forbidden fat, though not deliberately, then Rabbi Meier holds that their testimony can compel an offering based upon the KV of the death penalty, even if he doesn't admit wrongdoing.

The Sages reject this position and argue that an inconsistency would result from Rabbi Meier's position. In order to exempt himself from bringing an offering after witnesses testified that he acted negligently, a defendant could maintain that he deliberately ate the forbidden fat. The authenticity and integrity of the theocratic system would be compromised. Even if he acted negligently, the law would encourage him to state that he ate deliberately, for it would then

---

12. *Mishnah Keritut* 3:1.

relieve him from the added religious obligation.[13] Therefore, the Sages state that only a voluntary admission in the case of negligence can compel a guilt offering. The Gemara has thus far shown that WS does not have greater efficacy than ADM. Nonetheless, it continues now with two additional challenges to Rabbi Hiya's assertion.

C. Further Challenge: ADM Carries a Heavier Penalty Than the Rule of WS

Furthermore, ADM obligates one for a guilt offering [whereas WS do not]. Moreover, ADM renders him/her liable for an additional one-fifth penalty (in Hebrew termed a *chomesh*) to be paid to the Temple as part of the plaintiff's damages [WS do not carry this penalty].

Comment: The guilt offering and the one-fifth penalty are stated in Leviticus 5:20–26:

> [20] The Lord spoke to Moses saying: [21] When a person sins and commits a trespass against the Lord by dealing deceitfully with his fellow in the matter of a deposit or pledge, or through robbery, or by defrauding his fellow, [22] or by finding something lost and lying about; *if he swears falsely regarding any one of the various things that one may do and sin thereby*—[23] *when one has thus sinned and, realizing his guilt*, would restore that which he got through robbery or fraud, or the deposit that was entrusted to him, or the lost thing that he found, [24] *or anything else about which he swore falsely, he shall repay the principal amount and add a fifth part to it. He shall pay it to its owner when he realizes his/her guilt. [25] Then he shall bring to the priest, as his penalty to the Lord, a ram without*

---

13. The term "theocratic system" requires explication. Rabbinic Judaism has strong elements of democracy within it. *Halakhah* is determined by the majority. Dissent as to the nature of *halakhah* is permitted and strongly encouraged. The talmudic justice system has many parallels to Anglo-American jurisprudence. But the heart of this process is the Torah (as defined in chapter 3) and in this sense, it is theocratic. No individual, however, has the authority to claim personal access to the divine in contravention of the Torah. One has only the right of its interpretation.

blemish from the flock, or the equivalent, as a guilt offering [26] The priest shall make expiation on his behalf before the Lord, and he shall be forgiven for whatever he may have done to draw blame thereby.[14]

Rashi: *If he has sworn and denies that he owes the money and then later admits to it [then he is liable for payment and for the one-fifth penalty], for it is written in Scripture, "or anything else about which he swore falsely."*

Comment: The Sages argue that guilt in the religious context has a characteristic of self-acknowledgment often absent in litigation. In a legal proceeding, an individual may be found guilty but still maintain his/her innocence, as in the case of WS. In this situation, he/she remains exempt from the guilt offering because authenticity before God, as represented by confession and offering, is absent. Only when one actually admits guilt can these conditions be religiously required. Thus, ADM does have a greater impact than WS, for the former imposes more stringent religious obligations than the latter.

The Gemara will now respond to these challenges in the same manner.

D. Response: Rabbi Hiya Relies on the Same Minority View of Rabbi Meier

This is not a difficulty! Rabbi Hiya reasons as Rabbi Meier, for just as he [Rabbi Meier] held him [the defendant] liable for an offering based on the KV (that since the testimony of witnesses can cause the death penalty to be invoked, how much the more so should their testimony be able to enjoin the lighter penalty of an offering), he would also hold him [the defendant] liable for the one-fifth penalty based on the [same] KV.

---

14. *Tanakh*, pp. 159–160.

Comment: The Gemara has weakened the basis of the KV. Nevertheless, Rabbi Hiya's position is supported by the minority opinion of Rabbi Meier, and, therefore, the discussion continues.

E. Challenge: In Contrast to the Testimony of Witnesses, an Admission Is Not Affected by Evidence That Contradicts or Refutes It. Therefore, ADM Has Greater Legal Efficacy Than WS.

Rather, the distinguishing characteristic of ADM is that it is not subject to evidence that either contradicts or refutes it.[15]

Rashi: If a person admits that he/she owes money to the plaintiff and witnesses come and refute him by saying that he is not liable for anything, then he is not exempt in the matter [that is, he still owes the money], for [as we have previously seen in the Tosefta] the admission is the equivalent of one hundred witnesses.

Comment: If a person admits liability and then testimony is presented that exonerates him, the defendant remains liable because the admission of a litigant is equivalent to the testimony of one hundred witnesses.

But can you say the same for WS? For they are subject to contradiction and refutation.

Rashi: If two [other] witnesses come and contradict or refute them [the plaintiff's witnesses], this one does not pay compensation on the basis of the latter's testimony.

---

15. Contradiction and refutation are two different concepts in Jewish law. Witnesses are contradicted when independent evidence is presented that disputes their version of the facts at issue. In such an event, neither testimony is accepted. In contrast, refutation impeaches the credibility of the witness. For example, A testifies that a certain event occurred. B discredits A by swearing that A was somewhere else when the event took place and thus A could not possibly have witnessed the occurrence.

Comment: This presents a serious challenge to Rabbi Hiya's premise, for an admission results in the payment of monies even where other witnesses contradict or refute it. In contrast, the independent evidence proffered by WS remains subject to impeachment. When this occurs, no liability accrues to the defendant. Thus, the law of ADM is more powerful than that of WS because the former is irrefutable. Another aspect that renders this a considerable refutation is that the distinction occurs within the context of a legal proceeding. In the other challenges, the additional obligation that is imposed occurs outside the courtroom—that is, in the Temple. However, the result of a contradiction or refutation occurs entirely within the litigation process. Since WS may be contradicted while ADM cannot, the latter cannot be the minor premise upon which to formulate the KV for the former. For these reasons, this KV cannot serve as the basis for the rule in the Baraita. The Gemara will now formulate a new KV.

V. THE LAW OF THE SINGLE WITNESS
AS A BASIS FOR A KV

Introduction: A single witness (SW) may compel a defendant to deny under the oath the substance of the former's testimony.

The argument here begins simply but is subtle and becomes increasingly complex. You recall the hermeneutic rule of *Binyan Av Mishnei K'tuvim* detailed in the previous chapter, on the hermeneutics of the Talmud. The Gemara introduces this argument here to support the KV of the Baraita. Since a KV may not be based on the law of ADM, the rule of the SW might be the foundation for Rabbi Hiya's KV. The initial formulation is based on a comparison of the rule of the SW (the minor case) to that of WS (the major case) to show that they stand in relationship of minor to major importance.

The rule of the SW provides that the testimony of a single witness, while not having sufficient force to impose liability, nevertheless may compel the defendant to disavow such evidence. Thus the Gemara states:

A. Formulation of New KV Based on Rule of SW

It [the KV of Rabbi Hiya] is derived from the rule of the SW. If, in the SW case, his testimony cannot render a defendant liable for payment but may nevertheless compel an oath, how much the more so should the testimony of WS, which does result in liability, oblige an oath.

Rashi: The litigant claims, "money duly owing to me is in your possession." The opposing side responds, "I have nothing of yours" [that is, he/she denies liability]. Then [in the course of the trial] a single witness testifies that the defendant is liable. Surely this one may take an oath contradicting the single witness, for it is written in Scripture [Deuteronomy 19:15]: "A single witness may not validate against a person any guilt or blame for any offense that may be committed; a case can be valid only on the testimony of two witnesses or more" [Deuteronomy 19:15].[16]

[Rashi continues] With regard to all transgressions and sins, it (the testimony of a single witness) does not establish liability. But with regard to the oath, the testimony of a single witness does compel the defendant to take an oath and to testify in order to refute such evidence [Talmud Shavuot 40a].

Comment: The factual scenario of this rule is identical to that of the Baraita except that the plaintiff is able to produce only one witness to substantiate a part of the claim. Scripture does not establish the validity of the plaintiff's claim by such testimony (so long as the defendant takes an oath. If the defendant refuses, then he is liable to the extent of such testimony), but it does, according to the Talmud *Shavuot*, empower the court to impose an oath on the defendant for any portion to which such evidence applies.

Therefore, if a single witness, whose direct testimony does not result in liability, nevertheless compels an oath, is it not logical that WS, whose testimonies conclusively render him liable, compel an oath!

---

16. *Tanakh*, p. 304.

B. Challenge: The Single-Witness Rule Is Not Comparable to That of the Baraita

[There is an important distinction between the law of the SW and the WS.] What is essential about the rule of the SW is that, concerning those matters to which he/she [the SW] testifies to, he/she [the defendant] may take an oath [refuting the testimony]. But can you say [this principle] holds true for the case of WS—namely, that whatever he has denied [and though the denial has been contradicted by WS], he swears!

Rashi: That is to say, how can you derive the oath of two from the oath of a single witness? The essential point of the SW is that surely the defendant may contradict such testimony given by the the single witness. But can you say the same for the case of WS? In the oath of two witnesses, he/she cannot swear on that which they [the witnesses] have testified. However, [you say] concerning that which they have not testified to and which he has denied, he may swear, but not on their testimony. And from what source [in Scripture] do you derive such a stringency!

Comment: Bear in mind that the stringency to be applied is the oath. The reasons for its seriousness under Jewish jurisprudence is derived in significant part from Scripture [see chapter 7]. Rashi's understanding of the Gemara is that the laws of SW and ADM are not legally analogous to support a KV. A SW imposes the obligation on the defendant only to respond under oath to that portion of the plaintiff's claim to which the witness has testified. Two witnesses preclude the defendant from testifying on that evidence which they have given. Thus, the two cases are not legally analogous and therefore the SW cannot serve as a basis for supporting a KV on the issue of a disputed remainder in the case of WS.

C. Response: The Oath Imposed by the Single Witness May Serve as the Basis for Requiring the Defendant to Take the Oath on the Remainder

Rather, Rabbi Pappah said: [The KV] is derived from the rule that the oath [taken by the defendant] in the case of a single witness is "rolled over" [in order to compel the defendant to swear on any remaining claim brought against him by the plaintiff].

Comment: Given the issues of equality, egalitarianism, and the increasing charges of "sexism" and "discrimination" found in the Pentateuch, it is important to note at the outset that the following may offend feminist sensibilities. There simply is little way, short of "inventing" a new translation, to interpret the text in an egalitarian fashion. One might perhaps suggest that the Sages ought to have instituted an identical procedure for men. Suffice it to say that the biblical case of how the charge of adultery was to be handled serves as the basis for the principle of a "rolled-over oath."

One response, as we will see, is that the oath taken in the case of adultery was to remove all suspicion of wrongdoing and to restore trust in a relationship that requires it.

Rashi: The oath [taken by the defendant in the case of the SW] is rolled over: *If the defendant is obligated to take an oath on the basis of SW, as we have thus far said, and there is another claim in which [the obligation to take] an oath would not "fall upon" [the defendant], we "roll" it [this other matter] into this oath [caused by the SW] and he swears on both of them.*

This "rolled-over" oath is mandated by Scripture, as we learn in Talmud Kiddushin 27b from the biblical phrase, "and the woman shall say, 'amen, amen.'" Surely, he swears concerning those matters to which the single witness has not testified.

Comment: Under Jewish law, if a person is obligated to swear on account of one witness and there exists yet another claim upon which he would not otherwise be required to take an oath, the court is empowered to "roll" the oath onto any additional matters in dispute.

This legal concept of a "rolled-over" oath is scripturally mandated. It is derived from the biblical passages that concern a husband's suspicion of adultery. In such a case, Scripture requires the wife to appear before the priest, who then proclaims:

If no man has lain with you, if you have not gone astray in defilement while married to your husband, be immune to harm from this water of bitterness that induces the spell. But if you have gone astray while married to your husband and have defiled yourself, if a man other than your husband had carnal relations with you—may the Lord make you a curse and an imprecation among your people, as the Lord causes your thigh to sag and your belly to distend; may this water that induces the spell enter your body, causing the belly to distend and the thigh to sag. *And the woman shall say, "Amen, amen!"* (Numbers 5:19–22).[17]

The Talmud *Kiddushin* derives the law of the "rolled-over" oath from the prescription found in this passage: "Ulla said: How do we derive the law of the superimposed oath from the Torah. *'And the woman shall say Amen, Amen.'* To what does she say Amen? . . . Amen that she was not unfaithful by this man. Amen that she was not unfaithful by any other man."[18]

The significance of the term "amen" is derived from the religious setting. She is before the priest and God, and so her words are the equivalent of an oath. There is a suspicion regarding her integrity that can be removed only by her swearing in the name of the Almighty. The Talmud derives two oaths from the doubling of the "amen." One relates to the specific charge of adultery. The other is a general affirmation of her fidelity. Her oaths and actions before the High Priest and God fully resolve the distrust that exists within the sanctity of the marriage. Likewise, once one oath is administered in the SW case, it compels the defendant to deny liability on other claims in order to resolve all issues between them.

Thus, a KV might be established between the rules of the SW and WS. However, the Gemara will challenge this analogy.

D. Challenge: The SW and WS Are Not Legally Analogous and Thus No KV Can Be Drawn

What causes the oath to be rolled over in the case of a single witness is simply one oath causing another. But can you say the same thing for the case of WS for [their testimony] causes liability!

---

17. Ibid., pp. 213–214.
18. *Kiddushin* 27a.

Rashi: Simply one oath causing another: *SW compels an oath only on that to which he/she has testified, and it is that oath which is rolled onto another oath. But can you say the same thing for these witnesses! The fifty [zuzim] to which they have testified, obligate him to pay, but there is no oath imposed which can then be "rolled-over" onto the remainder.*

Comment: The two cases are not analogous. In the case of the SW, it is the fact that the defendant takes an oath on the remainder based on his/her initial oath that relates to the testimony of the SW. But in the case of WS, their testimony obligates him/her only for payment. He/she is precluded from testifying with respect to their evidence. Thus, there is no initial oath upon which to base a second one. Therefore, the law of the SW cannot be utilized as the basis for a KV to support the Baraita and a new KV must be developed.

VI. A KV DERIVED FROM TWO RULES: ADM AND SW[19]

A. A KV Based on the Common Element of Claim and Denial Found in the Cases of Both ADM and SW

The case of ADM will prove [the validity of the KV], for in the case of an ADM, certainly the defendant is not subject to contradiction. The case of SW will prove it [as well], for he/she [the witness] is subject to contradiction and [still] obligates him/her [the defendant] to take an oath. What is special about the rule of the SW is that certainly concerning those matters upon which [the witness] has testified, he/she [the defendant] may swear.

Rashi: *The one who partially admits the claim may swear upon that which he denies and [literally] his mouth does not admit.*

Comment: The Gemara is building a KV based on the two prior rules of ADM and SW. It will now incorporate the previous objec-

---

19. The reader is urged to reread chapter 3 relating to the hermeneutic rule of *binyan av mi'shnei k'tuvim* before commencing this section.

tions and respond to each based on the hermeneutic principle of
binyan av mishnei k'tuvim.

B. Repetition of Previous Objection of a KV Based on SW

But can you say the same for WS, namely, that concerning that
which he has denied, he is required to take an oath!

Comment: The rule of WS prohibits him from testifying on the
matter attested to by witnesses. Not so in the case of a SW.

C. Response: Support That Aspect of the KV by the Use of the Case of ADM

[If the basis of the objection to the KV is the SW, then] let the
case of ADM prove [that aspect of the KV].

Rashi: Let the case of ADM prove it. *He admits to part of the claim;
but on that part which he has denied and not admitted, he may swear.*

D. Challenge: The Argument Is Circular

The logic repeats itself. This aspect is not like this aspect and
this aspect is not like this aspect.

Comment: The case of the SW is distinguishable on one point from
that of WS; so alone it cannot support the KV. Therefore, in order
to meet that objection, the Gemara states, "cite the case of ADM
and the objection will be overcome." Well, when that happens, as
we have seen, objections are raised that render this KV insufficient.
Then the response is, cite the case of the SW to overcome those
objections, and thus the argument goes around in a circle. The
Gemara now "breaks" this aspect by showing that both SW and
ADM have a common element which is also shared by WS.

E. SW and ADM Share a Common Element that Is Also Found in the Case of WS, and This Might Serve as a Basis for a *Binyan Av* (an Extended Form of a KV) to Support Rabbi Hiya's Teaching

The common aspect that is found in them [SW and ADM] is that through the assertion of a claim and the subsequent denial, they come [before the court], and he/she [the defendant] then takes an oath. So too do I [perhaps a reference to Rabbi Hiya] bring the case of WS, for through a claim and denial, they [the litigants] come, and he/she [that is, the defendant] swears.

Rashi: Claim and denial: *[Because] this one claims and this one denies, they come before the court.*

Comment: Each law is insufficient by itself to form a basis for the KV for Rabbi Hiya's rule. Nevertheless, they share a common element. Both in the SW and partial ADM setting, the situation arose through the plaintiff's claim and the defendant's denial. In each instance, the defendant was permitted to take an oath on the disputed remainder. This same element is found in the Baraita. Witnesses testify because the defendant denied the plaintiff's claim. Just as in the cases of the SW and the partial ADM, in which the defendant is permitted to testify because of a claim and denial, so too in the case of WS should he/she be allowed to disavow the remainder.

The Gemara will now challenge this *binyan av* on the basis that there is an important element that is found in SW and ADM settings but is absent in the case of WS.

F. Challenge: A Presumption of Truthfulness Distinguishes the Cases of Both SW and ADM from the Case of WS

[It is true] that there exists a common element between them [the cases of the SW and the ADM], for surely there is no presumption that the defendant [in each of these cases] is a liar. [But] can you say the same [is true] for the case of WS, for surely there is a presumption that the defendant is a liar!

Rashi: [But] can you say same: *Since [the defendant] has denied everything, and they testified concerning the fifty [zuzim], there is a presumption that he is a liar, and it cannot be said that we have faith in him concerning the oath.*

Comment: In the case of the SW, there is no legal presumption of dishonesty. The case of ADM demonstrates some trust in the defendant. But after the testimony of the witnesses in the case of a total denial, there is at least some doubt as to the defendant's veracity. Thus, we should not trust him to take an oath and testify.

The Gemara responds:

G. Response: But the Defendant in the Case of WS Is Presumed Truthful So as to Testify in Other Cases

But in the case of WS, is he/she [the defendant] really presumed to be a liar? Certainly, Rabbi Idi bar Avin, citing Rabbi Hisdah, stated: A lender who denies a claim brought by his creditor remains a suitable witness [in other cases]. Only a bailee, [who denies possession of the bailment, and then witnesses establish the bailor's claim], is unfit to act as a witness [in a different case].

Rashi: The one who denies his lender: *Whether one denies the claim entirely or [whether one denies] a part of it and witnesses come and testify concerning that part of the claim to which he has not sworn, [we hold that] he/she remains a suitable witness [in other cases]. However, we do not say that he/she is a thief [and thus is prohibited from testifying in any case], as the Torah states: "You must not carry false rumors; you shall not join hands with the guilty to act as a malicious witness" [Exodus 23:1].[20]*

For since the lender gives permission to spend it [that is, the lender knows that the loan is going to be put to use], perhaps he/she [the borrower] had to spend it, and thus rationalizes, "until I have the funds, I will delay him, for if I admit [that I owe the money] to him now, I will immediately become destitute."[21]

---

20. *Tanakh*, p. 120.

21. Rashi, *Bava Metziah* 4a. The word יתבעני has the root בע ("to be empty, bare") in the *itpael* (reflexive) with a common singular suffix ["I"]. A literal translation might be, "I will lay myself bare immediately." (See Jastrow, *Dictionary*, p. 181.)

But in the case of the one who denies a bailment, even as to a por-
tion, when witnesses come and testify against him [even as to a part],
he is barred from testifying [in other cases], for how can it be that he
is [denying possession of it] for purposes of delay?

Now perhaps you might say that it was lost by him [the bailee]
and he seeks to delay him [the bailor] until he finds it? Further on in
this tractate [Bava Metziah 5b], we establish [the factual scenario
where the bailee is prohibited from testifying. It is the case] where
witnesses have come and stated that during the time it was in his pos-
session, he used it for his own purposes.

Comment: Prior to the taking of any oath, the borrower remains
an appropriate witness. This holds true regardless of whether he
has denied the claim in its entirety or has admitted to a portion of
it. Jewish law does not ascribe the legal status of a thief (who is
unfit to testify in all cases) to the borrower. The scriptural basis
for the rule pertaining to the thief is taken from the phrase found
in Exodus 23:1 "you shall not join hands" which is understood to
mean that those who rob cannot serve as witnesses.[22] In contrast,
since the purpose of a loan is for the borrower to utilize it (and the
lender expects him/her to do so), he/she probably has spent it out
of necessity.

The concern for economic preservation pressures the borrower
into an untenable position. Selfishness and greed are not the moti-
vating factors in the Baraita. The Talmud views the the fear of poverty as the primary force that causes the lender to deny the loan.
Therefore, the borrower, despite his initial denial, remains a
"kosher" witness to testify in other cases.

But the distinction made by Rabbi Idi with regards to the bailee
being unfit to take an oath needs further explication as well. As
Rashi explains, one might argue that just like the borrower, he seeks
to delay, not because of fraud or misappropriation, but rather

---

22. *Mekilta de-Rabbi Ishmael*, trans. Lauterbach, 1:162. The rabbinic understanding of this phrase is that those who are wicked shall not testify. This
would include robbers and men of violence. For further explication of this verse,
see chapter 7.

because of a personal embarrassment over having misplaced it. Thus, he rationalizes that until he finds it, he will deny having received it. As Rashi illustrates, this is not the case to which Rabbi Idi is referring. Instead, witnesses are prepared to testify that during the time the defendant was entrusted with the bailment, he made personal use of it—that is, he misappropriated it for his own needs. Combined with his/her initial denial and the presence of witnesses, he/she is the equivalent of a robber and thus unfit to testify in other cases.

H. Challenge: Unlike WS, ADM and SW Are Not Subject to the Law of Retaliation, and, Therefore, the *Binyan Av* Must Fail

Rather, refute [this *binyan av*] in the following manner. The element that both the ADM and SW share is that neither is subject to the law of retaliation, but can you say the same is true for the witnesses, for surely they are subject to the law of retaliation!

Rashi: Retaliation: *[This means] to pay a fine, for when [the testimony] of a single witness is refuted, he is exempt from the law of retaliation. And in the case of an admission, all the more so that there is no "connection" whatsoever to the law of retaliation. But can you say the same is true for witnesses: If they are refuted on the fifty that they testified to, they pay money.*

Comment: The law of retaliation provides that where witnesses have knowingly given false testimony, a penalty is imposed upon them. This consists of assessing them with the same monetary damage that the defendant would have sustained had their testimony not been refuted.

As stated in Deuteronomy 19:15–19:

A single witness may not validate against a person any guilt or blame
for any offense that may be committed; a case can be valid only on

the testimony of two witnesses or more. If a man appears against another to testify maliciously and gives false testimony against him, the two parties to the dispute shall appear before the Lord, before the priests or magistrates in authority at the time, and the magistrates shall make a thorough investigation. If the man who testified is a false witness, if he testified falsely against his fellow, you shall do to him as he schemed to do his fellow. Thus you shall sweep out evil from your midst; others will hear and be afraid, and such evil things will not again be done in your midst.[23]

Of course, a finding of malice is a prerequisite for the penalty to apply and thus precludes any fine for testimony which is merely impeached. (Otherwise, as a practical matter, who would ever testify as a witness in a case and risk such a loss?)

This rule does not apply in the case of the SW because such testimony alone cannot conclusively establish any issue at trial. (With an admission, the rule has no application at all.) Consequently, the common element that both ADM and SW share, unlike the case of WS, is that the law of *hazamah* (retaliation for false testimony) is inapplicable. Therefore, the *binyan av* does not underpin the rule formulated by Rabbi Hiya.

I. Response: The Law of Retaliation Is Not a Sufficient Distinction So as to Render This KV Invalid

This is not a difficulty! R. Hiya maintains that the law of retaliation is an insufficient basis [to refute the KV based on the hermeneutic principle of *binyan av mishnei k'tuvim*.]

Rashi: For him [Rabbi Hiya], this challenge [to the binyan av *based on the law of retaliation] is not sufficient, for [in a sense] the law of retaliation does apply in the case of the SW—that is, to nullify his testimony through the testimony of two witnesses. And we could say with respect to WS that [an aspect of] the law of retaliation is that [if they*

---

23. *Tanakh*, p. 305.

are refuted], they do not obligate the defendant to take an oath, then we could say as well with respect to the SW, that he/she [the SW] does not obligate the defendant to take an oath, for through the law of retaliation, his/her testimony is voided. And if [the objection to the binyan av *based on the law of retaliation] is because there is no payment of a fine [in the case of the SW who has now been refuted, unlike the case of WS], nevertheless this aspect does not render such testimony [any more] believable (that is, the fact that there is no fine does not make the testimony of the single witness any more credible. Indeed, such testimony is void, like that in WS).*

Comment: Rashi's commentary is quite lengthy because the Gemara's statement "for Rabbi Hiya, the law of retaliation is not a challenge" is not at all explained. First, he shows that the law of retaliation does apply in the case of the SW. If the SW is refuted, as in the case of WS, the most important effect is that his/her testimony is voided. Another aspect of the law of retaliation that both the SW and WS share is that, if the the testimony is refuted, the defendant does not have to take an oath. Finally, if one argues that in the case of the SW he does not pay a fine [which does occur in the law of retaliation, and therefore his testimony should somehow stand despite the rebuttal of other WS], this fact alone does not render his testimony credible, for the defendant may take an oath and refute this evidence directly. The lack of a fine in the case of a SW is a minor distinction insufficient to mount a challenge to the *binyan av*. The essential point is that in both cases, the most significant aspects of the law of *hazamah* apply. The testimony is canceled and no oath may be imposed.

Another way of explaining the Rashi and Rabbi Hiya's statement is that the distinction based on *hazamah* between the SW and the partial ADM, on the one hand, and the Baraita on the other, is inadequate to mount a challenge to his KV. First, the cases of the SW and the WS in the Baraita are both subject to the law of retaliation. In the case of the SW, the form of retaliation is that his testimony is voided. In addition, the defendant does not have to testify at all. Likewise in the case of WS, if other witnesses establish that the plaintiff's witnesses had falsely and maliciously testified, their testimony is canceled and the defendant relieved from having to testify.[24] Second, the status of all three cases contains an important element: that there exists a remainder which is subject to dispute. In both the SW and the partial ADM cases, the defendant is permitted to testify, thus resolving all issues before the court. Likewise, in the Baraita, where there exists a disputed remainder, the defendant should be allowed to take an oath and deny liability and thus settle all disputes between the parties.

With this response, the Gemara has concluded its exhaustive analysis of the *kal v'chomer* statement of Rabbi Hiya. (It will now discuss the importance of the phrase "and the Tanna of our Mishnah taught along similar lines.")

Let us now examine some features about the literary method of the Talmud.

OBSERVATIONS

The rationale of the Baraita is derived from the laws of the SW and ADM by the hermeneutic tool of *binyan av mishnei ketuvim*. A defendant may take an oath and testify on a disputed remainder where witnesses have confirmed only a part of the plaintiff's claim.

Clearly, the richness of the Talmud's analysis reflects a harmonizing and holistic approach in integrating scriptural and mishnaic sources within the context of its dialectic. In this aspect, the human characteristics of rationality and logic encounter that which is regarded as divine. The oath, and the laws of partial admission, witnesses, and single witness, as Rashi has illustrated, are all grounded in the Torah. Note, however, the lack of explication by the Gemara or even direct reference to the scriptural basis for these rules. In this regard, it seems as if the authors assume, as modern scholars have indicated, their readership to be well versed in these passages.

Another feature is the argumentative style of the Gemara. Neither the individuals making the challenges nor those respond-

---

24. Steinsaltz, *The Talmud: The Steinsaltz Edition*, Vol I, *Bava Metzia*, p. 34.

ing are identified. Anonymity in this regard gives a certain equality. Both the challenge and the response are important.

Finally, and perhaps most important, is that the Baraita is not explicitly covered by any of the scriptural rules cited. There is a "gap" in the law when it comes to WS who testify to only a part of the plaintiff's claim (a common occurrence in litigation). Thus, the Baraita becomes the symbolic arena between the reality of society—of the everyday struggle between people—and Torah. And just as people struggle with one another in court, so too did the Sages struggle to discern and to apply what God intended in a small but significant aspect of the divine blueprint for creation.

THE FUEL OF THE DIALECTIC

This striving to discern the divine intention must begin with an analysis of the central issue of this text, the oath, for it is the essential fuel of this dialectic. It underlies almost every argument, analysis, and formulation. Therefore, its scriptural treatment and its analysis in the corresponding literary rabbinic genres of the Midrash, Mishnah, and Talmud should be considered in order to fully appreciate the arguments of this passage from *Bava Metziah*.

The context of the dispute involves a lender and a borrower. The scriptural treatment of this relationship is therefore relevant to our discussion. Exodus 22:24 characterizes it in the following manner: "If you lend money to My people, to the poor among you, do not act toward them as a creditor: exact no interest from them. If you take your neighbor's garment in pledge, you must return it to him before the sun sets; it is his only clothing, the sole covering for his skin. In what else shall he sleep? Therefore, if he cries out to Me, I will pay heed, for I am compassionate."[25]

Deuteronomy 15:7–8 adds to the richness of the *mitzvah*: "If however, there is a needy person among you, one of your kinsmen in any of your settlements in the land your God is giving you, do

25. *Tanakh*, p. 120.

not harden your heart and shut your hand against your needy kinsman. Rather, you must open your hand and lend him sufficient for
whatever he needs."[26]

These two verses require a person to remain sensitive to the
needs of those who may require help. The *mitzvah* to lend is clearly
set forth. The midrashic exegesis of these verses will enrich the
understanding of the theological and ethical underpinnings contained in this passage from the Talmud.

The law of an admission played a critical role in this *sugya*.
Early in the passage, the Gemara asserted that the right to swear
on a disputed remainder in the case of an admission was provided
by Scripture. However, no citation to Scripture in support of
Rabbah's argument is made by the Gemara. Instead, as we will see,
its derivation is based on the phrase "this is it" found in Exodus
22:8: "In all charges of misappropriation—pertaining to an ox, an
ass, a sheep, a garment, or any other loss, whereof one party alleges,
'This is it'—the case of both parties shall come before '*elohim*': he
whom '*elohim*' declares guilty shall pay double to the other."[27]

The midrashic literature relating to this verse, as well as those
immediately preceding and following it, focus on issues of honesty and trust, suspicion and doubt, and God's role in resolving
disputes and promoting harmony between people.

Finally, the laws of both single and multiple witnesses play
an important role in developing the KV. These rules, provided for
in the *Sifre*, are based on Deuteronomy 19:15–20. Its analysis of
these passages provides much of the tension reflected in the dialectic.

Within the context of Scripture's characterization of the
lender–borrower relationship, the oath, admission, and witnesses,
will be combined to form a *scriptural foundation* that seems to provide the fuel which drives the talmudic dialectic in analyzing the

---

26. Ibid., p. 299.

27. Ibid., p. 119. Though the term *elohim* in many biblical passages is a
reference to God, in the legal sections of Scripture, the Midrash defines the term
as "judges." This has theological implications that are more fully treated in
chapter 7.

Baraita of Rabbi Hiya. These underpinnings illustrate that the talmudic process is neither disjointed nor irrationally associative in nature.[28] Instead, the scriptural foundation will reveal the inherent logic of the Talmud in its search for the divine will. As a corollary, their continuing search for the significance of God's revealed word, which transcends time, is fueled by the divine imperative of Sinai to explore the meaning of Torah and its application to the realities of human encounter.

---

28. The reader will recall from chapter 1 that the Talmud has been criticized on the basis that the Talmud appears disjointed and associative. Critics conclude from this apparent structure that the editors were far more interested in advancing their own agenda, that is, authority. In response, it may be the reader's own lack of familiarity with the literary antecedents relevant to the discourse that gives the Talmud this appearance. This work attempts to demonstrate that once this foundation is provided, the discourse is logical and is in essence an exegesis of Scripture.

7

The Scriptural Foundation
for the Talmudic Dialectic

INTRODUCTION

Numerous biblical passages have been either cited or alluded to in the course of the talmudic dialectic on the Baraita above. These scriptural elements provided the authority upon which the arguments were formulated and analyzed. Just as the authors of the Talmud were totally familiar with these sources, so too did they presuppose their reader's knowledge of their exegesis. The aim of this chapter is to provide the reader with this *scriptural foundation* and then to re-examine the Baraita and the Gemara in the light of this knowledge. In so doing, the reader will encounter the central issue of this text: the Talmud's reluctance to allow a rabbinic court to require an oath in the absence of a litigant's partial admission.

Three scriptural concepts were evident throughout this selection from *Bava Metziah*: oath, admissions, and witnesses. The requirement of the oath hinged on whether the evidence for the plaintiff was furnished by the defendant or, instead, by independent testimony. However, the text never explained the characteristics of this oath in its theological and human dimensions as developed by Scripture and its early rabbinic exegesis. By understanding its nature and function in humankind's relationship to

God and to one another, we may better comprehend the underlying theological and psychological aspects of the dialectic.

The second part of this chapter will show the process through which the law of admissions is exegetically derived from Exodus 22:8. When one examines this passage, the inference is not clear. Rather, the context, as indicated by the verses immediately preceding it, is a suspicion by a bailor of misappropriation by the bailee.[1] The laws pertaining to loans, however, are described in Exodus 22:24. The difficulty is that this latter verse does not provide for a remedy in the event of a dispute or a default by the borrower. Therefore, in order for the provisions of 22:8 to apply to the Baraita, one must demonstrate a sufficient analogy between the relationship of a lender to a borrower and the relationship of a bailor to a bailee. This can be accomplished only through an analysis of the rabbinic exegesis of these passages. The reader will, thereby, be exposed to a rabbinic philosophy that suggests that the function of litigation is as much the removal of suspicion and the restoration of trust in human relationships as it is to determine the truth of a matter.

The third section of this chapter examines the roles of both the single and multiple witnesses in litigation in the absence of an admission as described in Deuteronomy 19:15–21. The dialectic arises from the tension created by the legal definition of truth (according to Scripture) in the absence of such an admission. Legal certainty in such a case is determined by the testimony of two independent witnesses who are neither refuted nor contradicted. Whereas Scripture is clear that the testimony of two witnesses prevents the defendant from taking an oath altogether, the testimony of a single witness fails to meet the scriptural standard of certainty and truth. It is this uncertainty that creates a basis for imposing an oath in the case of a single witness. It also provides half of the necessary precedent to permit Rabbi Hiya's rule to be adopted. Thus, the *Sifre*'s analysis of this scriptural passage suggests a subtle shift in the perception by the court of the defendant's honesty and integrity in the absence of conclusive proof by the plaintiff.

---

1. A bailment is where X entrusts property to Y for safekeeping for a period of time. In the scriptural setting, the bailment has either been stolen or has been allegedly misappropriated. X now brings suit against Y.

Together, these elements will form a *scriptural foundation* that may enable the reader to consider more fully the scriptural concepts which the Talmud relied upon in constructing its dialectic. To this end, I hope to provide the reader with an opening through which he or she may peer beneath the surface of the text and into the rich theological and humanistic worlds created by God and humanity.

A. THE OATH AND ITS MIDRASHIC EXPLICATION

The Role of Intent

It is generally accepted within Jewish tradition that violation of a commandment requires intent. The oath is an exception, for Scripture considers both its deliberate and its inadvertent violation to constitute a transgression that triggers theological and practical consequences. Two passages, Exodus 20:7 and Leviticus 5:4, juxtaposed by the *Mekilta de-Rabbi Ishmael*, support this conclusion. These passages are:

"You shall not swear falsely by the name of the Lord your God; for the Lord will not clear one who swears falsely His name" [Exodus 20:7],[2] and

> [4] When a person utters an oath to bad or good purpose—whatever a man may utter in an oath—and, though he has known it, the fact has escaped him, but later he realizes his guilt in any of these matters—[5] when he realizes his guilt in any of these matters, he shall confess that wherein he has sinned. And he shall bring as his penalty to the Lord, for the sin of which he is guilty, a female from the flock, sheep or goat, as a sin offering; and the priest shall make expiation on his behalf of his sin. . . . [13] Thus the priest shall make expiation on his behalf of whichever of these sins he is guilty, and he shall be forgiven. [Leviticus 5:4–5, 13][3]

A tension exists between these two passages. The verse from the Decalogue is apodictic: "You shall not swear falsely in God's name."

---

2. *Tanakh*, p. 115.
3. Ibid., pp. 158–160.

No remedy is provided for its violation. God will hold one fully accountable. In contrast, the passage from Leviticus is casuistic. "When a person utters a false oath and realizes his guilt . . . then he shall confess, bring an offering, and God will forgive." There is a forum for redress and forgiveness in the Leviticus passage that is notably absent in the Exodus verse. Thus, the passages, when contrasted, seem contradictory.

The *Mekilta* addresses this dichotomy by interpreting Exodus 20:7 as addressing the situation in which one intentionally swears to a falsehood. In such a case, the phrase "for God will not acquit" renders ineffective any atonement offering. Instead, the punishment for its transgression (to be distinguished from forgiveness) is laches, which is instituted only in capital cases. Society reproves the offender.[4] In contrast, the *Mekilta* asserts that Leviticus 5:4 applies to the unintentional false oath. The person mistakenly believes *x* to be the case when *y* was the situation. At one time, the defendant may have actually known the truth, but at the time of his testimony, it was "concealed" from his consciousness. The individual, with the assistance of the religious institution, purges himself of this guilt through confession and offering.

Both passages assert that the individual is in an ontological state of guilt when false testimony is presented, regardless of intent. In the Exodus verse, "God will not acquit" implies the defendant's guilt, whereas the Leviticus passage makes the reference to guilt explicit.[5] The ability of the individual to rid himself of this state depends upon his intent, for the Leviticus passage provides a means for relief, whereas the Decalogue provides no such mechanism. As to this latter element, another dimension of the oath is to be explored before

---

4. In capital cases, Jewish law requires two witnesses to forewarn the defendant of the specific crime that he is about to commit and then these same two witnesses are to testify against him *before* punishment could be inflicted.

5. Guilt in Scripture suggests an ontological state, not one simply of emotion. A good analogy may be to modern law. One may be guilty of a crime, but not feel guilty. One is purged of this legal guilt through punishment imposed by the court. Likewise, the individual who incurs scriptural guilt could be cleared of this status only through the remedies that are provided. Thus, for intentional violations of Exodus 20:7, the absence of such a remedy is a serious matter.

approaching the midrashic understanding of atonement for swearing falsely: its relationship to holiness and profanation.

The Oath in the Context of Holiness

The oath functions in both contexts of holiness and profanation. Leviticus 19:1–12, commonly referred to as the "Holiness Code of Scripture," provides:[6]

> [1] The Lord spoke to Moses, saying: Speak to the whole Israelite community and say to them: [2] You shall be holy, for I, the Lord your God, am holy. . . . [11] *You shall not steal; you shall not deal deceitfully or falsely with one another. [12] You shall not swear falsely by My name, profaning the name of your God: I am the Lord.*[7]

The *Sifra* comments first on the importance of this chapter of the Torah: "The reason that Moses was to speak before the entire community was that the majority of underlying principles of the Torah are contained in it."[8]

According to the early rabbinic communities, this chapter is the core of the Torah. It is foundational, for it expresses a clear theology that holiness is the ontological state that is the object of religious practice. To remain in this state, there are specific standards of conduct which must be adhered to, one of which is the avoidance of a false oath. The *Sifra* articulates the conditional relationship between this ontology and behavior.

> "You shall be holy because I, your God, am holy" [Leviticus 19:2]. [The *Sifra* begins to expound:] This may be interpreted to mean "if you sanctify yourselves [by fulfilling these commandments], then I will consider you as if you are sanctifying me and if you do not sanctify yourselves [by following these *mitzvot*] I will consider you as though you are not sanctifying me."

---

6. The reader is urged to read all of Leviticus 19 in order to appreciate the relationship between holiness and human action.

7. *Tanakh*, p. 185.

8. *Sifra: Torat Kohanim*, p. 70.

[Rhetorically it asks] Or does it mean rather if you sanctify me, surely I will be sanctified and if not, I will not be sanctified? [No, for] Scripture teaches that the phrase "I am holy" is to be understood as follows. I am in my holiness whether you sanctify me or not. Abba Shaul stated: It is [similar to] a minister [in his relationship] to the king. What is his charge? To follow in the wake of the King.[9, 10]

Holiness characterizes the relationship between human behavior and its imitation of the divine. It is a state achieved through action that results in self-sanctification (holiness achieved through action). But this aspect is not one of egocentrism, for the *Sifra* implicitly rejects humanism. Action that leads to self-sanctification moves the religious person into the realm of the divine. Self-sanctification through righteous behavior corresponds to God's continual state of being, as it were, which is one of holiness ("I am in my holiness whether you sanctify me or not").

Similarly, unrighteous behavior does not mean that God is less sanctified. God's holiness is undiminished. Instead, righteous behavior is analogous to one who ministers to a king. His mission is to conduct himself with the appropriate protocol, which consists of acts that complement the king. For humanity, these proprieties are detailed in the Holiness Code of Leviticus and include the prohibition of lying, cheating, and swearing falsely.

The *Sifra* interprets these commandments as an interrelated series of events. "*You shall not steal, you shall not deal deceitfully, you shall not lie against your fellow man, and you shall not lie in my name.* If you steal, you will come to deal deceitfully. And if you deal deceitfully, you will eventually lie. And if you lie, you will come to swear falsely in my name."[11]

There are two ways in which to explain this midrash. The first is to take a specific event and show how, in the end, the offender will come to take a false oath. For example, suppose X steals from Y. X will come to deal deceitfully with Y by being evasive. Eventu-

---

9. *Sifra*, p. 70.
10. Jastrow, *Dictionary*, p. 460.
11. *Sifra*, p. 75.

ally Y will sense this deception and will confront X. X will then lie. Y will then bring X before a court, where the latter will be compelled to swear falsely because of his previous actions. The house of cards eventually collapses.

Another rendering of this midrash is that it describes the human personality that has embarked on the slippery path away from the state of holiness and towards its opposite, desecrating God's name. It leads from stealing to deceit to lying and finally even to being false to God. The person's course of moving farther from honesty and integrity culminates in his/her invoking God to further his/her own wrongful conduct.

The essential feature of this process is intention. Each of the acts involved—stealing, deception, lying, and invoking God's name to attest to a false matter—are deliberate. With regard to this last element, one might think there is a possibility of a loophole, which would be to swear in one of God's other names, rather than "the tetragrammaton."[12] The *Sifra* rejects this position.

> *You shall not swear falsely by my name*: What is added [by this verse] for surely it has already been stated "you shall not swear in the name of the Lord your God [in Exodus 20:7]"?[13] [Had this verse from Leviticus been omitted] I might have thought that I would only be liable for violating this commandment if using God's special name [that is, the tetragrammaton]. From where is it derived to include

---

12. The *Mekilta* describes that the oath was to be administered though the use of the tetagrammaton. Since both the *Mekilta* and the *Sifra* were edited subsequent to the destruction of the Second Temple in 70 C.E., this may reflect a response that since its name could no longer be pronounced (either because the Temple was destroyed or because no one actually knew how to pronounce it), the commandment against swearing falsely no longer applied. It may also support a thesis that the *Sifra* was compiled after the *Mekilta*, since the latter relies on the oath's administration by the tetragrammaton, whereas the *Sifra* does not. See *Mekilta de-Rabbi Ishmael*, trans. Lauterbach, 1:122.

13. The midrashic issue is that Leviticus 19:12 appears redundant in light of Exodus 20:7. This would contradict the principle that there is nothing extraneous or arbitrary in the Torah. In this regard, Ben Bag Bag states in *Avot* 5:22, "Turn and turn it [the Torah], for everything is in it."

all names [of God]? Scripture teaches [in this verse that the term]
"in my name" means any name that I have.[14]

The oath is not a technicality. Using any of God's names for a false
oath constitutes a transgression. Thus, intention, not behavior, is
the essence of violating these dictates—a point developed in this
chapter from Leviticus.

The act of taking God's name as an accomplice in order to
promote the individual's wrongful design renders the act a *hilul
hashem*, a defilement of God's sacred name. The *Sifra* concludes its
analysis: "And you profane the name of your Lord: [This verse is
teaching] that a false oath is a *hilul hashem*, a desecration of God's
name."[15] The intentional desecration of God's name renders the individual unholy and at the same time renders the Almighty and the
purpose of creation as a mockery before humanity. By placing the
intentional false oath in the category of a *hilul hashem*, Scripture and
the *Sifra* are emphasizing the seriousness of the transgression.

To summarize, thus far we have shown that the crime of swearing falsely is serious, whether intentional or unintentional. Its violation has an ontological effect in that it renders one unholy. For
unintentional violations, the remedy is confession, offering, and
restitution. But its intentional transgression renders the act a *hilul
hashem*, a desecration of God's name through which no immedi-
ate relief appears available.

The Perjurer Is the Moral Equivalent of a Thief

Given the halakhic categorization of the false oath as a *hilul hashem*,
it is important to consider the psychological dimension of the perjurer and its impact on his/her community. The parallel drawn is
to the scriptural treatment of the thief. The perjurer desecrates
God's name in a public forum, by attesting to a false matter. In a
sense, he is a thief who commits his crime secretly. Like the thief

---

14. Ibid., p. 75.
15. Ibid., p. 75.

who steals when no one is able to witness his crime, the perjurer also steals because he thinks no one will contradict or refute his testimony, which he knows is false. This argument finds support in the Mekilta's analysis of Exodus 22:6, in which it describes the mind-set of the thief.[16] "When a man gives money or goods to another for safekeeping which are then stolen from the man's house—if the thief is caught, he shall pay double."[17] The Mekilta implicitly equates the perjurer to the thief. It begins its analysis by contrasting the different psychological states of the thief and the robber, with the penalty more severe upon the former than the latter. It notes that if the thief is found, he must pay double the value of what he stole. However, a robber does not pay such a penalty. Rhetorically, it asks: "Why is the Torah more severe in its treatment of the thief than of the robber?"[18] The Mekilta then cites a mashal (parable) attributed to Rabbi Yochanan ben Zakkai, the founder of the rabbinic community at Yavneh. "The robber treats equally the servant and his Master. However the thief favors the servant over his Master."[19] Rabbi Yochanan ben Zakkai explains that the thief acts as if God's eyes and ears neither hear nor see the thief's transgression. The thief wrongfully believes that God simply does not take note of his actions. Three proof-texts are furnished: Isaiah 28:15, Psalm 94:7, and Ezekiel 9:9–10. The citation from Isaiah provides: "Ha! Those who would hide their plans deep from the Lord! Who do their work in dark places and say, 'Who sees us, who takes note of us?'" [Isaiah 28:15].[20]

The passage from Psalms requires a context, which is provided in the three sentences that precede the actual citation found in the Mekilta.

16. The reader should note that Exodus 22:6 is within the context of the main exegetical verse, which deals with the law of partial admission in which the individual is allowed to take an oath.

17. Tanakh, p. 119.

18. Horowitz and Rabin, Mekilta de-Rabbi Ishmael, p. 299.

19. Ibid.

20. Tanakh, pp. 676–677.

[1] God of retribution, Lord, God of retribution appear! [2] Rise up, judge of the earth, give the arrogant their deserts! [3] How long shall the wicked, O Lord, how long shall the wicked exult, [4] shall they utter insolent speech, and shall all evildoers vaunt themselves? [5] They crush Your people, O Lord, they afflict Your very own; [6] they kill the widow and the stranger; they murder the fatherless, [7], thinking, "The Lord does not see it, the God of Jacob does not pay heed."[21]

The Psalmist is appealing to God to take action against those who seek to destroy Israel. Those who utter "insolent speech" are also characterized as wicked. They erroneously think that the God of Jacob does not pay attention to it and thus deny God's omniscience.

Likewise, Ezekiel confronts God in the Temple regarding the latter's order to kill those who have committed abominations in Jerusalem. God responds: "[8] The iniquity of the Houses of Judah and Israel is very great, the land is full of crime and the city is full of corruption. [9] For they say, 'The Lord has forsaken the land, and the Lord does not see.' [10] I, in turn will show no pity or compassion; I will give them their deserts."[22] Rabbi Yochanan's analysis and proof-texts suggest a strong analogy between the characterization of the thief under this rabbinic model and the one who swears falsely. First, in each of these citations, thought and speech constitute the essence of the transgression. In Isaiah, it is the evil design in dark places in which they say, "Who sees us, who takes note of us?" According to the Psalmist, it is the insolent speech that incurs God's wrath. From Ezekiel, it is the corruption that has infested the city in which the corrupt say, "For the Lord has forsaken the Land, the Lord does not see." Both of these elements, evil design and speech, are present when one intentionally proffers false testimony. His/her conduct in both speech and behavior reflect an intent that states, "God does not see what I am doing."

But there is one element absent in the thief that is present in the one who takes a false oath in open court. The latter is done in

---

21. Ibid., p. 1220.
22. Ibid., p. 903.

a public forum. This element of perjury, absent in the thief, renders it a *hilul hashem* and will create a theological dilemma: whether God will forgive such a transgression during the lifetime of the perjurer even if he/she repents.

The Oath, *Hilul Hashem*, and Repentance

An open transgression of God's name, as has been shown thus far, is a serious offense. The *Mekilta* and parallel passages in the Talmud suggest that such a crime will not be forgiven by God until death. This possibility, that God will not forgive an intentional false oath because it constitutes a *hilul hashem*, presents a fundamental challenge to the Jewish notion of repentance in which all infractions against the Almighty are forgiven on Yom Kippur. This difficulty is illuminated in two passages. One is from the *Mekilta*. The other is from the concluding Mishnah from the Talmud *Yoma*. Within the context of this dialectic, the essence of the *hilul hashem*, a public display of arrogance against God, will be examined.

The author(s) of the *Mekilta* were troubled by the phrase "for God will not acquit the one who takes God's name in vain" (Exodus 20:7). If the verse is taken literally, then one will remain guilty forever. God simply does not forgive the one who violates this commandment. Such a position is disturbing from the rabbinic perspective, in which repentance and atonement are considered available in every instance.

Perhaps for this reason, the *Mekilta* analyzed Exodus 20:7 in conjunction with Exodus 34:6–7. The latter reads: "The Lord! the Lord! a God compassionate and gracious, slow to anger, abounding in kindness and faithfulness, extending kindness to the thousandth generation, forgiving iniquity, transgression, and sin; yet He does not remit all punishment but visits the iniquity of parents upon children and children's children upon the third and fourth generation."[23] The verse contains the verb *nakeh* (acquit). Thus, it appears that God forgives iniquity, transgression, and sin. On the

---

23. Ibid., p. 139.

other hand, it contains the phrase *lo yenakeh* (he will not acquit) to indicate that some transgressions may persist throughout generations. The author of the *Mekilta* concludes that repentance is the determinative factor in God's forgiveness. If the one who commits the transgression repents, God will pardon. If there is no repentance, then there is no acquittal.[24] This reflects the traditional Jewish position on sin and repentance.

However, the *Mekilta* limits the efficacy of repentance when it involves a profanation of God's name. "If one has profaned the name of God and repents, his repentance cannot leave the case pending, neither can the Day of Atonement bring him forgiveness, nor can sufferings cleanse him of his guilt. But repentance and the Day of Atonement both can merely make the matter pend. And the day of death with suffering preceding it complete the atonement."[25] The scriptural basis for this assertion is derived from I Samuel 3:14 and Ezekiel 37:13. According to the Book of Samuel, Eli, a priest at Shiloh, had two sons, Hophni and Phinehas. The Bible describes these two as scoundrels who treated the offerings brought by Israel with contempt. For this reason, they were despised by the people. In addition, they lay with women of ill repute at the Tent of Meeting, which housed the tablets of Moses. Eli argued with them: "If a man sins against a man, the Lord may pardon him; but if a man offends against God, who can obtain pardon for him?" When they ignored their father's admonition, God told Samuel: "And I declare to him [Eli] that I sentence his house to endless punishment for the iniquity he knew about—how they committed sacrilege at will—and he did not rebuke them. Assuredly, I swear concerning the house of Eli that the iniquity of the house of Eli will never be expiated by sacrifice or offering (I Samuel 3:14)."[26] This proof-text submits that those acts that are directly offensive to God and done publicly, such as lying with women of ill repute in the sanctuary or mocking the offerings of the community to God, are not forgiven through sacrifice or offering. These acts constitute a desecra-

---

24. Horowitz and Rabin, *Mekilta de-Rabbi Ishmael*, p. 228.
25. *Mekilta de-Rabbi Ishmael*, trans. Lauterbach, 2:250–251.
26. *Tanakh*, p. 422.

tion of God's Name. The result seems to be an endless form of punishment.

Ultimately, an unforgiving God is rejected by the *Mekilta*, which contends that death achieves complete repentance for profaning God's name. The *Mekilta* invokes the messianic vision of Ezekiel's dry bones prophecy.

> And therefore prophesy and say to them, so says the Lord God, surely I will open your graves and lift you up from your tomb and bring you to the land of Israel. And you will know, that I, in opening your graves and lifting you up from there, am God and that you are my people. And I will breathe my spirit into you and you will live and I will bring you to rest upon your land; and you know, that as I have spoken, so will I do, sayeth the Lord. (Ezekiel 37:13)[27]

Israel's exile from the Holy Land was viewed by the prophets as Divine retribution for its transgressions against the word of God. Yet, even in their exile, Ezekiel envisions redemption. God, regardless of the sin, does not forsake the community of Israel. Thus ultimate forgiveness and redemption will occur so long as one repents and observes Yom Kippur.

The concluding Mishnah from *Yoma*, which deals with Yom Kippur, challenges the *Mekilta*'s understanding of Exodus 20:7.

> . . . Transgressions between man and God—Yom Kippur atones. Transgressions between one person and another, Yom Kippur does not bring atonement until the man who committed the offense will seek pardon from his neighbor. And so Rabbi Elazar ben Azaryah would *drash* on the phrase, "From all your sins before God, you shall be purified" [Leviticus 15:30]; for sins between Man and his Creator —Yom Kippur effects atonement. . . . Rabbi Akiva stated: Rejoice, O Israel! Before whom may you be purified?[28] Who puri-

---

27. *Torah, Nivi'im, Ketuvim*, trans. author (Jerusalem: Koren Publishers, 1988).

28. The word מטהרין, though mishnaic Hebrew, is in the *piel*, which is an active, rather than passive, form. It reflects a strong, positive act. Thus, a suggested translation may be "before whom you do you cleanse [yourself from sin]? Who is it that purifies you? Your father, who is in heaven . . ."

fies you? Your father who art in heaven, as it is stated [Ezekiel 36:25]: And I shall sprinkle upon you purifying waters and you shall be purified; and as it states [in Jeremiah 17:13]: God purifies Israel; Just as the ritual bath cleanses one's sins, so too does the Holy One, Blessed Be He, purify Israel.[29]

This Mishnah posits that one who atones on Yom Kippur is cleansed of sins committed against God. Rabbi Akiva, who lived shortly after the destruction of the Second Temple and witnessed the crushing defeat of the Bar Kochba rebellion by Rome, proclaims to Israel in this passage that God will purify them, even in the absence of the temple cult. As proof-texts, he advises, rely on those prophets who witnessed the destruction of the First Temple.

But the Gemara to this Mishnah asserts that one who commits a *hilul hashem* is not forgiven on Yom Kippur. It relies on the same midrashic concept as expressed in the above passage from the *Mekilta* but cites a passage from Isaiah instead of Samuel as its proof-text:

> For the one who desecrates God's name, repentance is insufficient to leave the matter pending, Yom Kippur does not atone for it, nor does chastising purify. Rather all combine to leave the matter pending and death cleanses the person of the guilt. This is supported by Scripture. "Then the Lord of Hosts revealed Himself to my ears; 'This iniquity shall never be forgiven until you die,' said my Lord of hosts." [Isaiah 22:14][30]

The full context of this citation from Isaiah contains a popular verse. God has summoned Israel to observe a day of atonement by lamenting and donning sackcloth. Israel ignores this divine exhortation and instead celebrates by eating meat and drinking wine, all the while proclaiming: "Eat and drink, for tomorrow we die!"[31] The

---

29. *The Mishnah, Seder Moed,* with Commentary by Hanoch Albeck (Jerusalem: D'vir Publishing Company, 1988), p. 247.

30. *Yoma* 86a. This aspect of the argument appears nearly verbatim in the *Mekilta.* For a comparison, see Horowitz and Rabin, *Mekilta de-Rabbi Ishmael,* p. 227.

31. *Tanakh,* p. 660.

public display in which a society openly transgresses the word of God constitutes desecration of God's word. The Gemara to this Mishnah from *Yoma* develops this theme by exploring the meaning of "and you shall love the Lord, Your God" within the context of *hilul hashem*.[32]

> That the *Name of Heaven* shall be loved through your acts [the Gemara first describes one whose actions reflect his knowledge of Torah and how such a person is beloved by his/her community] . . . but the one who reads, studies, and serves scholars of the Torah but does not conduct his business affairs with honesty and his words are not comforting to his fellow-man, what do people say about him? Woe to the one who studied Torah and woe to his father and rabbi who taught him Torah for they see how crooked his actions and how repulsive his ways. And about such a person, Scripture states "[But when they came to those nations, they caused My holy name to be profaned, *in that it was said of them*] "these are the people of the Lord, yet they had to leave His land." [Ezekiel 36:20][33]

This Gemara suggests that the *hilul hashem* is not the act of corruption by one who is learned in Torah. Rather, it is the perception by other people that those who represent Torah have nullified its intent by unrighteous behavior. Such conduct renders Torah study meaningless, as well as the person's lineage and teachers. It demonstrates a profound lack of respect for God.

The violation of a commandment that falls into the category of *hilul hashem* thus has two elements. One is that it violates an express decree of the Torah. Second, it occurs in a public forum through which the observer concludes that God is unloved. The comment by Rashi not only illuminates this point but suggests an important historical underside to this problem of the perception of Jewish suffering incurred in the Diaspora by those who were non-Jewish:

---

32. Deuteronomy 6:5 provides in full: "And you shall love the Lord, your God, with all your heart, with all your soul, and with all your might."

33. *Yoma* 86a.

In that it was said of them, this is the nation: This verse describes the essence of desecrating God's Name. Just as an important person commits a transgression and punishment befalls him and everyone exclaims, [Look] what has happened to him, so too the one who sees the evil that has befallen the righteous and the wise, as it states, "and they desecrated my Holy Name."[34] And what is this desecration? Upon seeing these people of God dispersed among them, the gentiles say that God is not able to save them so that they would not be exiled. Hence, the Name of Heaven is desecrated and his glory diminished.[35, 36]

For Rashi, the *hilul hashem* is not only the perception of unrighteous acts. What is more important is that the non-Jewish world will view the suffering of the righteous as a sign of God's helplessness or God's abandonment of the Jewish people rather than as divine retribution for the unholy conduct of Israel that led to its fall and exile in 70 C.E.

To summarize: There is a difference between one who swears falsely through negligence and one who does so intentionally. As to the former, Yom Kippur, when combined with confession and offering, will entirely atone for the sin.[37] But the intentional violation constitutes a *hilul hashem*, which cannot be fully atoned for in one's lifetime. Ultimately, death will complete repentance and bring redemption. Perhaps for this reason, the *Mekilta* urges one not to swear at all, for only God knows what is in the heart—a God who

---

34. The wise and the righteous of subsequent generations suffer punishment from God because of the *hilul hashem* of their ancestors, which lead to the destruction of the Temple and the Diaspora.

35. *Yoma* 86a.

36. An implication of the *hilul hashem* is that it has the potential to confirm the argument of the gnostics: God, after creating heaven and earth, is no longer concerned with it. Thus, God is not going to intervene in the affairs of his "chosen people," or anyone else for that matter. It is theorized by historians that much of the literature of the tannaitic and amoraic period was a polemic against gnosticism.

37. Since the destruction of the Second Temple, as Rabbi Akiva indicates, complete atonement is effected on Yom Kippur through prayer and repentence.

becomes a judge who will not forgive the one who takes the God's name in vain during the lifetime of the penitent. Instead, such a person shall remain unholy.[38]

B. THE SCRIPTURAL DERIVATION FOR THE PARTIAL ADMISSION: EXODUS 22:6–8

Introduction

The derivation of the law of admission is from Exodus 22:6–8, which deals with the relationship created by a bailment. At first glance, these passages seem irrelevant to the Baraita of Rabbi Hiya. However, three important principles will be established. First, a bailment is a relationship of trust. When a suspicion arises that undermines this element, these verses suggest a mechanism for the resolution and restoration of the underlying association. The difficulty is that the lender–borrower relationship is not explicitly covered by this passage. Thus, the first task is to demonstrate that an adequate level of similarity exists between bailments and loans such that the latter should also be subject to Exodus 22:8.

The exegesis of Exodus 22:8[39] will show the following: First, the analogy between loans and bailment will support the rabbinic understanding that the failure to repay a loan would constitute a trespass on another's property. Second, a significant shift from ancient forums for eliciting truth occurs. The *Mekilta* will reject a suspected practice of consulting oracles for determining the truthfulness of an individual. In its place, the *Mekilta* will interpret the word *elohim* to refer to judges and, through a *gezera shavah*, will empower the court to administer an oath. Thus, instead of utiliz-

---

38. Horowitz and Rabin, *Mekilta de-Rabbi Ishmael*, p. 227.

39. For purposes of clarity [though the full citation is within the body of this work], Exodus 22:8 provides, "in all charges of misappropriation—pertaining to an ox, an ass, a sheep, a garment, or any other loss, whereof one party alleges, 'This is it'—the case of both parties shall come before God; he whom God declares guilty shall pay double to the other." *Tanakh*, p. 119.

ing divination, humanity must take responsibility for determining the truth of a matter. Third, the rendering of the phrase "this is it" is the source for the doctrine of partial admission that gives rise to the imposition of the oath. A Mishnah and supporting commentary by Rashi, taken from the Talmud *Shavuot*, will crystallize this analogy between the loan and bailment.

Finally, an important element, not present in either the Baraita or the Gemara of *Bava Metziah*, is discerned from this passage. There exists an obligation to accept the oath of the litigant by the other party.[40] This suggests that a primary goal of the scriptural litigation process is the restoration of the relationship from one grounded on suspicion and doubt to one of trust. Though important, a secondary purpose is to resolve the underlying dispute in the absence of independent evidence.

We turn now to the first goal of our discussion of these verses: to demonstrate the correlation between a bailment and loan. This is a necessary endeavor because the validity of the methodology depends upon demonstrating that scriptural support for *midrash halakah* is not arbitrary or the result of a strained or forced reading of the text. Instead, the verse in its full context clarifies the interdependency between the two sets of laws.

The Legal Analogy between Bailment and Loan

Exodus 22:6–8 provides:

> [6] When a man gives money or goods to another for safekeeping, and they are stolen from the man's house—if the thief is caught, he shall pay double; [7] if the thief is not caught, the owner of the

---

40. It should be noted that such terms as *adversary* or *opposing sides* do not adequately reflect the scriptural or talmudic characterization of the relationship of the litigants in court. The term used by the Talmud and later commentators is חבר, which connotes "friend." This is in keeping with the scriptural requirement that, where the defendant takes an oath, in the absence of other contradictory proof, the plaintiff is to accept it.

house shall depose before God that he has not laid hands on the other's property. [8] In all charges of misappropriation—pertaining to an ox, an ass, a sheep, a garment, or any other loss, whereof one party alleges, "This is it"—the case of both parties shall come before "*elohim*": he whom "*elohim*" declares guilty shall pay double to the other.[41]

A specific procedure must be followed in order to constitute a bailment. One, the bailor must deposit the article with the bailee. Second, he must state to the bailee, "Here it is; guard this article for me." If the bailor's language is informal (for example, if he states, "Keep an eye on it"), then the bailee is exempt from liability.[42]

In order for a claim based on a violation of this passage to be heard by a rabbinic court, certain requirements must be met. It must be subject to measurement, such as weighing or counting. Rabbi Natan defines "monies" to include those amounts that have been set aside for tithing. By focusing on the Hebrew word *lishmor*, Rabbi Natan expands the definition of "monies and vessels" to include any object that could be the subject of a bailment.[43]

In summary, a bailor (the one who deposits the item) and bailee (the one who accepts the item for safekeeping) have a relationship based on trust and a firm understanding. The bailor seeks protection of an article that has a definite value. The language that creates the legal relationship of a bailment is unequivocal. All of these factors—trust, understanding, specificity, and a transfer of the item into the physical possession of the bailee—must be present before a disputed claim that arises from this relationship may be brought before a court. These same elements must exist in the lender–borrower relationship in order for the *halakhah* that results in the imposition of an oath by a court to apply.

---

41. *Tanakh*, p. 119.
42. *Mekilta de-Rabbi Ishmael*, trans. Lauterbach, 3:113–114.
43. Horowitz and Rabin, *Mekilta de-Rabbi Ishmael*, p. 298.

The Duty to Loan

In this same chapter from Exodus, the requirement of lending to those in need is stated. "[24] *If you lend money to My people*, to the poor among you, do not act toward them as a creditor: exact no interest from them. [25] If you take your neighbor's garment in pledge, you must return it to him before the sun sets; (26) it is his only clothing, the sole covering for his skin. In what else shall he sleep? Therefore, if he cries out to Me, I will pay heed, for I am compassionate."[44] The *Mekilta* makes emphatic the obligation to lend money to those in need.

> Rabbi Ishmael states: Every "if" that is in the Torah renders [such a command] permissive [A person may either choose to fulfill its dictates or because of his own choice or action, may be subject to its directives. For example, the one who unintentionally swears to a falsehood is then obligated to perform certain acts] except in three circumstances, one of which is this commandment.
>
> [The *Mekilta* rhetorically challenges this statement of Rabbi Ishmael] You say [that the scriptural term] "if you loan money" renders it an obligation. Perhaps it does not? Rather [the phrase] is permissive. The *Mekilta* then answers: Scripture states [at Deuteronomy 15:8], "Thou shalt surely lend him" in order to render this *mitzvah* obligatory and not permissive.[45]

The full text of the Deuteronomy citation supports Rabbi Ishmael's interpretation that if someone seeks a loan, you *must* lend him funds. Deuteronomy 15:7–8 states: "[7] If, however, there is a needy person among you, one of your kinsmen in any of your settlements in the land that the Lord your God is giving you, *do not harden your heart and shut your hand* against your needy kinsman. (8) Rather, you must open your hand and lend him sufficient for whatever he needs."[46] Therefore, the lender is required to loan money to one

---

44. *Tanakh*, p. 120.
45. Horowitz and Rabin, *Mekilta de-Rabbi Ishmael*, p. 315.
46. *Tanakh*, p. 299.

in need. He cannot refuse without committing a transgression. The *Sifre*'s remarks:

> *Do not harden your heart*: There are people who will be in difficulty whether you give or not. *Do not shut your hand* (your heart): There are people who stretch forth their hand then close it. *Against your needy kinsman*: And from where is it derived that if you open once, you are to open [your hand] even one hundred times? Scripture teaches *for you must open your hand.*[47] *You shall lend him*: We give to him repeatedly and we collect it, these are the words of Rabbi Judah. But the Sages [state]: We say to him, "In the future we will collect it," but only to pacify his mind.[48]

The ethical values illuminated in this passage are a statement against the complacency of human nature to the poor. You are commanded to give, even though poverty will continue. There is an immediacy to lending, for the opportunity is lost if the moment is not seized, since the hands of those who are impoverished close quickly out of the embarrassment suffered by having to ask. And just as you give to a person who is in need once, surely you should extend yourself one hundred times. The obligation is endless.[49]

The legal right to consider it a loan indicates a dispute between Rabbi Judah and the Sages. Rabbi Judah's remarks reflect a relationship grounded in legality, for the one who loans the money has the right and expectation to collect it. But the Sages suggest that the characterization of the transaction as a loan is done only to pacify the borrower in order to preserve his sense of dignity and mutuality. Thus, the lender should consider carefully the pursuit of a legal remedy in the event of nonpayment. The duty to lend

---

47. The infinitive absolute form in the Hebrew פתח תפתח is understood by the *Sifre* to indicate a repetitive obligation.

48. *Sifre debi Rav*, pp. 98–99.

49. Notice the use of the term *one hundred* as a euphemism for "infinite." This same number was used to describe the efficacy of an admission when compared to that of witnesses.

should not create the automatic expectation of repayment. [50, 51] The *halakhah* follows Rabbi Judah.

Though establishing the obligation to loan monies without interest, Exodus 22:2, *et. seq.* is silent on remedies where the debtor has failed to repay. However, from the above, the same elements present in the case of bailment are found in the case of the loan. The lender trusts the borrower that at some point he will be repaid because, even from the Sages' perspective, it is the borrower who wishes to treat this as a loan. From the outset, the relationship will have an element of mutual respect at least in the mind of the borrower. There is an overt expression that concretizes the understanding in the borrower's mind that there is the expectation of and the right of repayment to the lender. A specific sum of money is transferred into the possession of the borrower from the lender. Finally, a dispute arises through the denial as to the amount owed, such that the lender suspects a misappropriation, as evidenced by the borrower's refusal to pay the balance claimed. Thus, the lender–borrower relationship is scripturally analogous to that of the bailor–bailee such that the provisions of Exodus 22:8 should apply. We now turn to the rabbinic exegesis of this pivotal verse.

Concerning All Matters of Trespass

This analogy between loans and bailments is further supported by the *Mekilta*'s exegesis of the opening phrase, "concerning all matters of trespass." The over-all structure of the verse invokes the hermeneutic principle of *k'lal u'phrat ukhlal*.[52] The *Mekilta* states:

---

50. This position might be evidenced by such statements to the borrower as, "I know you'll pay this back whenever you're able to," "Don't worry about it, when the time is right I know you'll pay it back," or "You don't have to sign anything, I know you'll take care of it whenever you're back on your feet."

51. For an extended discussion on the issue of loans to those in need, see *Bava Metziah* 31b.

52. The term *k'lal u'phrat u'klal* literally means "generalization, detail, and generalization." Where a scriptural verse begins with a general statement, followed by a detailed list of items, and concludes with a generalization, only items which have the same element as those contained in the detailed statement of

Concerning any matter of trespass: It is a general statement [in its description of items]; *concerning any ox, donkey, sheep, or clothing* are specific . . . *or any other loss* is a general statement. . . . Since the pattern is general, specific, and then general, only items which share the common element listed in the specified items can be included [within the rubric of chapter 22:8]. The elements common to each are that they are personal property and not subject to security. . . .[53, 54]

A specific interpretation is made of the term "concerning any matter of trespass" that renders it applicable to Rabbi Hiya's Baraita. Since trespass includes not only objects that are movable and not subject to mortgage but also monies, it theoretically could include the failure to repay a loan so as to constitute a trespass. This initial exegesis gives further foundation to the analogy between these two legal relationships used to support the applicability of Exodus 22:8 to the case of the lender.

The Meaning of "This Is It"

In simple fashion, the *Mekilta* defines the ambiguous phrase כי הוא זה (literally, "this is it") as constituting an admission to a part of the claim of the plaintiff's. It states: "that one says, 'this is it': that this one [the defendant] states, 'this is it,' and this one [the plaintiff] says it is not. From here, the (rabbis) reason that there is now an admission to a part of the claim." The case of partial admission has now been raised. The plaintiff claims against the defendant that the

---

the verse are subject to the scriptural mandate that follows. For a more extended discussion, see chapter 5 of this work and Steinsaltz, *The Talmud: A Reference Guide*, p. 153.

53. Horowitz and Rabin, *Mekilta de-Rabbi Ishmael*, p. 301. As an aside, this analysis is the basis for the *halakhah* in which a toraitic oath (one that uses the tetragrammaton) is not invoked in a claim based on real estate.

54. Personal property in modern law may also be the subject of security agreements, so long as specific statutory requirements are met (see Article 9 of the Uniform Commercial Code, adopted in all fifty states). However in common law, security agreements with respect to such chattel was not originally recognized. Only land was subject to such an agreement.

latter has misappropriated in some fashion an article that belongs to the plaintiff. The bailee or borrower either refunds a portion in open court (or both parties agree that a portion has already been returned) and in open court, he states, "This is it," referring to that which is refunded as being the extent of his liability. The plaintiff responds, "This is not the [entire] claim."[55] The Sages conclude that the status of the case is now one of partial admission to which there exists a disputed remainder.

"The Matter between Them Shall Be Brought before *Elohim*": From Oracles to God to Judges

The relationship of trust that preceded the litigation has now turned to one of suspicion, as represented by the term "all charges of misappropriation." The resolution of this suspicion begins with the *Mekilta* discerning the meaning of the phrase, "the case of both parties shall come before *elohim*." This term *elohim* is dealt with by the *Mekilta* in its analysis of the same term found in preceding verse. There, the *Mekilta* states: "I might have thought [that the term *elohim*] refers to the *urim v'tumim* [that is, oracles]. But since [in verse 8] it states, 'he whom *elohim* shall condemn,' it must refer to judges, for only judges may condemn."[56] The *Mekilta* may be reflecting a previous practice in which such disputes were resolved through oracles. Perhaps, at one time, this may have been the manner in which conflicts were settled where there was no independent evidence to support the claim of a party. Instead, the resolution of mistrust, which at its worst undermines a basic element necessary for a community or society to function, has now become a human duty.

There is a theological parallel as well. In the preceding section, it was established that, after one took an oath, God became a judge in determining whether a false oath had been taken inten-

---

55. One might infer that the text means the plaintiff to state, "This is not the claim in its entirety," though the actual wording of the text is, "This is not it." Horowitz and Rabin, *Mekilta de-Rabbi Ishmael*, p. 301.

56. *Mekilta de-Rabbi Ishmael*, trans. Lauterbach, 3:116.

tionally. Like their counterpart in heaven, judges determine the guilt or innocence of parties involved in a dispute, and thus the term is appropriate.

A logical consequence of defining the term *elohim* as judges would be to empower judges with the right to administer an oath. However, neither verses 7 nor 8 explicitly provide for this remedy. Because of its serious theological nature, on the one hand, and the human requirement to resolve issues of suspicion and mistrust, on the other, the authors of the *Mekilta* anchor their determination to impose the oath on the basis of the hermeneutic principle of the *gezerah shavah* (verbal analogy) to Exodus 22:10.[57]

The *Mekilta* notes that the phrase, "whether the defendant has sent forth his hand" is found in both Exodus 22:7 and 10. The latter verse provides in full: "*The oath of God* shall decide between the two of them that the one *has not laid hands on the property of the other*; the owner must acquiesce, and no restitution shall be made."[58] Since both verses contain the phrase "that he has not laid hands on the other's property," the halakhic (legal) requirements of Exodus 22:10 may be applied to Exodus 22:7. Since an oath of God is the remedy provided for in Exodus 22:10, it may be imposed in the case in which a party suspects another of misuse. Since the same term, *elohim*, is contained in verse 8, both its definition as "judges" and the remedy of the oath are proper constructions.

This contextual reading, based on the interdependent relationship between Exodus 22: 7, 8, and 10, is concretized in the Mishnah from the Talmud *Shavuot* and developed in the supporting commentary of Rashi. The Mishnah provides in relevant part: "Concerning the oath of litigants: . . . if [the plaintiff claims against

---

57. See chapter 5 for a detailed analysis of the *gezerah shavah*. Briefly, a *gezerah shavah* is a verbal analogy used in Biblical exegesis. If the same word or phrase appears in two places in the Torah, and a certain law is explicitly stated in one citation, then one may infer that the same law must apply in the other citation as well. It is often used not only to determine the meaning of words and phases, but to "transfer entire *halakhot* from one context to another." See Steinsaltz, *The Talmud: A Reference Guide*, p. 150.

58. *Tanakh*, p. 119.

the defendant] that the latter owes one hundred dollars and the [defendant] admits to fifty dollars, the defendant is obligated to take an oath denying liability on the remainder [and is thus relieved of any further obligation]."[59] This Mishnah from *Shavuot* begins specifically "the oath of litigants" and is therefore not limited to one group, such as a bailee.[60] Rashi writes: "*Concerning the oath of witnesses*: That the litigants swear on account of the admission to a part of the claim as derived from [Scripture] where one states, '*This is it*' [Exodus 22:8], as well as on the preceding [Scriptural passage] wherein it is written that '*the master of the house*' is brought before *elohim* to determine through the oath whether he *sent forth his hand*."[61] This reading of the Mishnah by Rashi is based on Exodus 22:8 in its full context to support or to derive the *halakhah* as articulated in the Mishnah. Any litigant, including a borrower, who is charged with misappropriation, wherein he states, "This is it," in order to indicate that he admits to a part of the plaintiff's claim, is to be brought before a court of law for the purpose of taking an oath in the absence of independent witnesses.[62] This Mishnah thus concretizes the analogy between the lender–borrower and the bailor–bailee. When the borrower is then charged with "misappropriation" and admits to a part of the claim, he is brought before the court and the oath administered.[63]

---

59. *Shavuot* 38b.

60. The previous section of the fifth chapter of *Shavuot* concerns the oath of one who accepts a deposit, that is, a bailee. Thus, the Mishnah from the main passage concerns the application of the oath in the context of general litigation and includes, therefore, the lender–borrower relationship.

61. *Shavuot* 38(b). See Rashi at שבועת הדיינין.

62. The reader will note that the full context of Exodus 22:10 indicates that there are no witnesses to testify as to the actual circumstances under which the loss of the bailment was incurred. There, the issue is negligence. Likewise, it appears that the *Mekilta* and the Mishnah assume the same lack of witnesses in the charge of misappropriation. Such an assumption would be appropriate given the parameters of the *gezarah shavah*.

63. This presumes that there is not evidence that is uncontrovertable, such as the testimony of two or more witnesses who can establish the entire validity of the plaintiff's claim. If this were the case, the defendant is prohibited from testifying.

The Requirement to Pay Double

However, the text still contains an ambiguity. Exodus 22:8 concludes: "[to whom the judges shall attribute guilt] such person shall surely pay double to his neighbor."[64] This verse, according to the opinion of Rabbi Shimon in *Mekilta*, appears to be in conflict with Leviticus 5:24. It provides: "Or anything that one has sworn to falsely, he shall repay the principal amount and add a fifth part to it. He shall pay it to its owner when he realizes his guilt."[65] The *Mekilta* reconciles these two passages as follows. The term "double" in the Exodus verse refers to two types of payment, rather than to an amount. The first payment is the requirement of restitution. The other is the one-fifth penalty. One who is obligated to pay the principal (because of false, even inadvertent, testimony) regarding a dispute must also pay the additional one-fifth penalty. Both verses cover the same situation. The court has determined that the individual has sworn falsely. Thus, he pays both the principal amount and the one-fifth penalty.

The Requirement to Accept the Oath

The *gezera shavah* that was used above, in addition, allows the remainder of the verse from Exodus 22:10 to be read as part of Exodus 22:8. This has the effect of imparting the purpose of the oath: to effectuate, if possible, the removal of suspicion and to restore a relationship that was initially based on trust. This segment provides that once an oath is taken: "[10] . . . the owner must acquiesce, and no restitution shall be made. . . . "[66] As a prelude to the analysis of this part of the verse, the *Mekilta* suggests that the oath functions to restore the original bond between these two litigants. The *Mekilta*, citing Rabbi Natan, provides: "That the oath softens the matter which affects both of them."[67] The Hebrew verb *hilah* means

---

64. *Tanakh*, p. 119.
65. Ibid., p. 160.
66. Ibid., p. 119.
67. Horowitz and Rabin, *Mekilta de-Rabbi Ishmael*, p. 303.

to soften, sweeten; to soothe, assuage.[68] An added dimension to the oath is thus intimated by the *Mekilta* in this rendering: that the jurisprudence of the Torah is fundamentally concerned with the restoration of the qualitative nature of the relationship that preceded the litigation. In other words, the oath becomes a tool through which human relationships may be preserved or restored through its removal of mistrust.

This theme of repairing human trust as a function of toraitic jurisprudence is further developed in the *Mekilta*'s interpretation of the phrase, "and the owner shall accept": "*And its owner shall accept and [the defendant] shall not pay.* From here, the rabbis hold that if anyone, upon whom an oath is imposed, swears, then he does not pay. But others hold [that the phrase he "shall accept" it] means that the owner takes the actual remains of the carcass."[69] The actual biblical phrase does not have a direct object for the verb לקח, which generally, depending on the vowels underneath the Hebrew consonants, means to take or to receive. The verb can also refer to a gift or lesson.[70] The *Mekilta* renders the direct object in its first interpretation to refer to the oath and, therefore, continues this theme of the duty to accept the oath of the defendant.

In this spirit, the plaintiff is "obliged" to accept the oath as one might receive a gift. The *Mekilta*, by its exegesis of Exodus 22:8, suggests a far different world of values from the one normally associated with the administration of the oath. Instead of the oath being connected to the issue of determining wherein the truth lies, its primary function is to restore a fractured relationship.[71]

---

68. Jastrow, *Dictionary*, p. 467.

69. *Mekilta de-Rabbi Ishmael*, trans. Lauterbach, 1:124. In the second interpretation, it refers to the owner's duty to literally take the carcass of the deceased animal, the remains of a bailment, which, through no fault of the defendant, was killed.

70. Jastrow, *Dictionary*, p. 717.

71. Of course, it also recognizes the reality of the disgruntled plaintiff by suggesting the other rendering, which is that all that he is required to accept are the remains tendered to him.

Summary

A theme that runs throughout these sections of the *Mekilta* is the value of facilitating trust and care in human relationships. The potential lender is not to harden his heart in response to those in need. The one who is disadvantaged and requires financial assistance does not seek charity. Instead, the *Mekilta* characterizes this borrower as one who seeks mutuality and respect. Thus, it is trust—indeed, one might even suggest faith—that should motivate the lender to extend his hand in support of his borrower.

But the reality is that sometimes a borrower cannot pay. Often, a suspicion of misappropriation arises, and there are no witnesses to the transaction. Exodus 22:8 provides a remedy: a legal proceeding which, though God's name is invoked, is a uniquely human enterprise. Human judges become the representative of a commitment to the divine scheme of justice as represented in the Torah. As the implementers of its jurisprudence, they become *elohim*, as it were, but not in the sense of those one engaged in divination or who furnish oracles. The search for truth is now an endeavor grounded in the realities of the interdependent connections between people.

Having examined the scriptural treatment of the oath and its purposes, let us now turn to the law of witnesses, which suggests, by prohibiting a defendant from taking an oath, that there are times when such a relationship between a lender and a borrower cannot be restored.

C. THE LAW OF WITNESSES: EXEGESIS OF DEUTERONOMY 19:15–20

In the majority of cases, there are witnesses to a transaction that gives rise to the dispute. As we have shown, an admission in the absence of independent evidence compels an oath to resolve disputed matters and to rejuvenate the underlying relationship. The authenticity of this goal is grounded in the reality that there is no other way in which to determine the truth. But where there are witnesses, suspicion as to the defendant's integrity is only heightened, for his denial is contradicted by their testimony. On the basis of reason alone, the inappropriateness of the oath in the case of witnesses seems self-evident.

Deuteronomy 19:15 provides the laws that determine the impact of the testimony of witness(es) upon a matter in dispute. "[15] A single witness may not validate against a person any guilt or blame for any offense that may be committed; a case can be valid only on the testimony of two witnesses or more."[72] The *Sifre* derives the rule of the oath in the single-witness setting from the phrase, "a single witness may not validate against a person any guilt or blame for any offense that may be committed":

> Rabbi Yose states: A witness cannot establish liability, but he can impose an obligation to take an oath. What is significant about the oath in the case of an admission? Surely, he pays compensation and on the basis of his acknowledgment, he is therefore permitted to take an oath as to the remainder. [Rhetorically, one could ask] should one take an oath on account of a single witness when, surely, the latter cannot impose liability? Scripture teaches [by use of the term] *any manner of guilt* that while the [single witness] cannot establish liability, he can impose an oath [upon the defendant to deny the charge].[73]

The *Sifre* notes the all-inclusive phrase "any manner of guilt." One could reason erroneously on the basis of a KV that his testimony could not compel an oath, for this type of evidence, unlike that of an admission, does not establish liability. Scripture, by using the term "any manner of guilt," is referring only to liability. In the absence of specific language directed towards an oath, it does not prevent the court from imposing this requirement upon the defendant.[74]

---

72. *Tanakh*, p. 305. The reader will note the omission of verse 21, which provides "nor must you show pity: life for life, eye for eye, tooth for tooth, hand for hand, foot for foot." The rabbinic exegesis of this phrase is that of monetary compensation for the loss of these items. See Talmud *Bava Kamma* 86a.

73. *Sifre*, p. 108.

74. As a practical matter, if the defendant refuses to take an oath, the plaintiff is awarded damages. The basis for the ruling is a combination of both the

The *Sifre* acknowledges the difference between the case of admission and that of the single witness. In the former, the defendant evidences honesty by his own conduct in which he admits liability. In the latter, the single witness has increased the level of suspicion. However the Torah places a limit as to the efficacy of this testimony. It does not establish liability for payment. It only permits the court to impose an oath. The Talmud *Shavuot* concretizes this rule in the following discussion:

> Rabbi Nachman in the name of Rabbi Yitzchak, quoting Shmuel:
> . . . but in the claim of a lender where the testimony of a single witness establishes only a *perutah* of the value of his claim [that is, a minuscule portion of the plaintiff's over-all claim, usually insufficient to establish any liability], the defendant is still obligated to take an oath. What is the reasoning? For it states, a single witness may not validate against a person any guilt or blame for any offense that may be committed [Deuteronomy 19:15]. For any transgression and for any sin, he cannot establish liability, but he can impose the obligation to swear as is taught in a Baraita: In any situation in which two witnesses can impose an obligation for money, one witness can impose an oath.[75]

Rashi develops this KV in his commentary to this passage from *Shavuot*: "The oath that is imposed in the case of a single witness arises from the fact that the borrower denies everything while one witness has testified that he is obligated for at least a portion of the claim. Thus, the defendant must take the oath even if his claim is only for a *perutah*, and he denies liability, since, if there were two

---

defendant's refusal to take an oath and the single witness's testimony. The presumption is that the defendant's refusal to take the oath is evidence that his testimony would confirm the single witness's account. The *Mekilta* provides that the court has no authority to compel the defendant to swear. See Horowitz and Rabin, *Mekilta de-Rabbi Ishmael*, p. 303.

75. *Shavuot* 40a. An example of the "chain of tradition," developed in chapter 2, is found in this selection. Rabbi Yitzchak is an *Amora* (the generation of scholars who followed the *Tannaim*) who cites tannaitic authority for his statement of the law with regard to the single witness.

witnesses, they would obligate him monetarily for this amount."[76] Rashi's insight provides the reader with the necessity for the construction of Deuteronomy 19:15 to impose an oath in the case of the single witness. If it were dealing only with liability for money, there would be no necessity for its inclusion because the last section of this scriptural verse states explicitly that liability could be imposed only in the case of two witnesses. The implicit question is thus, what does the first part of the verse come to teach us? It teaches that while liability cannot be imposed, the obligation to take an oath does result from the testimony of a single witness.

By the Mouth of Two or Three Witnesses

Liability can be imposed only by the testimony of two witnesses. The *Sifre* interprets this edict narrowly: "Not by a letter [to the court] and not through an interpreter."[77, 78] The witnesses must be present in open court. They cannot send a letter or affidavit stating what their testimony is. Furthermore, they must testify in a language that is understandable to the parties and to the court. Only in such an instance is their testimony regarded as valid. The law of WS may be viewed as an outside parameter which, if the situation warrants, precludes the taking of an oath.

Summary

The laws of the single witness and witnesses are grounded in Scripture. They confirm the other reality of the dialectic: that suspicion and doubt as to the integrity of the defendant is experienced where the extrinsic evidence contradicts his assertions. To allow for an oath where the evidence is defined as conclusive, as in the case of two witnesses, would not further the ends of scriptural jurispru-

---

76. *Shavuot* 40a.

77. *Sifre*, p. 108.

78. The Hebrew word מתורגמן is generally interpreted as a translator. Jastrow also renders the term "an interpreter." See Jastrow, *Dictionary*, pp. 860–861.

dence, and, therefore, no oath is allowed. But where there is proof, albeit not conclusive, an oath functions to remove the doubt. There is a line which, if crossed, precludes the taking of an oath. Thus, the right to an oath is not absolute. The Torah has defined, whether one agrees with it or not, the situation in which, if an oath were to be permitted, its integrity would be seriously compromised.

CONCLUSION

The blueprint of Torah often seems removed from the realities of the daily struggles between human beings for their economic survival. Nevertheless, relationships between people are the focus of Scripture. It functions to remove cynicism and mistrust where a dispute arises. Most important, its goal is to preserve the state of holiness in which God intended humankind to live. These rules of partial admissions, in which the duty to loan money without interest and to characterize it as a loan so as to maintain the dignity of the borrower, assert that people are worthy to invoke the name of the Almighty so that distrust may be removed from society. The fact that a person may invoke God's name dishonestly is a risk, but it alone would never justify a rule that would prohibit its practice. In that sense, the Torah expresses confidence in the basic honesty of people to use the name of God to increase holiness on earth.

Nevertheless, the purpose of a court is to determine wherein the truth lies. The Torah acknowledges that to permit an oath in the face of strong evidence could actually serve unwittingly to desecrate it. In light of this concern, the oath of a defendant is barred when the evidence is regarded as conclusive on an issue; that situation is defined as the irrefutable and noncontradicted testimony of two witnesses. At the same time, the testimony of a single witness does arouse doubt because this evidence is independent and contradicts the defendant's denial. Yet, it is not conclusive. Here, the court is allowed to impose the oath on this "gray area" of proof. It reflects a confidence that the defendant, sufficiently aware of

God's presence, will swear and testify truthfully or respectfully decline the obligation and fulfill the claim of the plaintiff.

And so, the role of the oath has a transcendent feature that extends beyond providing a methodology for determining the truth. This is to impress the solemnity of the moment by invoking God's presence. This feature serves to permeate the proceeding with holiness, so that the court may achieve its ultimate aim: the restoration and renewal of human relationships. If at all possible, the oath becomes a gift to the plaintiff that he is urged to accept. By doing so, he will fulfill the concluding command of the Holiness Code, referred to at the beginning of this chapter: ואהבת לרעך כמוך, אני יה׳ "Love your neighbor as yourself, I am the Lord."

8

The Synthesis of the Scriptural Foundation with the Talmud

INTRODUCTION

Having described a *scriptural foundation* to the Talmud's discussion of the Baraita of Rabbi Hiya in chapter 7, we now turn our attention to examining it as the essential fuel that drives the dialectic. This foundation provides three cornerstones. The first is the importance of the oath. The privilege of invoking God's name is a serious one for both the community and the individual. Both are at risk when an oath is taken, for one may conceal that which he knows to be the truth and thereby commit a *hilul hashem*; an act that endangers both the individual and those who witness it. For the latter, this threat consists of the loss of a religious community's most essential cohesive element, faith in the divine and a desire to strive towards that which is holy. For the one who proffers perjury, his loss is to suffer iniquity until death.

The second cornerstone is the lender–borrower relationship, in which the duty to lend repeatedly to those in need is explicit. A person who refuses to lend is regarded as a pharaoh—one who keeps people in bondage. Its characterization as a legal obligation is done only to promote the borrower's dignity and sense of equality. Yet, when the borrower refuses to pay and an action is instituted, the court has a duty to preserve the honor of the borrower

161

on the one hand, yet encourage a person to lend once again on the other.

The third cornerstone is the nature of suspicion and the role it plays in determining the right of an individual to swear in the name of the Almighty. If there is an admission, the court's role is clear. The defendant may take an oath denying the remainder. If witnesses testify, then their testimony is conclusive. But the Baraita deals with the gray area. Thus, the court must determine at what point is suspicion an adequate basis to prevent a litigant from testifying.

Each of these themes, as developed in the scriptural foundation, is relevant to the development of the talmudic dialectic on the Baraita of Rabbi Hiya. The purpose of this chapter is, thus, to integrate this scriptural foundation with the Gemara. Methodologically, it will take the following form. Each of the major thought units of the talmudic passage will first be summarized in order to reacquaint the reader with its main features and then analyzed in light of the foregoing cornerstones that comprise the foundation for the discourse. The analysis features subheadings wherein I relate a particular feature of this foundation to the dialectic (not all of the subheadings are commented on).[1] Nevertheless, in so doing, I hope to demonstrate that these literary antecedents of the Talmud are a prerequisite to a deeper understanding of the theological and human dimensions that the dialectic confronts in its effort to determine the role of God in a dispute between two who once trusted each other.

I. THE RULE AND RATIONALE
OF RABBI HIYA'S BARAITA

The Baraita's unique structure suggests that ADM and WS are equivalent in their impact. As we have seen, a KV rests on the

---

1. The term *thought units* has a precise definition. Chapter 6 set forth each of the major units of the discourse, delineating each by roman numerals. For example, the first major thought unit was "I. The Rule and Rationale of the Baraita." The second major unit was "II. The Necessity for the KV," and so on.

assumption that case A stands in a relationship of minor to major importance to case B. Thus, the Baraita should have been formulated: "That an admission has a lesser effect than the testimony of witnesses and that this statement is derived from a KV." Instead, the Baraita employs the phrase שלא תהא הודאת פיו גדולה מעדת עדים (that an ADM should not have any greater effect than the testimony of WS). This phrase suggests an equivalency between the two laws rather than a relationship of minor to major.

This comparability lies in the nature of the presumption that confronts the court. When one makes an admission, there is external evidence of the defendant's honesty. Thus, the dangers of a *hilul hashem* to the community and the transgression of taking a false oath are diminished. For these reasons, the Torah allows a defendant who admits his guilt to take an oath on the disputed remainder.

But, where witnesses are present, no such evidence appears before the court. The dangers of a *hilul hashem* resulting from a false oath are increased because witnesses have controverted the defendant's denial. Rabbi Hiya should have emphatically stated that the case of WS is far more serious than that of ADM.[2] However, he implicitly rejects this extreme that the defendant should be prohibited from testifying on a disputed remainder.

Therefore, the Baraita is making a significant theological, ethical, and legal statement. A rabbinic court can declare one unfit to testify only on the basis of unequivocal extrinsic evidence, and even then the defendant may still testify on any issue not covered by it. The borrower is still presumed fit to testify despite the presence of witnesses who contradict him as to a part of the plaintiff's claim. There is no increased danger of a *hilul hashem* to the community, nor an enlarged risk that the litigant would take a false oath. It is in this sense that the testimony of witnesses and admissions are equivalent, since neither threatens to violate any component of the scriptural foundation. In the case of both ADM and WS, the defendant is considered honest and thus competent to take the oath on the disputed remainder because there is no direct evidence on this aspect of the claim that would support an inference of dishonesty.

---

2. This might account as a reason for its exclusion from the Baraita.

As a corollary, the Baraita implies that a court can declare one unfit to testify, and thus avoid committing a *hilul hashem*, only on the basis of unequivocal extrinsic evidence, such as the testimony of two witnesses. Furthermore, no inference may be drawn as to the defendant's honesty or lack thereof on any issue beyond that evidence.[3] The Baraita seeks further support by stating that its rule is consistent with the Mishnah of "two holding onto the garment." The extrinsic evidence in this Mishnah is that both are holding onto the garment equally. Therefore, no inference may be drawn as to either party's dishonesty. Both may testify on the basis of what the issue is before the court—that is, the doubt as to the portion that the other is holding. This element is represented by each claiming, "All of it is mine."[4] The testimony consists of, "that I do not have less than a one-half interest in the whole," despite the other's implicit claim of misappropriation (because each claims that "all of it is mine"). The honesty of both is presumed because there is no extrinsic evidence on the doubt that would render the oath in this instance a *hilul hashem*. Thus, the phrase ותנא תונא (*v'tanah tunah*) may be read by the Baraita to stand for the following principle. Where there is no independent evidence as to a disputed portion of a claim, despite the presence of a doubt as to the honesty of litigant(s) caused by extrinsic evidence (such as the testimony of witnesses, or that of a partial admission, or where both have physical possession of a portion), such apprehension does not rise to the level of a suspected *hilul hashem* sufficient to prevent the defendant from taking an oath. The belief in the integrity of the litigant(s), the Baraita argues, is mandated by the Torah.

In short, the language of the Baraita, by implying an equivalency between ADM and WS, suggests to the reader to examine

---

3. There are some exceptions to this rule as we have seen. One who has been found guilty of being thief, a perjurer, or a bailee who has misappropriated a bailment for his own personal benefit cannot testify in a subsequent case. However, these offenses point to fundamental issues of character so as to impeach his credibility. The inability to pay a loan, as a matter of law, does not impugn the character of a borrower.

4. Rashi supports this interpretation of the phrase ותנא תונא in his commentary at *Bava Metziah* 3a.

closely each of these rules, to familiarize him/herself with the relevant scriptural passages, and to determine their nature as developed in the midrashic literature. Furthermore, the phrase *v'tanah tunah* indicates Rabbi Hiya's acknowledgment as to the necessity for harmonization with the Mishnah. By examining the scriptural foundation, the depth of the Baraita's claim that it be incorporated within the body of *halakhah* is understood *before* one confronts the intensive analysis by the dialectic. The Baraita is asserting that neither Scripture nor the *Mishnah* precludes the court from administering an oath in its case. In short, Rabbi Hiya claims that the Baraita harmonizes with both scriptural and mishnaic precedents.

II. THE NECESSITY FOR THE KV

An important distinction was made between ADM and WS. An ADM was extrinsic evidence of the borrower's truthfulness, though there was an inner tension in which he wanted to deny the claim entirely. The oath was allowed because the Torah asserts that no one would be so arrogant as to deny the claim of his lender.

At first, this statement seemed implausible. A person could deny the entire claim of a lender, whether in order to buy time or for any other reason. The audacity of the borrower could extend this far (and perhaps often does) in the everyday world of business relations. It seems more plausible than not that if the borrower did not have sufficient funds that he would deny the entire claim, rather than admit to a portion.

The Torah rejects this position. When one examines the scriptural scheme of lending described in Exodus 22:24 and its rabbinic exegesis, the rendering by Rabbah is readily understood. The loan is interest free and the refusal to lend is equated to a hardening of the heart. Thus, the lender is encouraged to extend credit to his neighbor many times over lest he become an oppressor similar to a pharaoh. In addition, the midrashic exegesis characterized this transaction as a loan at the behest of the borrower in order to "quiet" his anxiety that it might be perceived as charity. In light of this description and his subsequent admission, the presumption that the defendant would not be so arrogant as to deny the claim of his lender is convincing.

But in the case of WS, this presumption as to the borrower's lack of insolence is challenged by the Gemara.[5] Though the trans-actions that preceded the litigation may be identical, the defendant has demonstrated his arrogance by denying the entire claim such that the lender must produce independent evidence that substantiates only a part of it.

In this regard, the Gemara utilizes the scriptural foundation to assert its authority to define the parameters and hence the usage of the laws of Torah. If the rationale for the rule of imposing an oath on a disputed remainder is challenged (as in this case, where there exists extrinsic evidence of complete arrogance in the form of the defendant's own initial denial in the presence of two witnesses—a denial that is then conclusively contradicted at least in part by their testimony), then its applicability must be reconsidered. The contradiction of this underlying presumption justifies the suspension of the law that rests on it. This is a significant achievement in any system of advanced jurisprudence.

In such an instance, either the law's application would have to be rejected or a different underlying principle operative. It is interesting to note that the Gemara chooses the latter option as its path by developing and then challenging the subsequent KV formulations. In so doing, it accomplishes two objectives. One, it preserves the chain of tradition, for if the former option were followed, the Baraita would be discarded and probably forgotten. Second, while preserving as many links as is possible, it forges a new coupling to the reality of its present. No single aspect of the scriptural foundation satisfies the Baraita; that much is clear.[6] Nevertheless, the process of shaping this past tradition to the demands of the present provides the community with an authentic relationship between the divine Law and human needs. The chain is strengthened because of the Gemara's dialectic form, which con-

---

5. The Gemara is analyzing the parameters of the rabbinic exegesis of Exodus 22:24, which presumes the borrower's honesty.

6. One could easily reformulate the scriptural foundation as a dialectic.

tinuously questions the assumptions which underly the divine Law of Torah in the context of real-life circumstances.

In summary, the necessity of the KV rests on a finding of the inapplicability of the scriptural and midrashic characterization of the lender–borrower relationship. A rigid formula to determine the appropriateness of a rule is rejected because the Gemara reasons that if the underlying rationale is contradicted, then the law may not be automatically applied. It may be proved on another basis, and so the passage will continue in hopes of finding such a justification. To paraphrase the dialectic, "just because a transaction falls within the parameters of Exodus 22:24, it does not necessarily mean that the law of Exodus 22:8 and 10, despite the *gezera shava* that would result in the oath's imposition, should automatically apply. Instead, the appropriateness of scriptural law to a case must be carefully considered."

III. KV NUMBER 1

A. ADM and WS are Legally Analogous and Stand in a Relation of Minor to Major Importance

Structurally, this section of the *sugya* consisted of three steps. First, the KV asserted that an ADM is a less stringent criterion than WS in that the former did not obligate the defendant for "money," whereas the testimony of WS rendered him liable for payment. Since the oath was permitted in the case of ADM, in which liability could not be established, how much the more so in the case of WS, in which a defendant is obliged to pay, should an oath be rendered upon him. This KV was challenged on two bases. One is that the admission does obligate the defendant for monies. Two, an admission was the equivalent of one hundred witnesses and thus dispensed with the requirement of any additional proof on the matter admitted.

This led to the KV being reformulated to define monetary obligation as limited to a fine. Once an admission was made, no fine was imposed. However, in the case of WS, a fine was imposed, and therefore the law of WS was more stringent than that of ADM. If, in the case of the latter, an oath was permitted (even though no fine was imposed), then how much the more so should the oath be administered in the former case of WS (where a fine was imposed).

The Gemara does not challenge this new formulation. One possible theory is that the author(s) presume that its readership is acquainted with the scriptural derivation of the exemption from a fine which would defeat the KV. The right to impose a fine is a matter of statutory construction from the Torah which defines the court's jurisdiction. It has nothing to do with the nature of an ADM or WS or in determining whether they stand in a KV relationship. This relief from the payment of double restitution—one in terms of underlying liability and the other, a fine—is derived exegetically from Exodus 22:8, from the phrase "and the judges shall determine his guilt." The one whom the judges determine to be guilty shall pay "double." In the case of the ADM, the litigant, not the court, has already determined his own guilt. Thus, the judiciary has no authority to impose a fine based on this statutory construction of Exodus 22:8. Perhaps the reader is presumed to know the weakness of this formulation, since it is apparent from both Scripture and its midrashic exegesis.

Instead, the Gemara redirects its focus toward understanding the scriptural treatment of an ADM and WS in order to determine whether the two concepts stand in such a relation as to sustain a KV formulation.

IV. THE RELATIONSHIP BETWEEN ADMISSIONS AND WITNESSES

A. Challenge: An Admission Charges a Litigant with Greater Religious Obligations Than the Testimony of Witnesses

As Rashi indicated, this argument was premised on Leviticus 5:4, which detailed the sin of negligently uttering a false oath. According to Scripture, an individual who does so is in an ontological state of guilt. Through confession and offering, a person possesses the means to remove himself from this condition. However, when such an act is done willfully, no such remedy is provided. This is in keeping with the counterpart to Leviticus 5:4—that is, Exodus 20:7, in which it is stated, "thou shalt not take the Lord, thy God's name in vain." All that can be accomplished through confession and atonement for this latter violation is to leave the matter "pending." Complete forgiveness is granted only through death.

Scripture is silent concerning the effect of independent testimony that contradicts the denial of the defendant beyond establishing liability in a civil case. There are no references to offerings or sacrifices. It is in this arena that the dispute between the Sages and Rabbi Meier takes place.

Therefore, the challenge to the baraita's rationale rests on the assumption that WS, who are present in court when the defendant denies the claim, will contradict him, and that he knows they will, in fact, do so. Furthermore, despite this knowledge he still maintains his innocence. According to the Sages, such a person does not demonstrate a mental state sufficient to constitute "confession" so as to render him obliged to bring an offering.

Rabbi Meier's argument rests on characterizing the testimony of witnesses as indicating simply that the defendant is mistaken in his position. The only inference that may be drawn from their testimony (in the absence of an overt statement that indicates arrogance—that is, "I did it deliberately") is that the defendant is negligent in his position. Just as Scripture defines legal truth to consist of the testimony of two uncontradicted and irrefutable witnesses, Rabbi Meier would consider the requirements of Leviticus 5:4 satisfied in the case in which there are the independent testimony of two witnesses and the absence of a clear expression of defiance by the defendant, the defendant simply being "legally" negligent in his denial. He is in a state of guilt that requires atonement. For Rabbi Meier, there is no delineation between legal and theological guilt. Therefore, since WS, even in the face of a denial by the defendant, could impose the death penalty in a capital case, how much the more so should their testimony be powerful enough to impose the less stringent penalty of an offering. Rabbi Meier maintains the presumption of integrity, and his position is theologically benevolent.

This theological aspect (of bringing an atonement offering in the case of a negligent religious act) serves as a basis for sustaining the Baraita. Once again assuming the absence of defiance, the plaintiff has received restitution. He further observes the defendant making the requisite offerings according to the scriptural mandate for the removal of sin. Though they are not an overt expression of contrition, nevertheless, just as God accepts atonement offerings for acts which are done inadvertently, but nevertheless constitute an affront to God's honor, so too must the injured party infer that these acts, though ordered by the rabbinic court, are done so willingly in order to effectuate atonement. In conclusion, Rabbi Meier has equated the efficacy of WS and ADM within the context of negligent conduct regarding the act upon which the litigation is founded and the defendant's subsequent denial. Therefore, a KV could be sustained on this basis because it supports R. Hiya's position that ADM is not any more efficacious than the testimony of WS. The two are legally equivalent for purposes of atonement in the absence of verbal defiance.

E. Challenge: An Admission Is Not Affected by Evidence that Contradicts or Refutes It

This argument most seriously challenges the rationale of the Baraita. An ADM is irrefutable and noncontrovertible, even in the presence of witnesses who seek to demonstrate the innocence of the litigant. It promotes healing between the parties. The defendant is permitted to take an oath with regard to any other claim. The plaintiff is required to accept it. It accelerates the scriptural process of litigation towards a final resolution of the dispute. It is a significant column upon which to rebuild the relationship of trust.

Witnesses engender the opposite result. Their testimony fosters embarrassment upon the defendant. It generates anger upon the plaintiff for having been forced to produce independent evidence to sustain his claim. Furthermore, it encourages the adversarial nature of the proceeding in that these witnesses are subject to refutation and contradiction by other witnesses. In this latter case, the oath is administered to everyone. Thus, from a theological point of view, the name of God is being used not to promote holiness, but to determine wherein the truth lies. When applied to the lender—borrower scenario, the continual invocation of the oath creates the distinct possibility of forever discouraging such a lender from extending his hand to give another loan to a borrower. Thus, the fulfillment of a small portion of God's design for the world and the intended ontological state of scripture for humanity—holiness towards one another—are frustrated through this process.

This is an important challenge to the Baraita, for this analysis suggests that ADM promotes harmony and trust, whereas WS advance discord and alienation. The Baraita's premise that an admission has no greater effect than the testimony of WS is thus compromised ethically and psychologically. A new KV is required to sustain the Baraita's validity.

V. THE LAW OF THE SINGLE WITNESS (SW) AS A BASIS FOR THE KV

A. A Single Witness (SW) May Compel a Defendant to Deny under Oath the Substance of the Former's Testimony

The concept of the rolled-over oath in the SW setting is derived from two scriptural passages. From Deuteronomy 19:15, the rule is inferred from the construction of the verse. Since the passage is explicit in that the testimony of a SW could not impose liability, it is to be understood as permitting an oath to be enjoined on the defendant (otherwise what would be the purpose for its inclusion since the "b" part of the verse was clear that only the testimony of two or more witnesses could establish liability).[7]

---

7. A rabbinic axiom of scriptural exegesis is that there is nothing superfluous contained within Scripture. Every word has relevance. Theologically, this makes sense since it is regarded as divine in origin, and hence perfect.

The other passage was from Numbers and dealt with the suspicion of a jealous husband as to his wife's faithfulness. When she appeared before the priest, she would have to issue two denials. One was on the specific charge of adultery pertaining to an individual. The other was to deny having ever committed adultery.

The passage from Numbers is helpful in that it furnishes a basis for an analogy to be drawn from the husband–wife relationship in the context of adultery and applied to the lender–borrower relationship in the context of a denial of the loan. Both are grounded in trust. For the marriage, one aspect of this trust is the prohibition against adultery and the corresponding duty of faithfulness. Likewise in regard to a loan, the trust is affirmed when the lender generously provides the funds and the borrower promises to repay the money. In each instance, there is a suspected violation of a central component of that trust. In the case of the marriage, the oath is imposed to refute all doubt. Likewise, in the lender–borrower case, the SW has generated a significant level of doubt such that the oath could be used by a court. Thus, the oath is imposed not only on the specific aspect of his testimony, but on all other counts as well so that doubt is removed and the relationship repaired.

The introduction of the SW rule is appropriate from a scriptural perspective because it focuses on this underlying issue of doubt. The oath in this setting is used to quiet suspicions and promote harmony between the respective parties. Therefore, since the Baraita's difficulty arises within the context of witnesses, the law of the SW provides a foundation upon which to articulate a KV capable of withstanding the challenge that the scriptural perception of WS is that it promotes discord in its search for determining legal truth, whereas that of ADM promotes resolution and reestablishing trust.

Despite these parallels, there is a difficulty, which the Gemara articulates. The imposition of an oath in the SW case is based on an inference from Scripture. The decision to impose another oath on a disputed remainder is the product of a rabbinic ordinance built on this inference. To extend it now to serve as a basis for the facts of the Baraita is problematic, for the testimony of WS, unlike that in the SW setting, is conclusive. The doubt as to the defendant's integrity in the Baraita is far stronger because of such testimony than in the SW. Since there is no scriptural authority to impose an oath in the first instance, even though there may be a valid analogy to be drawn, no oath can be imposed on the remainder. Nevertheless, because of the similar scriptural issues of trust and doubt, it may serve as a partial basis for a KV.

VI. A KV FROM TWO RULES: ADM AND SW

A. A KV Based on the Common Element of Claim and Denial Found in the Cases of Both ADM and SW

Neither ADM nor SW are sufficient to formulate a KV. The Gemara, however, argued that the deficiency of one may be compensated for by the other such that together they may serve as the KV to support the Baraita. The element that each shares is that their respective status is that of a disputed remainder. This is the issue that is now being brought before the court such that the provisions of Exodus 22:8 should be operative.

In the case of a partial ADM, as we have seen, the defendant is subject to Exodus 22:8 on the basis of his admission. In the case of the SW, the oath in the first instance comes to nullify that portion of the plaintiff's claim under Deuteronomy 19:15. Now, there exists a disputed remainder that also renders Exodus 22:8 applicable. From the two together, a KV could be inferred that would establish the scriptural validity of the Baraita, for the issue in all three cases is that of a disputed remainder.

E. Challenge: A Presumption of Truthfulness Distinguishes Both the Single Witness and Partial Admission from the Baraita

The Gemara raises the fundamental objection to extending the oath as to the disputed remainder in the case of witnesses. Not only have witnesses established the conclusiveness as to a portion; unlike the case of the SW, the defendant can now be viewed suspiciously so as to prevent him from taking an oath and committing a *hilul hashem*.

F. Response: But the Defendant in the Baraita Is Presumed Truthful So As to Testify in Other Cases

This objection is confronted directly. A borrower who denies his lender is not to be viewed suspiciously. Instead, his circumstances, as detailed in the lender–borrower schema of Exodus 22:24, creates a presumption that the need for economic preservation compels him initially to deny the claim of the lender before the court. Thus, the law permits a borrower to be a fit witness in other cases.

The Gemara makes an important statement that supports the scriptural foundation developed in chapter 5 with regard to the analogy between the lender–borrower and the bailor–bailee. In this part of the argument, Rabbi Idi bar Avin seeks to distinguish the bailee from the borrower, for only the former is unfit to testify in subsequent cases. But this creates a serious problem of statutory construction because, as we have shown, in order for the provisions of Exodus 22:8 to apply to the lender, an analogy supported by Scripture must exist between a loan and a bailment. Rashi addresses this concern: "[In the case of a charge of misappropriation of a bailment] witnesses are prepared to testify that during the time the defendant was entrusted with the bailment, he made personal use of it."[8] His denial in the presence of witnesses stems from greed, which renders him the equivalent of a thief. For this reason, he is unfit to testify in subsequent cases. This motivation of greed, present in the bailee, is absent in the borrower.

There is a concept in modern law called a legal presumption. Essentially, it operates to allow a court to assume a certain fact to exist based on either the dictates of a statute or a common societal practice. The rationale that Rabbah affixes to the lender–borrower—that is, that only the necessity to avoid becoming des-

---

8. Rashi, *Bava Metziah* 4a.

titute forces him to make the initial denial, falls into the category of such a presumption. The presence of witnesses that contradict the borrower's denial only further evidences his desperate circumstance. The presumption still exists.

But such is not the case of the bailee cited by Rabbi Idi bar Avin. Hardship was not present when the transaction was created at the outset. The bailee was given the object for safekeeping. Witnesses are now prepared to testify that he has misappropriated it. The case of the bailee presented by Rabbi Idi renders operative the "b" portion of Deuteronomy 19:15, which prohibits him from testifying, since he is considered a thief. And as previously shown, the thief and perjurer share the common characteristic of intentional deception for selfish gain. By knowingly permitting such a person to testify, the rabbinic court would become involved in the process of furthering an individual to commit a *hilul hashem*, which brings harm to both the community and the bailee. Therefore, he is considered unfit to testify in subsequent cases.

However, as Rashi indicates, in the absence of this specific circumstance, the underlying analogy between the two legal relationships is still sustained. Thus the KV based on the *binyan av* remains valid.

G. Challenge: Unlike WS, ADM and SW Are Not Subject to the Law of Retaliation and, Therefore, the *Binyan Av* Must Fail

Another challenge was made against the *binyan av* of the SW and ADM by the Gemara. Utilizing the contextual approach,[9] it considered the Baraita in light of the entire section dealing with wit-

---

9. The term "contextual approach" is understood as follows: When a prooftext is utilized to formulate a halakhic position, such a verse must be considered in its full context. The remaining elements of the text may be utilized either to sustain or to reject the position. In this instance, the rendering of Deuteronomy 19:15 as pertains to the SW to form a part of the *binyan av* is being challenged on the basis of the remaining verses—that is, 16–21.

nesses—that is, Deuteronomy 19:15–21, in which the law of retaliation was contained. This penalty, quite severe, applied to witnesses who had maliciously given false testimony. If a conviction
or liability was established on the basis of their testimony and then
later the defendant's innocence was demonstrated, the witnesses
would suffer the same punishment that the defendant would have
incurred had their testimony been found credible.

This element is present in the Baraita, for two witnesses have
testified. If, later, their testimony is determined to be false and
malicious, they will incur a penalty. But this factor is not present
in the SW because no liability can be established. Clearly, it is not
available when the defendant makes an admission. Since this element is not shared by each case which forms the *binyan av*, the KV
is refuted.

The degree of analysis in which the authors utilize this contextual approach demonstrates their care in their use of Scripture.
Often, the rabbinic communities of this period are characterized
as "proving what they want to prove." Thus, their treatment of
Scripture is considered arbitrary in the sense that they use it to
advance their own agenda. Without debating this point, I would
suggest that, at least in this instance, the opposite is true. The proof-
text is being challenged by the Gemara on the basis of the context
in which it appears. It is attempting to disprove its "own" usage of
Deuteronomy 19:15 by referring to subsequent passages in advancing its challenge to the *binyan av*.

I. The Law of Retaliation Is Not a Sufficient Distinction So As to Render This KV Invalid

Rabbi Hiya regards this distinction as invalid. Deuteronomy 19:16,
et. seq., is penal in its intent. It is not evidentiary except to the limited extent of refutation. However, the laws of ADM and SW in the
scriptural setting have a pronounced evidentiary effect on the principal issues in the litigation. Each compel an oath to resolve all
issues that are in doubt. This factor is present in the Baraita as well.
There is a disputed remainder with no independent evidentiary
proof. Just as an oath was imposed in the scriptural settings of an

ADM in Exodus 22:8 and in the SW of Deuteronomy 19:15, so too should Exodus 22:8 apply to the factual setting of the Baraita.

CONCLUSION

The Talmud relies on scriptural and midrashic antecedents of which its authors presume its reader to have knowledge. In the commentary sections of chapter 6, which relied heavily on Rashi's citations to related scriptural, mishnaic, and talmudic passages, scriptural precedents were uncovered.

These scriptural provisions were identified and consisted of the following:

1. Exodus 20:7 is concerned with the seriousness of taking God's name in vain. For the offense of the intentional false oath, complete atonement is not possible in one's lifetime. This was the background that added an important dimension to the dialectic in understanding the Talmud's reluctance to adopt readily the rule of Rabbi Hiya.
2. Leviticus 5:4 implicitly provides for the administration of an oath by allowing for a remedy where false testimony is presented, but where such testimony was due only to negligence.
3. Exodus 22:8 details charges of misappropriation and the status of a litigated matter where there is a partial admission. The provision of the oath is considered to be applicable in this setting based on a *gezera shava* from Exodus 22:10.
4. Exodus 22:24 focuses on the lender–borrower relationship. It suggests that its characterization as a legal relationship is done at the behest of the borrower. This might account for the absence of a provision in this section for a legal remedy. Therefore, if a dispute would arise, relief would only be through the wording of Exodus 22:8.
5. Finally, Deuteronomy 19:15 describes the evidentiary impact of both the single witness and two witnesses. The lat-

ter is regarded as conclusive proof on the matter attested to. It serves as one of the principle arguments against the rule of the Baraita. In contrast, the former assists in establishing a *binyan av* from which the Baraita could be rendered harmonious with Scripture.

The Gemara does not cite any of these passages. Nevertheless, they (as well as others that may be unaccounted for) are the essential fuel that drives the Gemara towards its conclusion that the Baraita is grounded on these literary antecedents and thus within the corpus of *halakhah*.

The Values Embedded in the Scriptural Foundation

The Gemara utilizes the cornerstones of the scriptural foundation. These cornerstones may be analogized to the underpinnings of any system of jurisprudence. In the United States of America, the Constitution, the Bill of Rights, and perhaps the legal theory of Anglo-Saxon common law, serve as foundational to the courts. For the rabbinic communities of the tannaitic, amoraic, and saboraic periods, the Torah in its broadest dimension is the foundation upon which *halakhah* rests.

Having developed the scriptural foundation and seen its application in the talmudic discourse on the Baraita of Rabbi Hiya, we must now examine it and determine what theological and ethical conclusions, if any, may be drawn from it.

First, Torah attempts to serve humanity. God is there to be availed so long as humankind recognizes its limitation to invoke God as an aide to serve humanity's quest. A tribunal, which calls the integrity of human beings into question when presented with evidence and issues of doubt, is worthy of being referred to as *elohim*, for it is that role in which they are placed. It is a position to be shunned rather than sought after for God is holy and therefore judges are to follow the protocol of the King whom they serve and create an environment of holiness. Permitting even an inadvertent *hilul hashem* to occur would be a violation of its sacred task. It must protect the sanctity of God's name on the one hand while on the other promoting the integrity of each litigant. If at all possible, its role is to use the oath in its primary capacity, to restore trust in the world by removing doubt and suspicion in the minds of those who are before it.

The litigation which has come before the court arose out of the sensitive desire to perform the *mitzvah* of aiding and maintaining the dignity of one who was less fortunate and in need. But now, the relationship has turned because of a dispute. As crucial an issue as it is for the court to determine the truth, it must also question whether, through its proceedings, the plaintiff will ever perform this command or be hardened in his heart through this legal process. It must preserve the desire of the heart to do good, even when there is a sense of being taken advantage of. In essence, it must also create an environment within the lender to continue to loan without interest to those in need, lest society be divided between pharaohs and slaves.

As to the borrower, the Baraita promoted his dignity by permitting him to testify despite the presence of two witnesses who impeached his credibility before he takes the oath. The court must maintain a perspective of innocence and has no right to withhold the oath except in narrow, clearly defined circumstances. Its duty is not to look into the heart of a human being and determine if it is one that is seeking to do evil. Nor can it protect one from committing a *hilul hashem*. Rather, the judges must maintain a presumption of innocence in their minds. They are only the ministers to the King. And it is only the King who determines what is in the heart. Thus, a sensitivity must be present that recognizes the presumption of the borrower as being in a difficult circumstance such that he denies, on the one hand, but that he will either take the oath and honestly testify or decline the oath, on the other. The scriptural foundation and the Baraita express a unique faith in the fundamental goodness and integrity of humankind.

Finally, the Talmud is teaching that the right to the oath is ultimately in the hands of the borrower. There is the prohibition against taking God's name in vain. The penalties for intentionally violating God's name will extend into the grave. Even if he is negligent in his testimony, he will suffer through confession, atonement, offering, and restitution if he subsequently remembers facts that would indicate that his initial testimony was false. Ultimately, the duty to be honest is not between the individual and the court. Instead, it is between the individual and God. If this honesty is violated in open court, God is desecrated because the intention of the oath is to aid the development of holiness in society, not to promote distrust and discord. This will be the burden which the defendant will carry and which will perhaps be heavier than the debt of which he will be relieved. But by permitting the oath in this instance, despite the sometimes harsh realites, the Talmud confirms the essential goodness and trust in people, and expresses the hope that relationships can be restored and an environment rooted in holiness can be advanced with the help of the Almighty.

This last element, that God is to aid humanity, is expressed in the midrashic statement that the litigant is to accept the oath as a gift from the defendant. By doing so, the relationship is repaired and the ontological holiness described in Scripture as a state of being for an individual becomes the essential feature of human connection and of society at large.

9

Talmud and Scripture: Implications of a Scriptural Methodology in the Understanding of Talmud

THE PHILOLOGICAL METHOD: BENEFITS TO BUILD ON

This book began with a description of recent works that aim to provide access for the reader who wishes to engage the Talmud. The methodology that is used in these works is essentially philological: an approach that emphasizes the meaning of the passage in its syntactical and logical flow. The contributions by the authors who use this approach are enormous. Modern Jewry has a very real opportunity to study Talmud. Rabbi Adin Steinsaltz and others engaged in similar work have given those of us who lack the formalized years of *yeshiva* training a path in which to reconnect ourselves to a dialogue that is fundamentally concerned with Sinai and its meaning.

This methodology poses certain difficulties for the audience to whom these works are directed. The sheer quantity of material that is being furnished to the reader in each work presents a formidable challenge. No one ever claimed talmudic study to be an easy enterprise. *The Steinsaltz Edition: Bava Metziah* alone consists of five separate volumes. The reader may be overwhelmed by both the detail and the quantity of material in even a single volume.

The modern reader must also familiarize him/herself with the knowledge that the editors of the Talmud presumed its audience to possess: a thorough command of Scripture, its midrashic exegesis, relevant mishnaic passages, and even contemporaneous portions of the Talmud. Without this background, the reader has difficulty grasping the theological and human issues that are at stake in the talmudic discussion. The reader's "eye" must be trained to find the metaphysical and spiritual dimensions encoded in a passage. As a corollary, unless stated explicitly in the talmudic passage, underlying theological, ethical, and psychological issues are usually left unstated.

Thus, utilizing these texts is very helpful—indeed, essential. Nevertheless, from the above, one can see the inherent limitations (as with any methodology) of this approach. The following methodology, however, seeks to build on the achievements of those scholars who have undertaken the great task of furnishing modern Jewry access to this work.

SCRIPTURAL METHODOLOGY: AN APPROACH TO UNDERSTANDING THE TALMUD

This methodology calls attention to the historical and scriptural roots embedded in these texts. An axiom of this approach is that the Talmud is a symbol of the rational understanding of the relationship between the divine and humanity in its myriad circumstances. True, the problem of the Baraita in terms of its philology (the plain meaning of the words) is whether a person who denies his lender in the presence of witnesses should be permitted to take an oath on the disputed remainder. But another level of dialogue was revealed by an examination of the scriptural and midrashic antecedents—a level that focused on more fundamental issues of human and divine concern. To what extent may God play a role in restoring human relationships? Under what conditions does the Torah issue a psychological imperative for the individual and community to turn aside its suspicion and doubt as to the integrity and honesty of a person? How can a court of law create an environment of reconciliation so that the fulfillment of a moral law which provides aid for those disadvantaged may flourish? These are substantive issues which are represented in the Baraita and the talmudic dialectic that follows. The Talmud is thus symbolic literature.

The methodology is not difficult and is comprised of three steps. First, the *sugya* must be comprehended. A philological and contextual understanding is a prerequisite to any increased level of awareness of the underlying issues.

In the next phase, an analysis of a passage is then undertaken that will reveal central themes that occur repeatedly within the passage. In the selection from *Bava Metziah*, the oath, partial admission, single witness, and two witnesses are played out on the stage of the lender–borrower relationship. By focusing on these motifs, the reader begins the process of "taking a step back" from the dialectic in order to develop a sense of its human and divine dimensions. In this phase, the reader might ask the following:

1. What do Scripture and Midrash contribute to the understanding of the lender–borrower relationship?
2. What is the significance of the oath in Scripture and in the subsequent rabbinic literature that precedes or is contemporaneous with the Talmud?
3. What are the scriptural and midrashic supports for the laws of admission, single witness, and witnesses, and their rationales?

Once such issues are identified, the most difficult part of this methodology is then engaged: examining the treatment of these topics by the literary antecedents of the Talmud. These consist of scriptural passages and their midrashic exegesis, relevant *mishnayot* and *baraitot*, and contemporaneous literature, such as related talmudic passages. At this level, the assumption of the editors, that its reader is knowledgeable of these topics in their scriptural and rabbinic contexts, is satisfied.

The interrelationships of these various themes are more fully realized in the scriptural foundation than in the talmudic dialectic. The divine and human dimensions are treated directly in theory. Thus, the reader is able to appreciate the necessity for the dialectic approach that the Talmud adopts, as well as the historic antecedents upon which each talmudic position rests.

Finally, the passage is reread in light of the scriptural foundation in order to "discern" the divine intention within the particular human issue that the Gemara confronts. For example, there is a nexus between the oath, which represents the invocation of the divine, and the right of a person to make use of it, even if suspected of being less than forthright. The Baraita tells the community that not only has it no right to withhold the oath from a defendant (but for a few narrow exceptions), but that it must let go its suspicions and accept the oath of the defendant as one would accept a gift, and thus conclude the matter. The Baraita and the Gemara teach that the divine, within the parameters of certain definitive exceptions, presumes the essential integrity and honesty of people. Because of this fundamental view by God of humanity, a person is entitled to use the name of God to affirm his/her character.

IMPLICATIONS OF THE METHODOLOGY

The Meaning of Talmud

This methodology expresses philosophically the concept that the Talmud is an extension of the Written Torah and the Oral Torah. These are the Talmud's foundation, upon which it builds. By amplifying these texts, the Talmud falls within the divine imperative of Sinai. Just as there are conflicting passages within the Tanakh which, when contrasted as the midrashic literature so often does, gives the appearance of a miniature dialectic, so too does the Talmud engage in its own dialectic. The result in each instance is a synthesis and a deeper appreciation for the nuances of each work as it struggles to resolve the human and theological issues that are presented.

Torah is not simply the scroll that is in the ark, or the Mishnah, or the collection of *midrashim*. Instead, Torah is that which preceded creation. Talmud is another step toward reaching that ultimate perfection because of its demand for a rational comprehension of the paradoxical nature of the human condition. The meaning of Talmud is that it extends the path towards an understanding of the divine wish for humanity.

The Function of Talmud

Once the meaning of Talmud is grasped as a structure that rests on Torah, its function becomes clear. If Scripture is a partial expression of Torah, then it must serve some over-all purpose of life. Rabbi Akiva defined the central tenet of the Torah as "love thy neighbor as thyself." But this verse must once again be placed in context. It appears in the Holiness Code in the Book of Leviticus. It is holiness in everyday life that the Torah and by extension Talmud is attempting to discern.

To be able to "love thy neighbor as thyself" after a person has refused to acknowledge his debt is generally beyond the capability of most of us in the absence of a mechanism for resolution. It might even be considered naïve to expect an individual ever to loan money again once he/she has been taken advantage of. But Torah and its subparts—Scripture, Midrash, Mishnah, and Talmud—search for a way in which to restore trust and kindness in the ontology of the human condition. Holiness is the state that Torah always beckons humankind to enter. The Talmud functions to carve a path within the concrete realities of life in order to allow humankind to be holy and thereby to adhere to the protocol of God.

The Challenge that Awaits Us

The *scriptural foundation* in this work consists of three cornerstones. A building, however, is comprised of four. It is for the reader to construct the fourth cornerstone, then to build the walls and to furnish the interior. The work awaits us. Each of us is challenged to construct our own cornerstones, indeed our own homes, by using the gifts that were presented to us centuries ago at the foot of Sinai. The foundations and cornerstones may never be complete. However, when they are, surely there will exist a dwelling place on earth wherein the name of God shall reside.

Glossary

These terms are gleaned from the sources identified in the bibliography of this work, with particular reference to Strack and Stemberger, *Introduction to the Talmud and Midrash*, and Rabbi Adin Steinsaltz, *The Talmud: A Reference Guide*.

Amoraic Period: Divided into seven generations, beginning in 220 C.E. and concluding circa 475 C.E. In the sixth generation, Rabbi Ashi [d. 425 C.E.] is believed to have begun writing the Gemara.

Amoraim: Refers to those rabbinic scholars who lived during the amoraic period. Their work is recorded in the Gemara sections of the Talmud in explicating a Mishnah or Midrash. Their pronouncements are not considered as authoritative as those of the Tannaim. Amoraim lived in both Palestine and Babylonia.

Babylonia: A country that existed in antiquity in what is now Iraq. At the time of the first exile, the Jews went to Babylonia. There, they established communities and academies of Jewish learning, where the Talmud Bavli was written. It was the leading Jewish community in the Diaspora until the beginning of the eleventh century.

Baraita: [plural, baraitot] A general term used to describe a tannaitic teaching or ruling that was not incorporated into the Mishnah.

Binyan Av Mishnei K'tuvim: (בנין אב משני כתובים) A hermeneutic rule in which two cases, A and C, are analogous such that a certain stringent rule of law applies in each case [in our case it is the imposition of the oath on a disputed remainder]. A and C are then analogized to case B [in our *sugya* it is WS] so that the stringency in A and C is applicable to case B.

Central Conference of American Rabbis: The organizing body of Reform rabbis in the United States.

Columbus Platform of 1937: A statement of principles adopted by the Reform Movement, in Columbus, Ohio, in 1937.

Conservative Movement: A movement within Judaism that regards Talmud as part of the revelatory process and defines *halakhah* in the sense of norms. It regards *halakhah* as binding but possibly subject to change when historical demands warrant it. However the burden rests on the one advocating such change to demonstrate the necessity for it.

Dayo: [literally, "It is enough"] A rule that limits the applicability of a *kal v'chomer* to the stringency that is applied in the minor case. *Dayo* prevents one from arguing that if, in Case A, a certain stringency is applied, how much the more so in Case B, which is far more serious, should a greater stringency be found.

Drash: [Hebrew] To explore deeply the meaning of a particular scriptural passage or word.

Gemara: [Aramaic] Literally, the "finishing" or "study"; that portion of the Talmud that comments on the Mishnah. It is found in the center column of any standard edition of the Talmud and begins with the designation "גמ." The authorship of the Gemara is attributed to Rabbi Ashi (d. 425) but is regarded by scholars as having been completed between 550 and 600.

Geonic Period: The period from 600 to 1000 during which the talmudic academies in Babylonia were acknowledged as the authority for the understanding of *halakhah*. Jewish communities throughout Northern Africa and Europe would submit questions to them, and their answers would be regarded as binding. Their writings have been compiled into a work entitled *Sh'ālot U'Tshuvot* [appropriately titled "Questions and Answers."]

Geonim: A reference to those scholars who lived during the period from circa 500 to 1000 in the academies of Babylonia [*see* Geonic Period].

Gezerah Shavah: (גזרה שוה) A comparison of similar expressions: If the same word or phrase occurs in two Pentateuchal passages, and in one passage such word or phrase is defined while in the other it is not, then its construction and usage in one may be applied to the other, so long as one has received the rule within the chain of tradition.

Hachashah: A form of impeaching the testimony of witnesses by showing that the witnesses did not witness the events to which they have testified (for example, they were somewhere else when the event took place and thus could not have witnessed the event).

Halakhah: [literally, "the way"] In the rabbinic sense, *halakhah* refers to the law concerning a matter of Jewish jurisprudence or praxis. In Orthodox Judaism, *halakhah* is regarded as binding. In Conservative Judaism, *halakhah* is binding, but the methodology for its determination is regarded as retaining a greater measure of flexibility. Reform Judaism regards *halakhah* as nonbinding.

Hazamah: A form of impeachment in which the testimony of witnesses is refuted by a second set of witnesses testifying to the same matter differently.

Hermeneutics: The science of logic. In Talmudic study, hermeneutics represents a collection of rules of logic from which *halakhah* may be derived or discerned. In rabbinic literature, there are thirteen such rules [referred to as שלש עשר המדות—*shelosh esreh medot* (thirteen rules)]. The first seven are attributed to Hillel and the remaining six to Rabbi Ishmael.

Hilul Hashem: [Hebrew] A term used to identify an act that desecrates God's Name. For example, when one knowingly testifies under oath to a matter which he/she knows to be false, such conduct, since it is done in public, is regarded as a *hilul hashem*. In much of the rabbinic literature, a *hilul hashem* can be fully atoned for only with repentance, suffering, and death. One reason for this harsh view is that, since the conduct is public, it has the potential for undermining the community's belief in God.

Hukim: [Hebrew; law, rule custom, assigned share or mark] Used in many contexts to indicate a divine rule that is followed purely on the basis of faith and as a sign of obedience. In the citation from the *Sifra* in chapter 3, it refers to all of the halakhic *midrashim*.

Kal V'Chomer: (קל וחומר) An *a fortiori* inference. A hermeneutic rule that expresses the idea that where two cases are legally analogous and stand in a relation of minor to major importance, and in the case regarded as minor, a certain stringency is applied, how much the more so should the same stringency be applied in the more serious case. The use of the *kal v'chomer* is limited by the principle *dayo* (literally, "it is sufficient"). Once the inference is made, the stringency to be applied in the more serious case is limited to the one used in the minor case.

K'lal uphrat ukhlal i attah dan ella ke-ein ha-perat: (כלל ופרט וכלל אי כעין הפרט אתה דן אלא): Literally, "general, particular, general; you can only rule like that of the particular." Where a general rule is first stated, then followed by a series of specific illustrations, concluding with a restatement of the general, then the general rule may be applied only to an item which shares the common characteristic of the specific articles contained in the passage.

K'lal Yisrael: A reference to all Jewry. It expresses the idea that Jews, all over the world, are one community.

Kinas: A fine—for example, where one has negligently testified to a matter that is false and later learns or "recalls" the truth, a fine may be imposed.

Law of Partial Admission: מודה במקצת [abbrev. ADM] Where a debtor admits to a part of the claim of his/her creditor, he/she may then take an oath on the remainder in the absence of independent evidence and be relieved of further liability. This rule is not stated explicitly in the Torah, but is exegetically derived by a midrash in the *Mekilta de-Rabbi Ishmael*. It is regarded as toraitic.

Law of the Single Witness: [abbrev. SW] This toraitic rule provides that where a single witness testifies, though such evidence is not conclusive as to liability, such testimony does impose an oath upon the defendant to deny such testimony. It also serves as the basis for a "rolled-over" oath, in which the defendant is then entitled to swear on all matters brought against him/her by the opposing party.

Law of Witnesses: [abbrev. WS] This toraitic rule states that where two witnesses have testified on a particular matter and the opposing party offers no independent testimony by two other witnesses that contradict or refute such evidence, then the opposing party is prohibited from taking an oath and attesting to the truth of his position. Their testimony is regarded as conclusive on the matter.

Lidrosh: [Hebrew] The Hebrew infinitive of the root *drash* (see above).

Mamon: Aramaic for money.

Mekilta de-Rabbi Ishmael: A collection of halakhic *midrashim* on Exodus 12:1–23,19; 31:12–17; 35:1–3. While the focus is on the legal sections, it includes narrative portions as well. It is considered by many to have been compiled 250–300 C.E.

Meseket: [plural, *mesektot*] A volume [tractate] of Talmud.

Mesoret: A handing down of the tradition from one generation to the next.

Midrash: From the Hebrew root דרשׁ, which means to study in a deep and penetrating manner. A collection of rabbinic writings that probe the deeper meanings and implications of scriptural texts and words, of which there are two types: *midrash aggadah* and *midrash halakhah*.

Midrash Aggadah: A type of midrash that elucidates a scriptural passage or passages, or word[s], and which is part of a narrative (for example, the story of Abraham).

Midrash Halakhah: A type of midrash that seeks to probe the meaning of scriptural passages and that is in the form or nature of a command (for example, "Thou shalt . . . ").

Mishnah: [plural, mishnayot] The redaction of the Oral Law by Rabbi Judah HaNasi and his colleagues in circa 200 C.E. Structurally, the Gemara section of the Talmud is a commentary on the Mishnah.

Mishneh Torah: A code of Jewish law based on an exhaustive study of the Talmud by Moses Maimonides, which he completed in 1178.

Mishpatim: [Hebrew, statutes or laws] Generally, it refers to laws. In the citation from the *Sifra* in chapter 3, it is defined as the hermeneutic rules used in *midrashim* to derive *halakhah*.

Mitzvah: A commandment found in either the Written or Oral Law. Also used in a generic sense of a good deed that helps another person.

Nasi: An office held by the one whom the Romans recognized as the religious and political spokesperson for the Jewish people during their period of occupation after the destruction of the Second Temple. (Rabbi Judah HaNasi—literally, "the prince"—held this position).

Oral Law: Those laws which, according to rabbinic tradition, were given orally by God to Moses, who then taught them to the seventy elders, who then passed them on to each successive generation. In the year 200 C.E., these laws were organized by Rabbi Judah HaNasi and his colleagues into a work known as the Mishnah.

Orthodox Movement: A movement of Judaism that regards *halakhah*, as determined in the Talmud and its later codification in the medieval period, as binding. The understanding and implementation of *halakhah* is vested in the rabbinic leadership of the movement.

Pentateuch: A Greek word meaning "five books." It refers to the Five Books of Moses, or what is commonly referred to as the Torah. The five books are *Bereshit* [Genesis], *Shemot* [Exodus], *Vayikra* [Leviticus], *Bamidbar* [Numbers], and *Devarim* [Deuteronomy].

P'shat: [Hebrew] A term used to designate the "plain or intended" meaning of a scriptural passage or rabbinic text in contrast to a midrashic or homiletical understanding. According to some rabbinic scholars (for example, Rashi), sometimes the "plain or intended" meaning of such a passage or word is its midrashic explication.

Reform Movement: A movement of Judaism that regards the rabbinic literatures of Midrash, Mishnah, and Talmud, as part of the revelatory process, but whose adherents are under no religious obligation to follow them simply based on that status alone. Revelation in the Reform Movement is ongoing, and, thus, what may have been the revealed truth in one generation may differ for the next. In contrast to the Orthodox and Conservative theology, the individual is granted the autonomy to decide his/her religious praxis. Such autonomy carries with it the ongoing commitment to Jewish learning. The role of the rabbi is solely that of a teacher and counselor who has no inherent authority over the individual's religious ideology or praxis.

Saboraim: A group of anonymous scholars who lived in Babylonia after the amoraic period [beginning c. 475 C.E.]. It is believed by some that they finished the writing of the Talmud circa 550 to 600 C.E.

Sages: [Hebrew *Chachamim*] Generally, the term is used in the sense of the majority opinion with respect to a halakhic matter, particularly during the tannaitic period.

San Francisco Platform of 1976: A statement of principles adopted by the Reform Movement at a convention in San Francisco in 1976.

Sanhedrin: This was Israel's primary religious and legislative body during the Second Temple period. It consisted of seventy-one judges, and its pronouncements and decisions were binding upon Israel. It met in a designated chamber located in the Temple courtyard.

Scriptural Foundation: A term used to describe the collection of related passages found in Scripture, Midrash, and Mishnah that underpins the topic the Talmud is discussing.

Scripture: The biblical canon as defined by Judaism, consisting of the Pentateuch, the Books of the Prophets (for example, the Books of Isaiah, Jeremiah, and so on), and the Books of Writings (for example, the Books of Ruth, Psalms, Proverbs, Job, and so on).

Sifra: A term used to describe a collection of *midrashim* on the Book of Leviticus, more formerly known as *Torat Kohanim*. The core text is believed to have been in place by the second half of the third century.

Sifra debe Rav: Another term used to describe the *Sifra* in which the Talmud attributes its authorship to Rav, who, after studying in Israel during the tannaitic period, returned to Babylonia and established the first academies.

Sifre: A collection of *midrashim* on the legal passages from Exodus, Numbers, and Deuteronomy. *Sifre Numbers* is regarded as having been compiled after the middle of the third century. *Sifre Deuteronomy* is regarded by many scholars to have been redacted by the end of the third century.

Shalshelet Hakabbalah: The chain of tradition. Embedded in this expression is the notion that each Jew is linked to a chain of tradition that extends back in time to the revelation at Mount Sinai.

Sugya: [Aramaic] Term referring to a selected portion of Talmud.

Talmud: [literally, study or learning] It refers to the collection of writings, dating from between 425 C.E. and 600 C.E. in the academies of Babylonia, that commented on the Mishnah. Essentially, it is composed of two parts. One is the Mishnah. The other part is the Gemara [literally, the finishing], which is a commentary, in the form of a dialectic, to the Mishnah. It often includes references to Scripture and both antecedent and contemporaneous rabbinic literatures of Midrash, Baraitot, and Tosefta, as well as received teachings of rabbis who lived during the tannaitic period (100 B.C.E. to 220 C.E.) and the amoraic period (220 C.E. to 425 C.E.).

Talmud Bavli: The Babylonian Talmud, which was compiled circa 425 C.E. to 600 C.E.

Talmud Yerushalmi: The Palestinian Talmud, composed circa 400 C.E. in Palestine. This text, while predating the Bavli, is not as commonly used because of the abbreviated nature of the writing, though its infrequency of use is not to be confused with lack of importance.

Tanakh: A Hebrew acronym for the three major divisions of the Jewish Bible; *Torah, Niviim,* and *K'tuvim*—the Five Books of Moses, the Books of the Prophets, and the Books of "Writings" (for example, Chronicles).

Tannaitic Period: The period of time in which the Tannaim lived. Their pronouncements are of high authority, for they were either contemporaneous to or preceded the redaction of the Mishnah. The period is generally divided into five generations, beginning in circa 10 C.E. and concluding at 220. Some scholars regard the period between 200 and 220 as a transitional period between the Tannaim and the Amoraim.

Tannaim: Refers to the group of rabbis who lived from circa 10 C.E. to 200 C.E. Among those who are more well known are Hillel and Shammai, Rabbi Akiva, and later, Rabbi Judah HaNasi.

Torah: Generally defined as the sacred scroll that consists of the Five Books of Moses. In rabbinic literature, the Torah consists of three elements. One is the Written Law as contained in the Pentateuch—that is, the Five Books of Moses. It also is comprised of the Oral Law, as represented in the Mishnah. In the Talmud, this definition is expanded to include the *midrashim* and the hermeneutic rules as well. According to modern scholarship, the written Torah was completed by the year of 425 B.C.E. when the Israelites returned from their exile in Babylonia to Israel.

Torah Sh'baal Peh: [*See* Oral Law]

Torah Sh'bichtav: [*See* Written Law]

Torot: [Hebrew plural for Torah, referring to instructions, teachings, or laws] In much of the midrashic literature, wherever the word is found in the written Torah and it is possible to read it as a plural (for example, *torahtechah* in an unpointed text can be translated as either a singular or a plural; thus, "your torahs"), the term is understood as proof that both the Oral Law and the Written Law were revealed to Moses at Mount Sinai.

Tosefta: [literally, additions] A collection of pronouncements, contemporaneous to the redaction of the Mishnah, that were not included in the latter. Often the Gemara will discuss the meaning of a particular tosefta in relationship to a mishnah.

Tractate: A volume of Talmud.

Written Law: A reference to those laws that are regarded by the Sages as being either expressly stated in Scripture or derived from it through Midrash.

Bibliography

PRIMARY SOURCES

Epstein, Isodore, ed. *Hebrew-English Edition of the Babylonian Talmud*. Trans. Maurice Simon. London: Soncino Press, 1960. 28 vol.

Maimonides, Moses. *Commentary on Pirkey Avoth*. Trans. Paul Forcheimer. Jerusalem: Feldheim Publishers, 1974.

Mekilta deRabbi Ishmael. Ed. H. S. Horowitz and I. A. Rabin. Jerusalem, 1970.

Mekilta de-Rabbi Ishmael. Trans. Jacob Z. Lauterbach. Philadelphia: The Jewish Publication Society, 1933.

Midrash Rabbah. Jerusalem: Jerusalem Press, 1970.

Midrash Rabbah: Genesis Volume I. Trans. H. Freedman. New York: Soncino Press, 1983.

The Mishnah: Seder Kodashim. Commentary by Hanoch Albeck. Tel Aviv: Dvir Publishing House, 1988.

Mishnah: Seder Moed. Commentary by Hanoch Albeck. Tel Aviv: Dvir Publishing House., 1988.

Mishnah: Seder Zeraim. Commentary by Hanoch Albeck. Tel Aviv: Dvir Publishing House, 1988.

Siddur Rinat Yisrael: Ahskenaz Diaspora Version. Edited and annotated by Shlomo Tal. Jerusalem: Moreshet Publishing Company, 1982.

Sifra Torat Kohannim [printed edition].

Sifre debi Rav [printed edition].

Steinsaltz, Adin. *The Talmud: The Steinsaltz Edition.* Vol. I , *Tractate Bava Metzia.* New York: Random House, 1989.

Talmud Bavli (Vilna edition). New York: Otsar HaSefarim, Inc. 20 vols.

Tanakh—The Holy Scriptures: The New JPS Translation According to the Traditional Hebrew Text. Philadelphia: The Jewish Publication Society, 1988.

Torah, Nivi'im, K'tuvim. Jerusalem: Koren Publishers, 1988.

REFERENCE MATERIALS

Encyclopaedia Judaica. Jerusalem: Keter Publishing House, 1972. 20 vols.

Jastrow, Marcus. *Dictionary of the Targumim, Talmud Babli, Yerushalmi, and Midrashic Literature.* New York: The Judaica Press, 1985.

Steinsaltz, Adin. *The Talmud: The Steinsaltz Edition, A Reference Guide.* New York: Random House, 1989.

The New Jewish Encyclopedia. Ed. David Bridger. New York: Behrman House, 1962.

SECONDARY SOURCES

Albright, W. F. *The Biblical Period from Abraham to Ezra.* New York: Harper Torchbook, 1963.

Ben-Sasson, H. H. *A History of the Jewish People.* Trans. George Weidenfeld and Nicholson Ltd. Cambridge: Harvard University Press, 1976.

Bright, John. *A History of Israel.* 3d ed. Philadelphia: Westminister Press, 1981.

Cohen, Shaye J. D. *From the Maccabees to the Mishnah.* Philadelphia: Westminster Press, 1987.

Emet Ve-Emunah: Statement of Principles of Conservative Judaism. New York: Jewish Theological Seminary of America, Rabbinical Assembly, 1988.

Feldman, Aharon. "Learning Gemara in English: The Steinsaltz Talmud Translation." *Tradition* 25:4 (Summer 1991).

Halivni, David Weiss. *Midrash, Mishnah, and Gemara: The Jewish Predilection for Justified Law.* Cambridge: Harvard University Press, 1986.

Jacob, Walter. "Standards Now." *Reform Judaism* 21:1 (Fall 1992).

Kraemer, David. *The Mind of the Talmud.* New York: Oxford University Press, 1990.

Lerner, Michael. *Jewish Renewal.* New York: G.P. Putnam & Sons, 1994.

Meyer, Michael A. *Response to Modernity: A History of the Reform Movement in Judaism.* New York: Oxford University Press, 1988.

Mielziner, Moses. *An Introduction to the Talmud.* New York: Bloch Publishing Company, 1968.

Neusner, Jacob. *Invitation to the Talmud.* San Francisco: Harper & Row, 1984.

————. *Judaism: The Evidence of the Mishnah.* Chicago: University of Chicago Press, 1981.

Neusner, Jacob. "Method and Substance in the History of Judaic Ideas, an Exercise." In *Jews, Greeks, and Christians*, ed. R. Hamerton-Kelly and R. Scroggs. Leiden: Brill, 1976.

Safrai, Shmuel. "The Era of the Mishnah and Talmud." In *A History of the Jewish People*, ed. H. H. Ben-Sasson, trans. George Weidenfeld and Nicholson Ltd. Cambridge: Harvard University Press, 1976.

Seltzer, Robert M. *Jewish People, Jewish Thought: The Jewish Experience in History.* New York: Macmillan Publishing Company, 1980.

Strack, H. L., and Stemberger, G. *Introduction to the Talmud and Midrash.* Trans. Markus Bockmuehl. Minneapolis: Fortress Press, 1992.

Unterman, Isaac. *The Talmud: An Analytical Guide to Its History and Teachings.* New York: Bloch Publishing Company, 1952.

Wellhausen, Julius. *Geschichte Israels*. Berlin: G. Reimer, 1878.

Werheimer, Jack. *A People Divided: Judaism in Contemporary America*. New York: Basic Books, a division of HarperCollins Publishers, 1993.

Index

Abba Areca (Rav), 59–60
Abraham, and Isaac, 82–83
Academies, 45, 63–64, 66
  Babylonian, 15, 19
Acceptance, of interpretations,
  96
Admissions, 94–95, 104–105,
  125
  in *binyan av mishnei k'tuvim*,
    84–87
  and guilt-offerings, 68
  in *kal v'chomer*, 78–80
  partial, 144, 149–152, 165–
    166, 173
  in relation to witnesses, 79–
    80, 98–110, 128, 162–
    165, 167–170
  and single witness, 115–119,
    156–157
Adultery, 112–113, 172
Akiva, Rabbi, 57, 59, 61, 70, 140
Albeck, Hanoch, 57, 60
  on Mishnah, 65, 68–69
Alfasi, 70

Alfasi commentary, 16, 24
America, Judaism in, 6–11
Amplification, of Torah
  imperative of, 31–32, 42–43,
    184–185
  methodology for, 90
Arrogance
  in denial of debt, 99–100,
    165–167
  against God, 137

Babylonia, 24
  academies in, 15, 19
Bailment relationship, 128
  misappropriation in, 88–
    89
  testimony in, 118–120
  versus borrower–lender,
    128, 143–145, 148,
    152, 174–175
Baraita of Rabbi Hiya, 52, 93–
  126, 162–177, 182–184
  on bailment, 143–145
  challenges to, 168–171

Baraita of Rabbi Hiya
    (*continued*)
    and hermeneutic rules, 173,
        178
    rationale for, 162–165
    values of, 179, 183
Baraitot, 27, 32, 70
Bava Kamma, 78, 102
Bava Metziah, 84–85, 97–98,
    101, 124
Bavli Talmud. *See* Talmud, the
Ben Yose the Galilean, Rabbi
    Eliezer, 74
Ben Zion Wacholder, Dr., 24–
    25, 69
Berakhot, 81
Binyan av Mishnei K'tuvim
    (hermeneutic rule), 74,
    84–87, 110, 116–117,
    120–123, 174–176, 178
Blessings, for Talmud study,
    81–82
Bomberg, David, 17
Bomberg edition, 17–19

Chain of tradition (*shalshelet
    hakabbalah*), 3–4, 10, 32,
    43–44, 166–167
Charity, 34; *see also* Lending,
    duty to loan
Commandments. *See* Mitzvah
Commentaries, Talmud, 15–
    24
Confessions. *See* Admissions
Conservative Jewry, 6–7,
    11
Creation, Torah in, 33, 36

Dead Sea Scrolls, 55
Desecration. *See* Hilul hashem
Deuteronomy, 38, 173; *see also*
    Sifre
    on law of retaliation, 120–
        121, 176–177
    on witnesses, 124–125, 155–
        159, 171
Dialectic, talmudic, 90–91,
    123–126, 183–185
    scriptural foundation for,
        125–162, 184–186
Diaspora, 45, 141–142
Discrimination, and adultery,
    112–113
Divine intention, 33–36, 81
    struggle to discern, 90–91,
        124
Divine will, 52, 82–83
    struggle to discern, 28–29,
        37
Dwelling house, for divine
    will, 91, 186

Editions, of the Talmud, 14–
    24
Ein mishpat ner mitzvah, laws
    in Talmud, 19
Eli, 138–139
Elohim, as judges, 143–144,
    150–151, 178
Emet V'Emunah: Statement of
    Principles of Conservative
    Judaism, 6–7
English, translation into, 20–
    23
Epstein, I., 20

Epstein, J. N., 66
Evidence, 96, 98
    and admissions, 109–110
    needed to deny testimony,
        163–164
    of single witness, 111, 115
Exile, as punishment, 139,
    141–142
Exodus, 87, 151
    on admissions, 168, 173
    on bailment, 143–145
    on lending, 165–166, 174
Ezra, and Torah, 50–52

Fines; *see also* Penalties
    obligated by admissions,
        167–168
Finkelstein, Louis, 61
Forgiveness, for false oaths,
    130, 137–143, 169

Galilee, Jewish learning in,
    64
Gamliel, Rabban, 38, 64
Gemara, 17, 62, 141, 172–
    173
    on admissions, 125, 168,
        173–176
    on Baraita of Rabbi Hiya,
        95–96, 107, 109, 166–
        167
    kal v'chomer in, 80, 98–103
    nature of, 83–84
    on single-witness rule, 110–
        111, 114–118
Genesis Rabbah, 82
Geonim. *See* Babylonia

German, translation into, 19
Gezera shavah (hermeneutic
    rule), 74, 87–88, 143–
    144, 151, 153–154
God
    creation by, 33, 36
    human relation with, 53, 81,
        90, 182–183
    and oaths, 129–130, 132–
        143
    omniscience of, 135–136
Goldschmidt, Lazarus, 19
Greeks, and hermeneutic
    rules, 75
Guidance, for Israel, 53, 54
Guilt
    and false oaths, 168–169
    offerings for, 68, 103–108,
        169

Hadasi, Judah, 75
HaGaon, Sherira, 44–46
Halivni, David Weisse, 54–56
HaNasi, Rabbi Judah, 41, 147–
    148
    redaction of Mishnah by, 32,
        44–45, 64–66
HaNasi, Rabbi Yehudah, 60
Hebrew, commentaries in, 21–
    22
Hermeneutic rules, 25, 27, 39,
    47, 59, 73–91, 148–149;
    *see also Binyan av Mishnei
    K'tuvim; Gezera shavah;
    Kal v'chomer*
    in Mishnah, 68–69
Hezekiah, Rabbi, 40

Hillel, Rabbi, 61
and *halakhah,* 44–45, 56, 64
hermeneutic rules of, 73, 75
Hilul hashem (defilement of God's name), 134, 137, 140–141
avoidance of, 163–164, 178–179
false oaths as, 137–143, 161, 179–180
Hiya, Rabbi, 60, 70, 176–177; *see also* Baraita of Rabbi Hiya
Hoffman, D., 57, 60
Holiness, 131–134, 161, 185
preservation of, 159–162, 171, 178–180
Holiness Code, 131, 160, 185
Holocaust, effects of, 3–4

Identity, Jewish, 4–6
Idi bar Avin, Rabbi, 118–120, 174–175
Importance, weighing. *See Kal v'chomer* (hermeneutic rule)
Intention, 76–77, 105–107; *see also* Divine intention
and oaths, 129–130, 133–134, 142–143
Introduction to the Mishneh Torah (Maimonides), 41–42
Introduction to the Talmud (Mielziner), 54

Invitation to the Talmud (Neusner), 5
Ishmael, Rabbi, 57, 58–59, 73–74
Israel, 50
guidance for, 53–55

Jacob, Rabbi Walter, 8–9
Jewish people, 46, 50, 63
punishments of, 139–142
Jewish People, Jewish Thought: The Jewish People in History (Seltzer), 15–16
Jewish Renewal: A Path to Healing and Transformation (Lerner), 4–5

Kal v'chomer (hermeneutic rule), 74, 76–84, 98–103, 105–123
on admissions and witnesses, 68–69, 162–165, 167–177
Kiddushin, 112–113
K'lal u'phrat ukhlal (hermeneutic rule), 74, 88–89, 148–149
Knowledge. *See* Rationality; Torah study
Kraemer, Dr. David, 90–91

Languages, in the Talmud, 13–16, 19–23
Lauterbach, Jacob Z., 53, 59

Laws (*halakhah*), 6–7, 19, 40–
    41, 64, 66, 69–70, 75–76,
    166–167; *see also Midrash
    halakhah*
  applicability of, 80, 85–87
  conflict over, 8–9, 44–46
  derivation of, 25–26, 39,
    87
  justification of, 54–55, 78
Leadership, of Jewish people,
    64, 77–78
Lending and borrowing, 124–
    126, 128, 172, 174–175;
    see also Bailment
    relationship
  duty to loan, 146–148, 161–
    162, 165–166, 179
Lerner, Michael, 4–5
Leviticus; *see also Sifra*
  on guilt offerings, 103–105
  on oaths, 129–131, 168–
    169
  on one-fifth penalties, 107–
    108
Limitations, on laws, 78, 87
Lineage, and accuracy of Oral
    Law, 43–44
Literary style
  of Gemara, 123
  of Mishnah, 66–68
  of *Sifra*, 59
  of Talmud and
    commentaries, 25
Liturgy, daily, 3, 73–74
Logic, 14; *see also*
    Hermeneutic rules;
    Rationality

Maharsha commentary, on the
    Talmud, 16
Maimonides, Moses, 41–42,
    45, 59–60
Maimonides commentary, 24
Mamon, as fines, 102–103
Marriages, trust in, 112–113, 172
Material things, and Torah,
    34–37
Mego (legal formulation), 100
Meier, Rabbi, 41, 64, 67–68, 70
  on contradictory testimony,
    169–170
  as minority opinion, 105–
    109
Mekilta of Rabbi Ishmael, 129–
    130, 146, 148–151, 155
  compared to *Sifra,* 60–61
  hermeneutic rules in, 87–89
  on *midrash halakhah,* 57–59
  on truthfulness, 135–140,
    143–144
Memory, and recitation of Oral
    Law, 63, 67–68
Mesorah edition, 24, 26
Mesoret (received tradition),
    9–10
Methodology
  scriptural, 182–185
  of Talmud, 2–3, 13–14, 27–
    29; *see also*
    Hermeneutic rules
Midrash, 2, 39
  definition of, 40–41, 52, 53
  development of, 32, 54–55
Midrash, Mishnah, and Gemara
    (Halivni), 54

Midrash halakhah, 53–57
Midrashim, 38–39, 61, 125
  against false oaths, 132–
    133
Midrashim aggadah, 55
Mielziner, Moses, 54, 62, 70
  on hermeneutic rules, 79–
    80, 89
Mihaly, Dr. Eugene, 69
Mind of the Talmud: An
    Intellectual History of the
    Bavli (Kraemer), 90
Minority opinions
  in Baraita of Rabbi Hiya,
    105–109
  in Mishnah, 66–68
Miriam, 77–78
Mishnah, 27, 55–56, 60–62,
    69, 144, 151–152
  and Baraita of Rabbi Hiya,
    95–98
  definition of, 62–63, 65
  and Midrash, 40–41
  redaction of, 32, 44–46,
    69–70
Mishnaic midrash, 56–57
Mitzvah, 1, 8–9, 47
  about lending, 124–126,
    146–147
  and holiness, 131–134
  Talmud study as, 1–2, 4
Moses
  and Ezra, 51–52
  and Miriam, 77–78

Nasi (political office), 64
Negligence, 169–170, 179–180
  in bailments, 88

Nehemiah, 70
  Book of, 50–51
Neusner, Jacob, 5, 59, 60, 66
Numbers, Book of, 77, 172; *see*
    also Sifre

Oaths, 104, 143–144, 145,
    178–180
  acceptance of, 153–154, 170
  false, 163–164, 168–169
  and hermeneutic rules, 78–
    80, 85–89, 99–101
  requirements for, 99–100,
    172–173
  rolled-over, 112–113, 171–
    172
  significance of, 127–143,
    150–151, 161
  and witnesses, 94–95, 97,
    110–115, 121–122,
    155–160, 168
Omniscience, of God, 135–
    136
Oral Law, 38–39, 54; *see also*
    Mishnah
  accuracy of, 43–44, 89–90
  Mishnah as, 61–63, 69–70
  redaction of, 44–46, 64–65
  relation to Written, 40–43,
    45, 62
Oral tradition, and writing of
    Mishnah, 32
Orthodox Jewry, 6, 11

Pagination system, in Bomberg
    edition, 17
Palestine, academies in, 45
Pappah, Rabbi, 112–113

Payment
  double, 87–89, 153
  obligated by admissions,
    101–102, 167–168
Penalties
  and law of retaliation, 120–
    122
  one-fifth, 107–108, 153
Pentateuch, 32, 37, 55–58, 58–
    59
  hermeneutic rules for, 75–
    76, 78 ·
  importance of, 49–52
  and laws, 54–55, 60–61
  and Mishnah, 66–67, 69
  and oaths, 112–113, 124–
    126
*People Divided: Judaism in
  Contemporary America, A*
  (Wertheimer), 10–11
Perjury, 134–137
Pharisees, and Oral Law, 54
Philological method, 181–182
Presumptions, underlying,
    166–167

Rabbeinu Asher commentary, 16
Rabbenu Hananel
  commentary, 19
Rashi, 15–16, 41, 82–83
  on bailments, 144, 174–175
  on Baraita of Rabbi Hiya,
    95–103
  on oaths, 151–152, 168–169
  on punishment, 108, 141–
    142
  on single witnesses, 111–
    115, 157–158

  on witnesses, 109–110, 120–
    122
Rashi commentary, 17–18, 22–
    23
Rationality, 76, 185
  relation with God through,
    81–84, 90–91, 123
  in the Torah, 33–34, 41
Rav (Abba Areca), 59–60
Rava, 82–83
Reform Jewry, 7–11
Relevance of Talmud, to
    modern life, 2–3, 14, 25
Repentance, for false oaths,
    137–143, 169
Retaliation, law of, 120–122,
    175–177
Revelation, divine, 6–7, 90
Rolled-over oaths, 112–113,
    171–172
Romans, 63–64

Sadducees, 75
  and Oral Law, 54, 89–90
Sages
  on guilt-offerings, 68
  on loans, 147–148
  on preexistence of Torah, 33
Sanctification. *See* Holiness
Sanhedrin (court), 54, 59,
    83–84
Schools, talmudic, 16; *see also*
    Academies
Scriptural foundations, 27–28,
    185–186
  for talmudic dialectic, 125–
    160, 161–186
  values in, 178–180

Scriptures. *See* Pentateuch
Second Temple period, 50, 53,
    54, 63
Seltzer, Robert M., 15–16, 51
Shammai, debate with Hillel, 64
Shammai, in conflict over
    halakhot, 44–45
Shimshon, Rabbeinu, 34–35
Shlomo ben Yitzchak,
    Rabbeinu (Rashi). *See*
    Rashi
Sifra, 38–39, 41, 57, 59–61
    on holiness, 131–134
Sifre, 38, 41, 60–61, 125, 147
    on *midrash halakhah,* 57–58
    on single witnesses, 156–158
Simeon, Rabbi, 61
Simon b. Jochai, Rabbi, 61
Sinai, 2, 42, 65
    Torah given at, 33, 37–39
Single-witness rule, 110–117,
    156–158, 171–174
Sins, 103–107, 107–108, 129–
    130
Siphra debe Rav. See Sifra
Soncino edition, 20–21, 24, 26
Sophrim (scribes), 54
Stare decisis, 96–97
Steinsaltz, Rabbi Adin, 5, 21–
    22, 61–62, 96
*Steinsaltz Edition: Bava Metzia,
    The,* 25–26, 182
Steinsaltz Hebrew
    Commentary, 21–22, 24
Strack, H. L., 57, 60, 63, 70
Suspicion. *See* Trust
Syntax, of the Talmud, 13–14

Talmud, the, 9–10, 32
    importance of, 5–6, 184–185
    obstacles to comprehending,
        13–24
    and Torah, 40, 51
Talmud *Avot,* 43–44
Talmud *Berkhot,* 81
Talmud *Shavuot,* 144, 157
    on oaths, 111, 151–152
Talmudic study, 15
    blessings for, 81–82
    methods for, 26–27, 181–
        185
    texts for, 16–17, 20–21, 27
Tanna, and Baraita of Rabbi
    Hiya, 96
Targum, 55
Temple, Second, 50–51
    destruction of, 45–46, 63
Temple Scroll, 55
Texts
    antecedents of Talmud,
        183–184
    of branches of Judaism, 6–
        11
    engagement with, 90–91
    for talmudic study, 16–17,
        20–24, 27
Theocratic system, 106–107
"This is it" (meaning of), 149–
    152
Torah, the, 32, 123–124, 164
    definitions of, 6–10, 37–43
    on holiness, 131–134
    of Moses, 49–51
    preexistence of, 33, 37, 185
    reading by Ezra, 50–51

Torah study, 2, 8, 59, 141
  functions of, 3–4, 33–34,
    36–37
  relation with God through,
    35–36, 52, 90–91
  and Talmud, 5–6, 11
Torat Kohanim. See Sifra
Tosefta, the, 16–17, 24–25, 27,
  32, 69–70
Tradition, 3–4; *see also* Chain
  of tradition
Transcendence, struggle for,
  4–6
Translations. *See* Languages
Transmission of Torah, 37–38
Trespass, 148–149
Trust, 143–145, 150, 172
  preservation of, 159
  restoration of, 112–113,
    128, 144, 153, 170,
    185
Truthfulness
  determination of, 143–144,
    150, 159
  presumption of, 117–118,
    128, 163–164, 169–
    170, 173–175

Understanding, 2, 39, 91
Unterman, Rabbi Isaac, 89

Values, of scriptural
  foundation, 178–180
Vilna edition, of the Talmud,
  17–20

V'tanah tunah (harmonizes),
  95–97, 165

Weiss, A., 60
Wertheimer, Jack, 10–11
Wiesel, Elie, 3
Witnesses, law of, 68, 108, 125
  and hermeneutic rules, 78–
    80, 85–87
  ill effects of, 170–171
  and law of retaliation, 120–
    122, 175–177
  and oaths, 111–112, 155–159
  in relation to admissions,
    94–95, 97–110, 128,
    162–165, 167–170
  single, 110–117, 110–118,
    171–174
  truthfulness of, 117–120
Written Law, 37–39, 54; *see
  also* Oral Law;
    Pentateuch; Torah

Yehudah bar Ilai, Rabbi, 59
Yeshivot, in Jewish tradition,
  3–4
Yochanan, Rabbi, 40–41
Yochanan ben Zakkai, Rabbi,
  63–64, 135–136
Yom Kippur, and forgiveness,
  137, 139–142
Yoma, 139–141

Zimmerman, Rabbi Sheldon,
  9–10

ABOUT THE AUTHOR

Edward Boraz is the rabbi of Congregation Bnai Tzedek and co-founder of its Creative School of Jewish Learning. He received a Juris Doctor from Loyola University and practiced law for ten years. Awarded a Wexner Fellowship, he was ordained at Hebrew Union College–Jewish Institute of Religion in 1993. Currently, he is a doctoral candidate at the college–institute in the field of rabbinics. He resides with his wife, Shari, and their two children in Cincinnati, Ohio.